Small Media,
Big Revolution

Small Media, Big Revolution

Communication, Culture, and the Iranian Revolution

Annabelle Sreberny-Mohammadi
Ali Mohammadi

University of Minnesota Press

Minneapolis

London

Parts of this book previously published in the article "Small Media for a Big Revolution: Iran," *International Journal of Social, Cultural and Political Sciences* 3,
no. 3 (Spring 1990), are reprinted with permission of Human Sciences Press, Inc.
Parts of this book previously published in *Quarterly Review of Film and Video* 12,
no. 4: 33–59, are reproduced with permission from Harwood Academic Publishers
GmbH. Parts of this book previously published in the article "Communications in
Persia," E. Yarshater, ed., *Encyclopaedia Iranica,* vol. 6, fascicle 1, are reprinted
with permission of Mazda Publishers, Costa Mesa, California.

All photographs in the book were taken by Annabelle Sreberny-Mohammadi

Published by the University of Minnesota Press
2037 University Avenue Southeast, Minneapolis, MN 55455–3092
Printed in the United States of America on acid-free paper

Library of Congress Cataloging-in-Publication Data

Sreberny-Mohammadi, Annabelle.
    Small media, big revolution: Communication, culture, and the Iranian
  revolution / Annabelle Sreberny-Mohammadi and Ali Mohammadi.
        p.   cm.
    Includes bibliographical references and index.
    ISBN 0-8166-2216-7 (alk. paper)
    ISBN 0-8166-2217-5 (pbk. : alk. paper)
    1. Mass media—Political aspects—Iran.   2. Iran—History—Revolution,
  1979.   3. Communication—Political aspects—Iran.   4. Islam and state—Iran.
  5. Freedom of information—Iran.
  I. Mohammadi, Ali.   II. Title.
  PN95.82.I7S68   1994
  302.23'0955—dc20   93-46191

We dedicate this book
to Sara and Leili,
daughters of the revolution

Contents

IV. The Revolutionary Process

Acknowledgments

We want to thank all those friends and colleagues in the United States, Britain, and Iran who have discussed various of the ideas and read sections of this work over the past decade. We would particularly like to thank John Downing, Rick Maxwell, and an anonymous critic for helpful comments about the manuscript. We would also like to thank the good people at the University of Minnesota Press for their help: Janaki Bakhle, for believing in our work; Robert Mosimann, for keeping up the pressure; and Laura Westlund, for bringing order out of our disorder. We alone stand responsible for the final product.

Prolegomenon

This book is not only an analytic account of the role of media in the Iranian revolution, but also the story of our—the authors'—lives. Having talked for years about revolution, we actually lived through one. It dramatically affected our own lives, but we were merely two of the millions involved in its process. Yet, if an essential element of the revolutionary mobilization in Iran was its spontaneous, unscripted, small-scale escalation, its movement of countless individuals into political agents, then our small actions were at some level a mimicry of the actions of others and were mimicked by many others in this extraordinary moment of social solidarity that toppled a shah, and thus our experiences are precisely what need to be described. The political and the personal are always mutually implicative; in such a moment of social crisis, even more so.

In this initial section, we will provide a brief overview of our lives in Tehran and our own inscriptions into the social and political environment of 1977–79. In other parts of the book, we elaborate on specific experiences and stories that not only help develop an intellectual understanding of the revolutionary process, but also provide a deeper, empathetic taste of what being there was like. Analytic writing tends to overlook the fact that revolutions are psychologically electric moments, full of emotional charge and somatic intensity, which social scientific jargon is woefully inept at presenting (and theory rarely considers worthy of analysis).

Completing this long-overdue project, fourteen years after the revolution, is a way of remembering for each of us and a way of trying to make sense both of the broader political processes and of our own lives, and of the implications of each for the other.

It also seems appropriate at the beginning of this book to clarify that this is a volume of/from two voices. One prefers the voice of a speaker, and the other is more the writer: orality and literacy, the very tropes we shall discuss later. One author prefers Persian, and one prefers English. This text embodies their personal and political involvements and struggles over twenty years. Both are here.

It is evocative of the disjunctive global moment in which we live that I, Annabelle, a Londoner, came to experience the Iranian revolution and now write a book about the process; that as a Jew, I write about an Islamic movement; that as a woman, I write about a highly patriarchal context in which the "problem of women" always threatens to spoil the prevailing order; and that born a first-generation Briton because of the Jewish Diaspora, I write this in the context of another, political, exile.

Ali was the first member of his family to attend university, gaining his political baptism as a student in Tehran during the last democratic politics of the Mossadeq period in the 1960s. He was the only one of his family to go abroad to study, to obtain graduate qualifications to take back and use in Iran. We met as graduate students in the United States, both of us unattached from our "own" cultural moorings. I was at American University in Washington, D.C., teaching probably one of the first courses in a U.S. university on "Terrorism and National Liberation Movements" with Abdul Aziz Said. I returned to London to teach high school, but after a year of international correspondence and travel Ali and I both decided to move to New York. We lived together in Morningside Heights and worked on doctoral degrees at Columbia University.

In 1976 we married in London, quickly, en route to Iran. The marriage certificate is redolent with the mixing of many worlds: my father, the Polish doctor, British army major, part of the Jewish Diaspora; Ali's father, the Isfahani farmer, literally rooted in traditional Iranian life. We, the products, were already part of the global mixture with my Western lefty anti-imperialism and interest in Third World cultures, and Ali's delight in due process, political freedoms, and functioning technology, countering my arguments against technological dependency with evocations of the joys of electricity. So I "married in" and came to love Iran, its people, and culture as many Westerners have done before me. If Iranians were *gharbzadeh*, "Weststruck," I would joke that I had become *sharghzadeh*, "Eaststruck."

I was both insider and outsider to the Iranian revolution, but perhaps so was Ali and many of his contemporaries. Schooled in the West, well-read in Marx, Dewey, and Freud as well as Saadi, Hafez, and Mowlana, mine/his/our/their vision of the post-Pahlavi Iran was of a democratic, socialist, open society. Or at least the fragments about the future that we discussed suggested this, for, thinking back, this was very much a movement in negativity, with only a vaguely articulated vision of the new collective future to which it would lead. The Shah always seemed to cast an enormous shadow, obscuring the shape of the visions of the future; he had to be toppled in order to let in the light. I taught sociology at Damavand College and National University, conducted media research, and edited an English-language quarterly journal called *Communications and Development Review*. Despite the ever-present fear of SAVAK in the classroom, I always found some scope for introducing critical ideas without directly mentioning the clearly taboo topic of the Shah or the taboo name of Marx. (My sociology books were retained in customs because local bureaucrats confused Max Weber with Karl!) There was also some space in which to publish interesting materials, at least in English, for an international audience. Indeed, coming abroad for conferences during that period, I was often asked how the *Review* could be as critical as it was; my only answer was that because it had little resonance inside Iran, it was probably a useful exercise in repressive tolerance for the regime. The research institute where I worked, Iran Communications and Development Institute (ICDI) under the directorship of Majid Tehranian, managed to bring in many of the top international scholars in communications during a brief dynamic period from 1977 to 1978. It was a unique moment and place for debate and analysis about the prospects of communications for development, the dilemmas of cultural contact, and the problems of rapid modernization. Many scholars conducted "research," gave lectures, interviewed high officials, wrote analyses (some very flawed), and left. Because I was the only permanent non-Iranian researcher, the visitors were given the dubious honor of sharing my office, and I was able to dispute at length with Ithiel de Sola Pool, Daniel Lerner, Percy Tannenbaum, and James Halloran, among others, and to be privy to much discussion about the role of communications in development in the Third World.

Ali helped to establish the research and planning department of ICDI and then left to direct a new graduate program in communications and culture at Farabi University. He also taught at the Tehran Institute of Political and Social Science. We worked within the system, presumably in one schema of analysis operating as low-level parts of the "problem," but we became active parts of the popular attempt at "solution."

Life in Tehran in the mid-1970s partook of an exquisite schizophrenia. Many of us were caught between two—or even more—worlds. How can we give you a taste of the beauty and passion, the confusion and excitement, of that period? Let's take up a vantage point in the foothills of the Alborz Mountains, against which northern Tehran nuzzles. The highest peaks, snow-covered much of the year, offer a cool vista over the heat and bustle of the rapidly expanding city. The edifices that stand out in the panorama of the capital exemplify the tensions on the ground. There is the Hilton Hotel, square and squat, the most banal of Western architecture, the American hyperreality of air-conditioning, midday gloom, and flowing whiskey that spans the globe, home to besuited businessmen waiting to cash in on the overflowing petrodollar boom. There is the dome of the mosque in Tadjrish, with its round minaret providing appealing curvatures in the angular view, the most indigenous of forms. Then there is the proliferation of residential housing lapping over the edge of the mountains, overflowing city boundaries, a building boom based on foreign contract labor and rising middle-class aspirations, exemplifying a huge range of Western styles and Iranian fantasies. In the south of the city—too far to see from our lookout point in the mountains—the shantytowns of sheet-metal housing reveal the underside and urban underclasses of the northern boom . . . a city without a sewage system, hovering perilously close to its own mire.

We rented the top floor of an old house in the northern part of the city, once the summer residence of a wealthy family. We heated the apartment with a big kerosene stove, a *bokhari*, used an old sitz bath, and enjoyed the tall persimmon trees in the garden. One salary paid the rent; the other salary hardly covered food and other expenses. I bargained in my best Farsi for fruit and vegetables in the market in Tadjrish, but inevitably Ali would assure me later that I'd been robbed blind in the price I paid for cucumbers. The new supermarket on Pahlavi Street carried French cheeses, smoked salmon, and even American diapers, expensive luxuries for the Westernized elite.

We strolled in the new municipal parks such as Park-e Mellat, with its lake and elaborate stone steps; we wandered down Manouchehri, enjoying the clutter of handicrafts and antiques; we mooched in carpet shops and bought a couple of rugs. Regularly on Fridays we climbed with friends in the hills to the north, going out on the trails beyond Darband or Jamaran, and sat outside in the ramshackle cafés to eat kebab and drink tea or *dough*, a salty yogurt drink. We walked and talked politics endlessly, the mountains providing a special kind of free space. We skied at Abali, where the elegant Tehrani elite mingled with the brilliant local village skiers. We queued up with the hoards of young men and the occasional girl to see Iranian, sometimes Western, movies and spit sunflower-seed husks all over the cinema floor. Rudaki Hall, the only modern concert hall in the center of town, provided occasional symphony concerts and opera or theatrical performances. Bagh Ferdows, an old Qajar palace set among magnificent cypresses in the north of the city, offered traditional Iranian music. We ate out at Khansalar (later destroyed by a bomb), Paprika, Xanadu, and Hatam chicken-kebab house. We munched greasy hamburgers standing in fast-food places on 24 Esfand Square, and delighted in ice cream flavored with rose water. We sat in cafés with pianists playing Satie, while outside the itinerant builders ate bread and onions straight from newspaper laid on the pavement. On many weekends we would take our lives in our hands to endure the nightmare of Iranian driving and visit Isfahan to enjoy my mother-in-law's cooking and be enveloped by the tribe of Ali's family, lazing in idyllic flower gardens that walled off the rest of the world and the growing social commotion.

Life was increasingly expensive, particularly for government or public employees on fixed incomes; paying for housing and running a car absorbed the bulk
of a salary. I never got used to the number of servants (maids, cooks, gardeners)
that the upper middle class required, and although these domestic workers were
often part of enduring family ties and responsibilities, I still do not feel comfort-
able with the practice. Many of our friends were also "mixed couples," sometimes
so mixed that they had to communicate in a third language. We were assorted
academics, professionals, and artists, a secularized Western-educated middle-
class intelligentsia, part of the process of modernization yet critical of it, disen-
franchised, discontented.

In my letters to friends in Britain during our first year in Iran (1976), I wrote
that there were four staple conversations in Tehran: the first was where and how to
buy a car; the second, where and how to buy a house or apartment; the third, how
to find a wife, sometimes a husband; and the fourth, how to get out of Iran. Social
discontent was palpable, and individual frustration and malaise much discussed,
yet that was rarely transformed into overt political discussion. There seemed to be
nothing to talk about. One year later, however, there was only political discussion,
and individual problems, though not solved, were no longer the focus of collective
energy.

From early 1977, the atmosphere changed dramatically. Women I knew began
covering their hair and attending prayer meetings, which I also visited. Criticism
of the regime became more overt, debate in classrooms more edgy, television
more sarcastic. Friends and students began to talk about political parties and
groups that were emerging, about organizing. Leaflets started to circulate, demonstrations were called, and, as the movement took off, we too became involved.

We visited London during the summer of 1978. Ali returned to teach in
Tehran, and I stayed in England, waiting for the birth of our first child, for the
thought of giving birth in my fractured Farsi was more than I could tolerate. Sara,
like the revolution, arrived too fast, a long bony being shoving her presence into
the world to become our daughter of the revolution. Ali later had to wrench me
away from the fears of family and friends in England, as well as from my own,
infected as we all were by the dramatic images of the popular mobilization broadcast on the British nightly news.

In the autumn we marched in many demonstrations in Tehran, some of which
were the largest gatherings of human beings ever and certainly the most massive
groups in which I have participated. Among the first sounds our elder daughter
mumbled, as she brandished a chubby fist, were "Marg bar Shah," Death to the
Shah. We talked with numerous Western scholars who came to Tehran to see first-
hand what was happening, and we argued that the Shah was finished. Ali became
an active member of the Organization of University Professors and helped to
write and distribute their alternative newspaper *Hambastegi* (Solidarity). Under
the Islamic Republic, he was implicated in the internal political effects of the

takeover of the U.S. embassy, and was labeled along with many others as a "spy" because he had talked with Americans. Indeed, this domestic political dynamic was probably at least as important as the international process of the "hostage crisis," for it effectively extinguished what remained of the secular opposition inside Iran.

We left Iran in the spring of 1980 when the universities were closed and the secular opposition eclipsed, and when the hunt for fresh eggs, meat, and toothpaste occupied most waking hours. Yet exile does not end the frustrations of the educated middle class, who seemed to have no political role under the Shah and even less role in the Islamic Republic. For Iranians, as for many others, to live in "exile" is to live in limbo, to be tugged in many different directions, but to preserve a strong identification with an emotional "home" far from one's actual place of residence. It is a hard way to live, made more difficult by the simple fact that everyday life is remarkably mundane after the intense excitement of living the revolution.

Annabelle
New York, Summer 1992
Leicester, Winter 1994

Introduction

The Iranian revolution ranks as one of the most tumultuous popular revolutions in history. It differed significantly from other Third World revolutions and movements of national liberation in several fundamental ways. Unlike the Chinese, Vietnamese, and Angolan struggles, for example, which were based on peasant mobilization in the countryside, the Iranian movement had an urban dynamic (Halliday, 1988). It was a popular and populist movement, its solidarity cutting across lines of class. It was strongly based on the traditional urban propertied class of the bazaar and the clergy, together with modern urban groups such as the salaried middle class, intellectuals, students, and workers. Their combined ranks were swollen by numbers of recently arrived urban migrants. It was a movement in negativism, the strongly stated antipathies of the movement toward the Shah's regime and U.S. neocolonialism creating common ground while the politicization of Islamic rhetoric provided further cultural glue.

It was essentially an indigenous movement, not precipitated by war or any particular external threats. It was a revolution in an oil-rich nation that had already undergone significant and very rapid social change to produce "pseudomodernization" (Katouzian, 1981) and highly uneven socioeconomic conditions. But it was a revolution against dependency in a nation never directly colonized but in which the increasingly visible signs of economic and cultural dependency and a growing myth of foreign involvement were strong causal factors.

It was a revolution in the television era, in which the mass media, far from helping to legitimize an unpopular regime, in fact revealed in a boomerang effect its lack of substance beyond a mimetic Westernization. It was a profound identity crisis in which the processes of cultural Westernization and desacralization were themselves felt to be part of the problem. It was an extremely rapid, popular movement united under radicalized Islamic slogans against a royal dictatorship supported by the West.

The Iranian revolution was very much a late-twentieth-century product, the result of various kinds of uneven development that characterize many current Third World formations. Its religious ideology and traditional leadership are partly the by-products of dictatorship and lack of political development and possibilities for political participation, the extreme mimesis of the West, and the social and cultural strain of rapid social change. Retraditionalization around religion provided an indigenous, political, and populist rhetoric that was the basis for a massive political mobilization. Thus political and cultural issues were causes of discontent.

In a context where the political sphere was controlled by the regime with few opportunities for participation, the rapid and massive nature of popular participation was quite remarkable in itself. But equally as surprising an element of the mobilization, for many Iranians and non-Iranians alike, was the nature of the leadership and organizing ideology of the popular movement. The mobilization was coordinated by the religious leaders using traditional networks of social communication, which were enhanced and extended by an innovative use of various contemporary "small media," including photocopied leaflets and audiocassette tapes.

What we are most centrally concerned with in this book is to present a case study of the communications dynamic of popular revolutionary mobilization, because it is in this area that the Iranian movement revealed some of its most unique features. Its model of "organization" was one of communications, with no revolutionary party or tight cadre of revolutionaries, but rather a preexisting politico-religious leadership orchestrating the movement through the distribution of religious commands to an audience already predisposed to listen.

Many different conceptual models have been used to understand the Iranian revolution, but there is still no systematic attempt to utilize the tools of analysis of communications to analyze the process. Communications is one of the most synthetic of disciplines. Its study implicates many other themes, such as power, authority, influence, and the central concerns of politics; symbolic meaning and the reproduction of social life; the nature of expressive culture, and the forms of sociability and communication; the interaction between different cultures, both at the national and interpersonal levels. If no single discipline can adequately explain social transformation, then too no single element of communications analysis can explain the fascinating and intricate phenomenon of the Iranian revolution. But perhaps a synthesis of various approaches can lead toward the construction of a communications model of revolutionary mobilization. In this volume we argue that the Iranian revolution appears to present a new, alternative,

"Third World" model of revolutionary process: populist, urban, and based on "small media."

Revolutions have rarely beeen thought of in terms of communications. From attempts to build general models based on class, or deprivation, or conflict, clusters of models have developed that focus predominantly on behavioral, social psychological phenomena (Gurr, 1971; Johnson, 1966; Brinton, 1965) or on essentially structural processes, particularly weakened state formations (Tilly, 1978; Skocpol, 1979a). Increasingly, the focus is on conjunctural events, analysis of the specific set of factors that cause social dislocation and unrest (Skocpol, 1979b; Goldstone, 1980). When communicative elements are recognized, it has been primarily as epiphenomena, the detritus of the political process rather than central to it. Yet perhaps it is communications that is able to link the social psychological and the structural in novel, conjunctural ways.

In many of the brief popular and powerful movements of recent years, there has been a clearer sense of the contribution played by mediated communications, particularly small media. Fax machines were used in the popular struggle in the People's Republic of China, community video played a role in Poland, and the television station was a site of struggle in Romania. Western analysts have begun to talk about the role of media in social change within authoritarian political systems. John Kifner (1989: 1) describes the "videocracy" that replaced the dictatorship of Ceausescu, and quotes the claim that the Romanian movement was "the first revolution on live television." Another piece occasioned by the dramatic events in Eastern Europe, entitled "Prime-time Revolution" and written by Jonathan Alter (1990), focused on the amazing potential power of the media to foster change. A *Koppel Report* on ABC television in 1991 called *Television: Revolution in a Box* ran briefly through a litany of such examples.

Significantly, these discussions frequently mention the role of communications in the Iranian revolution of 1978–79. Kifner discusses power in the electronic age, saying that once those who plotted revolutions took aim at radio stations, but "in the Iranian revolution, new technology spread the word of Ayatollah Ruhollah Khomeini, first through tape cassettes telephoned from abroad and played over mosque loudspeakers" (1989: 1). Alter too uses the Iranian case as his central example, noting that "the Ayatollah Khomeini distributed thousands of cassette tapes when fomenting his despotic [*sic*] revolution against the Shah" (25). Similar singular sentences can be found in academic works on various aspects of contemporary media, including Ganley and Ganley (1982), Boyd et al. (1989: 12, which contains a bizarre argument about the role of video in the revolution that appears to be quite incorrect), and Larkin (1989). Yet this has by now become a cliché that is too often the extent of common knowledge about the phenomenon, leading to the far too easy conclusion that small media can make revolution. At the same time, numerous volumes on the Iranian revolution mention the use of cassette tapes en passant, as an interesting aside, as though communications systems, messages, and dynamics have little to offer the study of actual revolution (Stempel, 1981; Keddie, 1983; Lewis, 1988: 116). We hope to show the extremity of both positions.

There is still no detailed account of the Iranian revolution that specifically examines communications in the revolutionary process, especially the role of small media, and attempts to explain how and why the particular kinds of small media were effective. Closer analysis of the causes and dynamics of the Iranian revolution reveal mediated communications as central to both: the media as state institutions promoted the Shah's modernization program and the media were the culture brokers that introduced Iranians to Western cultural consumption. The popular movement grew around the twin concerns of hostility to dictatorship and to cultural dependency, creating a collective identity crisis that energized the movement. The widespread availability of consumer electronics, international telephone lines, and recording devices brought the authoritative voice of Khomeini into Iranian homes to mobilize the popular movement, and a variety of "small media" forms carried oppositional messages and fostered participation against the regime. Small media created a political "public sphere"; they were channels of participation, extended preexisting cultural networks and communicative patterns, and became the vehicles of an oppositional discourse that was able to mobilize a mass movement. They must be seen as technologies or channels of communication, but also as the web of political solidarity and as the carriers of oppositional discourse. Very modern media, the spoils of dependent development, became the mouthpiece of a retraditionalizing popular movement. This was in many ways a (post)modern revolution, where, as Halliday (1988: 36) so neatly suggests, "the originality of the Iranian revolution resides neither in its 'traditional,' nor in its 'modern' character but in the interaction of the two." In short, only a rich, historically inflected cultural approach to such communication can transcend a narrow, technologically biased understanding to situate small media in a complex net of economic, political, and cultural relations.

Revolutions are among the most evocative moments when structure and agency confront each other, when power discovers its opposite. Our intention is to try to explain *how* a specific contemporary revolution happened, *how* a people rebelled in a context where rebellion, even if desired, seemed impossible. Analysis of communications would seem to be an ideal way to explore revolutionary dynamics, because it implicates the way opposition can and does develop within a repressive state formation. Against the historical development of big state and big media structures in Iran, we will explore the development of oppositional structures of communications (the forms of small media), their cultural location (embedded in traditional cultural practices), and their discursive formations (the oppositional ideologies).

No adequate conceptual model exists regarding the role small media can play within politically repressive conditions and the reasons why they are such an important tool in political mobilization and change. The political literature on revolution focuses on cause rather than dynamics, and often suggests in hindsight an overdetermined causal logic that makes revolution necessary. The political communications literature often examines rhetoric abstracted from historical process.

The revolutionary experiences of Nicaragua and the Philippines, and recent movements in Poland and elsewhere in Eastern Europe, suggest similar populist and culturalist dynamics to those of the Iranian movement, although with different configurations of political actors, channels, and ideologies. Three features that distinguish all these recent movements are their speed, their spontaneity, and their populism. It appears that repressive regimes go out not with a whimper but with a bang, as massive pent-up popular dissatisfaction suddenly finds its blowhole via small media. Where formal political activity is disallowed, informal cultural spaces may become politicized particularly through the effective use of small media and group communication. Even so-called authoritarian and totalitarian systems are contradictory, perforated systems in which crevices to locate resistance can be found.

Not all resistance is revolutionary, however, and neither is all resistance successful. But, in general, the dynamics of contemporary revolutionary mobilization and the creation of solidarity, trust, and resistance have received far less attention than has the mapping of the instruments of repression. The structural relations between the various sets of actors—particularly between state and society—and the resources, flexibility, and will of the state are crucial variables in any revolutionary situation. Yet at the risk of not taking the power dimension of the state seriously enough, we want to argue that structures have legitimacy as long as they are endowed with legitimacy, they have power as long as people allow them to have power. At some point in the Shah's rule, the "power" the regime had reputedly had over people, in their fear of SAVAK and the military, their concern about their salary and position, their self-censorship, broke, and people were not frightened anymore. *Iman-e-Bozorg va Dastha-ye Khali*, a people armed only "with a great faith but with empty hands," became an important slogan of the revolution.

All revolutions write their own scripts, and their media are part of the process. In such contexts, communication and politics are not separate acts, for the altering of public affect, the mobilization of opinion, and the promotion of further participation are part of the revolutionary process. This volume examines one revolutionary context, the Iranian revolution, and attempts to show in detail how this process worked. If history is constructed through many different narratives, then the development of big media and the counterclaims of political and cultural opposition is one narrative that still needs to be told. That story is in itself insufficient to explain the Iranian movement, and thus this book walks a fine line: it is both a book about media forms that uses Iran as a case study, and a book about Iran that uses communication models to explain some of the sociopolitical events of the recent past. We have tried to write a multidimensional culturalist account of the dynamics of the Iranian revolution that recognizes both external forces and internal dynamics and seeks to understand the impact of each upon the other; that situates narrowly political phenomena within a wider cultural framework of lived experience and social ritual, which give meaning to collective life and thus define political action; and that allows the richness of the material of the revolution to speak itself.

Indeed, this "speaking" of the revolution implies that this political process is also and perhaps even more fundamentally a communicative process: a people communicating with and to itself; contending leaderships communicating with putative followers; political "messages" of various kinds circulating and provoking other political action; competition as to which contending image of the "community" will prevail. Communications in itself does not function as a simple organizing perspective, but rather allows us to focus on a number of different levels of analysis and pose a variety of interrelated issues.

This book begins with two theoretical chapters. In the first, we critique the assumptions of both modernization and dependency paradigms about the advent of "big" media, essentially broadcasting, to the Third World, and the "big" effects these media were expected to have, including their deployment in support of "big" autocratic states in the process of development. We explore newer models of globalization and disjuncture that provide a more complex picture of international economic and cultural relations, and consider how these relations might precipitate an identity crisis in Third World systems. We look at the connections between mass media and national identity, analyze how collective identity is established and challenged, and discuss how tradition may be reconstituted as the basis of collective identity and thus work to create a popular movement as in Iran. In the second chapter we develop a model of "small" media as the resources of such an opposition movement in a highly repressive context and suggest how they can promote popular mobilization.

Having established the political and cultural tensions between the state and a popular movement, we then examine each of these sets of forces in turn. In chapters 3 and 4, we present a detailed historical account and analysis of the development of mass media in Iran in the context of interimperial rivalries and external interests in Iran, the dynamics of dependent development, and the requirements of a royal dictatorship. Media are seen as central institutions in the project of Pahlavi development, but also become the targets of political and cultural concern as an opposition movement unfolds in the late 1970s.

In chapter 5 we describe the evolution of both secular and religious oppositions. In chapter 6 we explore the manner in which religious culture is interwoven with many facets of Iranian social life and collective identity, as well as the political resources—institutions, social authority, political discourse—that the religious forces brought to the political movement.

Ideological struggles are essentially discursive struggles about whose definition of the community and whose rhetorical authority is the most compelling, so chapter 7 examines the languages of the revolution and develops an argument as to how and why clerical authority and rhetoric could overcome both the claims of the regime and those of the secular opposition. This chapter shows how the clerisy was eclipsed as an independent alternative force to the Pahlavis, either having to acquiesce to religious leadership or become marginal actors in the mobilization. Chapter 8 examines the different kinds of small media used and their specific agitational purposes.

A narrative of the revolution in chapter 9 tries to provide a sense of the excitement and urgency of the brief, intense revolutionary mobilization. It examines in detail those moments when communications played a crucial role in the insurrectionary process.

Chapters 10 and 11 survey communication and cultural policy since the establishment of the Islamic Republic. We explain how some central motifs of Iranian political life are distressingly repeated with the emergence of a new, Islamic, repressive state while new dynamics of resistance are developed. The last chapter elaborates on the theoretical utility of bringing communications-based analyses to the study of revolution and summarizes some of the possible lessons of the Iranian case, both for theorizing Third World revolutions and for practicing them.

Any model occludes as much as it reveals, and no single narrative can hold the richness and complexity of a phenomenon like a popular revolution. The weakness of our approach is that in its focus on mobilization, participation, and ideology, it privileges agency and makes the process sound highly willed and intended, and thus tends to relegate issues such as the crisis of the state, regime reactions, and alternate scenarios, including other possible international reactions. One of the biggest problems in any historical writing is our working backward from the outcome to its inception, which tends to make the process appear so overdetermined that one wonders how it could possibly have come out otherwise. The alternative options of the Pahlavi state, and alternative international responses—particularly from the United States—have been dealt with by analysts of political science and international relations (Cottam, 1984). While the political outcome of the Iranian revolution did not have to be this way, we do want to show why the dynamics of popular mobilization took the form that they did and how communications played a particular role as cause and effect, as the tools of systemic power *and* as the resources of agents making a revolution.

I
Media, Modernization, and Mobilization:
Theoretical Overview

Chapter 1
Mighty Media, Big States, and Modernization: Big Identity Crises

The central logic of this volume is that media developments have radically altered our understanding of political dynamics, specifically, here, mass mobilization into a revolutionary movement. Media are frequently part of the structures of power of authoritarian states in the Third World, yet also the tools of resistance against those states. Looking at the dynamics of media use can help us understand breakdowns in regime policy and ideology but also the mobilization of alternate identities and resources to fight against the state, helping to explain how subjects of strong states become agents in their demise. The focus of this chapter is to examine how media have become the weapons of strong states and to present the theoretical models and expectations that flow from that development.

For our case study, the Iranian revolution cannot be seen simply as a structural crisis in which a nexus of factors such as economic dislocation and political illegitimacy combined to undermine the state, and the clergy, waiting in the wings, emerged as the new/old leadership after a religious coup d'état (Arjomand, 1988). The revolution also needs to be seen as exemplifying a deep collective identity crisis that has to be understood in terms of the long and complex integration of Iran into the contemporary world capitalist system and the mixed and disjunctive effects that process has had on Iranian political, economic, and cultural life. The structural crises must be linked to changing perceptions and alternate identities that empowered Iranians to act to make a revolution. If the logic of our argument gives a certain primacy to political activity and ideological struggle over structural collapse, we always try to locate these elements within broader national and international structures, and to see the activities and ideologies as creative adapta-

3

tions to the political possibilities of the moment—indeed, as part of the complex conjuncture of forces that work to make a revolution.

The slippage between the notion of the "Iranian revolution" and that of the "Islamic revolution" is one indication of the struggle around identity and "naming the community" that was a central part of the revolutionary process. This identity crisis was not a simple conflict between modernity and tradition but between a highly dependent and dictatorial process of modernization and a retraditionalizing rhetoric based on indigenous culture in which competing communicative structures offered different definitions and visions of the national community. Culture and communication were part and parcel of the process of dependent development as well as elements in its overthrow, and this volume will attempt to develop a political economy of communications and culture in Iran and discuss their role in the Iranian revolution.

Media in the Third World

For development theorists, the postcolonial experience of Third World states posed a challenge, that is, why newly independent political states found it so hard to achieve economic development. Development was equated with modernization, and modernization was seen as a process of diffusion of Western social structures and values. Hence if the obstacles to this process in Third World countries could be ascertained and solved, then they too could march on toward development. Theorists such as Rostow and Hagen isolated different problems or lacks in Third World systems, for example, the lack of capital to support economic "takeoff" to sustained growth or a lack of entrepreneurial motivation. But once modernization came to be seen as the diffusion of Western social and cultural attitudes, then it was only a short step to proposing that mass media were important channels of diffusion and powerful tools for development. They could help to create the empathetic "mobile personality" and promote economic consumption and political participation that development required (Schramm, 1964, 1972; Lerner, 1958). Lerner further proposed that media development was a secular trend of global importance, the assumption being that traditional societies did not possess distinct or elaborate systems of communication.

However, the notion that there is no distinct, organized system of public communications or class of professional communicators in traditional societies has been challenged, especially for the Middle East. Fathi (1979) and Borthwick (1965) have argued that the function of the Islamic pulpit was, and still is, a medium of public communication, not only for specifically religious messages but also for "defending certain policies, stirring public emotion, or spreading propaganda" (Fathi, 1979: 103). The mosque was the location of the weekly communal prayers but also the center of the community, much as the forum was to Rome or the agora to Greece. There were distinctions between preacherly roles: the *khatib*, or religious man, delivered a strictly religious sermon and the *va'ez*, or storyteller, was often more directly political and developed a considerable following and influence. In Iran the pulpit has played a considerable political role at key historical moments, particularly during the constitutional movement and again in the recent mobilization. But however much the model of communications and development has subsequently been critiqued as linear, historic, technologistic, and so on, its wholesale adoption by UNESCO in the early 1960s meant that it was the basis for media development in many parts of the Third World and a perspective that supported the massive development of Iran's state broadcasting system in the 1970s. Big media became the tools of big authoritarian states.

An alternative theoretical approach operated on very different premises. Instead of fostering independence, modernization based on high technology was seen to create new ties of dependency, and, instead of autonomous development, a mimicry of the West was encouraged. Concerns about media imperialism and cultural synchronization grew.

For Iran, the various strands of political dependency (Cottam, 1979, 1984), economic dependency (Saikhal, 1980), and cultural dependency (Motamed-Nejad, 1977) have been explored and documented but rarely have been woven together to explore their mutual impacts. Here, our specific interest in the advent of mediated communication to Iran is narrated within the context of broader political dynamics of dictatorship and economic patterns of dependency that it helped to reinforce, as described in the historical materials of chapters 3 and 4.

Ironically, there is actually a great deal of similarity as to how these opposing theoretical perspectives conceived of the media. Both the models of modernization theory, in the form of communications and development models, and of dependency theory, in the form of cultural imperialism arguments, anticipated "big" effects from the "big" media. In both approaches, the preexisting "traditional" culture and social formation would be irreparably altered in the direction of modernizing, Westernizing tendencies, a process that was greeted with either delight or dismay, to be promoted or prevented. The preexisting culture was perceived as capable neither of resistance to incoming influences nor of reconstitution by selectively adopting foreign values and practices.

Changing global realities, particularly in mediated cultural production and flow, and alternative theorizing (in poststructuralist, postmodernist mode) invite a far more nuanced look at the encounter of "tradition" and "modernity," and imply more disjunctive relations and hybrid outcomes than the older models deemed possible. In the radically altered global economic and political environment, with the demise of the Second World of state socialism and the rapid industrial development of certain countries of the periphery, we are increasingly forced to confront the notion of the "end of the Third World" (Harris, 1987; Ahmad, 1993). Center-periphery, metropolis-satellite, and even world-system models with their comparatively clear power relations and unequal economic dynamics are being challenged by models of globalization and new world disorder that suggest a new level of complexity and multiplicity of interactions that we are just beginning to recognize and theorize.

The newer models of globalization describe the intensification of worldwide social relations linking erstwhile remote places. This "time-space distanciation" (Harvey, 1989) helps to create what Giddens (1990: 64) has called "complex relations between *local involvements* (circumstances of co-presence) and *interaction across distance* (connections of presence and absence)" (emphasis in the original). These models acknowledge the powerful global webs of communication/ information that have fostered such a collapse of space and time, which have been developed as integral parts of the global expansion of capitalist relations but which are not exactly congruent with economic flows and impacts. Appadurai (1990) particularly stresses the *disjunctures* between the five scapes of interaction that he argues constitute the "global cultural economy": the ethnoscape, technoscape, financescape, ideoscape, and mediascape.

Some proponents see the new situation as partaking of a radically new economic-cultural structure called "postmodernity" (Harvey, 1989); others see recent developments only as the supreme development and natural extension of global capitalism and prefer names that stress continuity, such as "late capitalism" (Jameson, 1990) or "high modernity" (Giddens, 1990). Significantly, the newer theorizing recognizes the centrality of communication and cultural flows and actors in the emerging structures of global relations.

The media environment of the 1990s is far more complex than that of the 1960s, the epoch when the earlier models were conceived and in which they now seem frozen (Sreberny-Mohammadi, 1991). Radio has a global reach and television is close behind, so that by 1988 only the smallest and poorest countries and territories did not have any nationally based television service (UNESCO, 1989). Not only are more countries wired for picture, but more have become sizable producers of programming. Although the international consumption of Western cultural products is still considerable, if not rising, there is also growing international interest in and consumption of Indian film (Dissanayeke, 1988), Brazilian *telenovelas* (Olivera, 1990; Antola and Rogers, 1984), Egyptian television programming (Tracey, 1988; Boyd, 1984), and Rai and other kinds of world-beat music (McMurray and Swedenburg, 1991). More mediated producers, more products, and more hybrid genres are flowing than ever before. This can partly be linked to the increased movements of people internationally, as immigrants, refugees, exiles, tourists—the diverse cross-cultural encounters of Appadurai's ethnoscape. Thus not only is there considerable "deterritorialization" (to borrow Deleuze and Guattari's term) of signs in terms of images and texts, but also of peoples, creating a highly mobile, nomadic, restless global environment.

New theorizing, demanded by new global realities, has undermined or rather exploded the stark either-or logic of the older models: either center or periphery, either modern or tradition, either wealth or poverty, either First World or Third World. We are starting to recognize that there exists, to quote Trinh Minh-Ha (1987: 139), "A Third World in every First World, a Third World in every Third World, and vice versa."

The growth of multiple sources of media products and the complexity of the cultural flows have led to a revisionist perspective that challenges the putative hegemony of Western cultural products and the one-way flow of these products (McNeely and Soysal, 1989). In what Hannerz (1989) has labeled the new "global cultural ecumene," the countries of the periphery, alias the Third World, are recognized as possessing old and complex cultures that mediate and interact with imported First World cultural products to create local meanings, hybrid cultures, new social identities. "Modernity" and "tradition" do not meet suddenly, in pristine condition, but rather have been encountering each other for decades if not centuries, and mutating in the process. The disjunctive development and interplay of Appadurai's "scapes" radically question center-periphery models of international power, but also suggest uneven levels of development of the various scapes within the Third World. Iran, for example, experienced quite rapid economic development, very limited political development, and a nonexistent civil society, together with a relatively open mediascape filled with Western cultural products. The disjunctures between these internal scapes help to explain the structural crisis and show why identity issues become paramount. Such theorizing is also useful in that it challenges the empty abstractions of modernity and tradition and requires that we analyze the *particular* forms and mutations of each that existed in Iran. It also stresses the *interactions* between these competing social and cultural forces—especially, for our purposes, the uses of the media in the Shah's modernizing project and reactions to that, and how preexisting cultural practices were utilized to resist that project.

What becomes problematic in some formulations is that the terms of the encounter often become obscured, and the political and economic force fields within which cultural interactions take place are ignored. Although we want to acknowledge the centrality of cultural and ideological questions, they must not be allowed to become disconnected from political and economic structures and dynamics. We must be wary of analysis (even our own) that seems to suggest that cultural issues have an autonomous, idealist life, allowing that connections, mediations, and determinations among and between these various social spheres seem to dissipate. There is no center to hold. Clearly, this is a danger for work in the field of cultural studies but one that can be dealt with by keeping the specific historical and social-structural contexts of any cultural phenomena in mind (as the work of Stuart Hall and Raymond Williams alerts us to do). We try to do this in our Iranian case study as we examine various sources of cultural *power* that the monarchy, the clergy, and the clerisy could wield (the institutionalized patterns of communication, the kinds of legitimacy and authority that competing leaderships could build on, and the communicative and discursive forms that were most accessible to the population) and consider how these are interwoven with political and economic power.

Modernization and Identity

At the same time as the "subject" seemed to disappear in postmodern theory, we have witnessed an explosion of concern about rootedness, centeredness, the re-rise of nationalism, and the reconstruction of identities. We cannot do justice to this huge explosion of theory, other than to explore the utility of issues of individual and collective identity for understanding the Iranian case and the role played by communications in identity formation.

Identity was a major concern of both the development and dependency approaches to communications. Communications and development assumed that mass media would help to legitimize new states and create a sense of national identity. One of the central dimensions of the transition to modernity was felt to be the development of affiliations with and attachments to communities larger than family, locality, tribe, religion. Thus, an acute problem facing "new" nations emerging from colonial domination was the establishment of an "integrative revolution" and a new cohesive identity that would combat the fragmenting forces of previous "primordial" identifications (Geertz, 1973). The implication was that the stable continuity of a formal state requires popular identification with the notion of a "nation" that the state embodied, and media were thought to play a crucial role in developing this sense of "national identity."

Critical models, however, argued that the manner in which mass media have been introduced in Third World countries has frequently posed a threat to preexisting cultural identities without providing coherent alternative systems of values, beliefs, and practices to supersede the past. Modern media may thus be a disintegrating force, undermining the powerful solidarizing meaning of old cultures, and, with a considerable amount of Western cultural products to fill the schedule, may play little role in fostering the new, modern sense of "national identity." This process may lead to extreme cultural anxiety and a desire to return to the values and habits of the past, when things were settled and familiar. In fact, this position became enshrined as a kind of international orthodoxy in the *MacBride Report* (1980: 159), which describes this dilemma neatly: "With the speed and impact of the media explosion, certain harmful effects have been observed. For many people, their conception of reality is obscured or distorted by messages conveyed by the media. The rapid increase in the volume of information and entertainment has brought about a certain degree of homogenisation of different societies while, paradoxically, people can be more cut off from the society in which they live as a result of media penetration into their lives . . . at the extreme, modern media have trampled on traditions and distorted centuries-old socio-economic patterns."

Dependency theorists seemed to separate national political identity from cultural identity and be more concerned with the erosion of the latter than the lack of democratic practice of the former. This orientation produced the irony of the debate for a New International Information Order in which some of the most autocratic states in the Third World denounced Western cultural penetration.

It appears that tradition need not be overwhelmed by processes of modernization, although in the encounter the naive taken-for-granted tradition is irreparably altered when it becomes conscious of itself and seeks to fight external impacts by reclaiming "indigenous" identity. But there is also the danger of an "identity crisis" (Pye, 1971) when the community discovers that what it had unquestioningly accepted as the physical and psychological definitions of its collective self are no longer acceptable under new historical conditions. This could be provoked through internal processes of national reorganization and redefinition (witness the bloody breakup of Yugoslavia) but can also be precipitated from outside as new images and horizons of action circulate. Thus the global cultural and political ecology increasingly impinges on internal politics and notions of collective identity.

One brief example of how nondomestic rhetoric opened up a field of action in Iran would be the human-rights rhetoric of U.S. president Jimmy Carter. Though in itself deeply flawed and limited, indeed at times quite hypocritical, within Iran it suddenly provided a new kind of discursive space to be explored and exploited by secular groups that began publicly to criticize the Shah's dreadful human-rights record and sent letters to Western rights-monitoring organizations (described in detail in chapter 5).

Other theorists have focused on the impact of a Western industrial model of modernity on non-Western cultures. Gellner (1984:viii) describes the predicament quite graphically: "These societies are torn between 'westernization' and . . . populism, that is, the idealization of the local folk tradition . . . The emulation of the developed world flows from the desire to steal its sacred and power-conferring fire; the romanticism of the local tradition, real or imagined, is a consequence of the desire to maintain self-respect, to possess an identity *not* borrowed from abroad, to avoid being a mere imitation, second-rate, a reproduction of an alien model." For both Gellner and Geertz, these two forces—what is local, known, and valued, and what is foreign, modern, and partly desired—are historic processes fought out in the material transformations that the social structures of new states experience. In the case of Iran, we might wryly note that many of the anti-American demonstrators outside the embassy in Tehran wore American T-shirts, and one of the most famous cartoons of the revolution showed a door of the U.S. embassy being opened and an embassy official shouting to a flag-waving demonstrator, "Mr. Hossein, your visa for America is ready now!"

In Iran, one "primordial" identity—religion—came under threat from a number of forces at once: rapid development, a development strategy heavily dependent on the West, and a repressive regime that tried to undermine this traditional identity further. When religion became politicized, it became perhaps abnormally powerful as an ideological/political force, summoning a solidarity that few secular ideologies have been able to challenge.

Yet the notion of "primordial identity" is not transparent or self-evident. Phylogenetically, social identification with religion or tribe occurred historically prior to identification with a "nation," but such identities are themselves "discursive formations," constructs created, maintained, and called upon in various cultures, especially in times of conflict. (And might not gender, omitted from Geertz's list, be ontologically the most primordial?) Thus it is vital to explore which identity is summoned during a period of political mobilization, and how that identity interacts, cancels out, or reinforces other possible collective identities that might be so utilized. For the most part, modernization theorists assumed a relatively unproblematic national identity maintained or manipulated by state structures or structural crisis in which purely political definitions of the polity might be in contention. Indeed, although nation-states as structures have often been taken to be the apotheosis of modernity (Giddens, 1985; Gellner, 1983), that does not mean that the practices of such states reinforce a national identity, or that any such national identity is fully accepted by the peoples bounded by this state structure (Schlesinger, 1991). Rather, as Appadurai (1990) notes, the "nation" and the "state" are each other's projects, and the relations between these two terms and two levels of reality remain complex and problematic, as the numerous regional wars of the early 1990s bloodily attest.

In Anderson's (1983) discussion of the role of print in promoting vernacular languages and hence the rise of national consciousness, he develops the powerful notion of the nation as an "imagined community": "*imagined* because members of even the smallest nation will never know most of their fellow-members, meet them, or even hear of them, yet in the minds of each lives the image of their communion" (15). He suggests that "all communities larger than primordial communities of face-to-face contact (and perhaps even those) are imagined. Communities are not to be distinguished by their falsity/genuineness, but by the style in which they are imagined" (15). The "imagined community" is a discursive structure, developed and argued in and through language, and the particular "national" variety that comes to dominate the political structure may be only the triumphant version in the competition among alternative visions of the collectivity. Anderson focuses on the "birth" of nations, but within any nationally bounded political structure, different versions of the "social imaginary" (Castoriadis, 1987) may constantly compete to define the collectivity.

Iran is not a new political entity, and the Anderson problematic of the emergence of an idea of the "nation" that will ground a new state is not at issue here. Even if the physical boundaries of the Persian empire and the Iranian nation-state have altered over time, some deep and real political continuity exists, played on by the Pahlavi shahs in their reconstruction of 2,500 continual years of monarchy.

Iran was never directly colonized by any single colonial power, yet its history is a history of colonial interventions and external powers vying for influence. This foreign intervention left behind a legacy of "psychological dependency" in Iran, a diffuse mythology of the power of colonial nations sometimes in excess of their actual or even potential role within Iran. The Pahlavi rhetoric of "national identity" was increasingly belied by the actual relations of, and growing social perceptions about, the Pahlavi state, which was restored to power through Western intervention and was highly dependent both economically and culturally on the West. Thus despite itself, and its attempts to develop a nationalist rhetoric and utilize the media for its dissemination, the regime never really enjoyed populist legitimacy. Instead, it came to be seen as the embodiment of antinationalist forces. What became an issue, at a conjunctive moment of crisis for the Pahlavi state, was competition about ways of defining the collectivity—as "nation" (*mellat*) or "community" (*ummat*)—that undermined the state formation. The different versions of collective identity proposed by the royal dictatorship, the clergy, and the clerisy are discussed at length in chapter 6.

Islam came to Iran in the eighth century, and the religious identity of Shiite Islam has dominated since it was established by the Safavids in the sixteenth century as the state religion. Currently, 98 percent of the population is defined/ identified as Shiite (the remaining 2 percent of religious minorities includes Zoroastrians, Jews, Armenians, and Assyrians). Religion provided an extremely "inclusive" identity, which actually overflowed national boundaries into the broad concept of the *ummat*, the community, of Islam beyond Iran, a religio-imperialism that has come to frighten the West.

Orthodox approaches to modernization failed to comprehend and thus underestimated the power of traditional cultural, particularly religiously derived, identities. The cultural crisis that contemporary modernization brings was also underestimated. While traditional allegiances may be fragmenting forces, they may also become powerful influences for national cohesion; a so-called primordial identity might actually share boundaries with the nation-state identity and be a more popular basis of collective identity than the latter, as Shiism came to challenge the modernizing rhetoric of monarchical Iran.

What has also been overlooked in modernization paradigms—and in their critical opposite, "cultural imperialism"—is the potential boomerang effect of Western cultural penetration and dependent development, which may operate to undermine (not legitimate) a state formation. Here an "identity" crisis may take on both political and cultural dimensions. It is an internal crisis of the state, with internal political competitors, but it is also a rejection of external influence on that state, so that the claims for alternative collectivities take on enormous resonance. Islam could be claimed as an indigenous cultural identity that had not been contaminated by foreign cultural values and which had historically acted as a defense mechanism against alien cultural penetration, as in the Tobacco Revolt at the turn of the twentieth century, and had long warned of its dangers.

"Traditional Society" and Retraditionalization

The general assumption that the less traditional a society is, the more it is capable of sustained growth may be incorrect. The disruption of traditional lifestyle may lead to disorganization, anomie, and alienation; the adoption of modernizing institutions and lifeways also implies acquiring their various social pathologies. Further, the Third World manifests a lack of codevelopment of the various social spheres. For example, India presents low social mobilization but still maintains a viable modern polity. Iran under the last shah had rapid urbanization and a high level of exposure to mass media, but exhibited low political development. Frequently there is disjuncture between the political and economic spheres, so any typology of codevelopment based on a heavily idealized Western experience simply does not fit the historical experiences of Third World nations.

For both modernization and dependency paradigms, tradition often appears as a hypostatization to be altered (toward modernity) or protected (as some frozen authenticity) but rarely does it appear as a live cultural response to the current global environment. Tradition can be mobilized, politicized, utilized in defense of some putative "indigenous" identity (which can, of course, be the site of intense local disputation), a process that is necessary only when the tradition is already brought into question and alternative discourses are available. This is what Geertz (1973: 219) calls "ideological retraditionalization," the politicization of tradition to combat forces that seek to weaken and dissolve it. This process cannot be a naive "return to tradition," for the context has eliminated the possibility of naive recuperation; rather, retraditionalization is a self-conscious defense of traditional norms. Bourdieu (1962) recognized this process as part and parcel of the colonial experience, specifically French colonialism in Algeria. He argues that "traditional traditionalism meant following a tradition that was considered . . . the only possible tradition" (1962: 155), whereas the discovery of the existence of another tradition leads to a new understanding of one's own tradition as merely one choice among several, or as conventional and arbitrary as all the others. When the colonial power attempts to impose its cultural patterns, a language of refusal develops, expressed in symbolic fashion; for example, women's wearing of the veil signals the emergence of a "new traditionalism" as a culture of resistance.

Arjomand (1984: 195) has termed this process simply "traditionalism," which he neatly describes as designating "the type of social thought, action or movement which arises when a tradition becomes self-conscious either in missionary rivalry with competing traditions or in the face of a serious threat of erosion or extinction emanating from its socio-political or cultural environment." This develops in conscious opposition to a rival set of beliefs and mode of conduct, and tradition is idealized against the alien norms of the rival belief system. Arjomand argues that such traditionalism in twentieth-century Iran "has been a general movement for the defence of Islam against Western influence led by the Shi'ite ulema" (1984: 197).

The Shiite *ulama* are part of a descending class (Germani, 1981) for whom time was running out; they had to mobilize to protect their own influence and the traditional socioreligious life they embodied. In political and ideological terms, the "use of tradition is an instrument rich in possibilities for the manipulation of the popular masses still recently incorporated into industrial society, still bearing traditional attitudes, and who, above all, continue moving for the most part within the norms corresponding to this traditional ascendant type of society" (Germani, 1981: 172). Clearly, the clergy manipulated an identity of politicized Islam for its own interests, and when the "tradition" in question is a holistic religious culture central to definitions of individual and social identity, its politicization is likely to have enormous coercive power. Yet we will argue that the destruction of a civil society with a public sphere under Mohammad Reza Pahlavi meant any other more progressive/modern collective identities were very weakly elaborated.

The utility of a notion of "retraditionalization" is that it overcomes any simple bifurcation of tradition and modernity, and instead throws light on the complex interplay between the two, suggesting how and why traditional culture becomes the font of reconstructed political identities. It also begins to make problematic some of the new rhetoric of international communications, such as an easy support for "authentic" "indigenous" cultures. Long histories of cultural contact complicate the excavation of the "authentic" culture, and its moment of constitution as a political pole against Westernizing influence is also its moment of reconstitution into a new phenomenon, one that already partakes of hybridization and synchronization.

Religion and Ideology as Political Discourses

In this process of "retraditionalization," religion itself is irrevocably altered as it enters the fray of ideological politics. Some theorists have argued a radical separation between religion and ideology, suggesting that the latter is a particular form of modern political discourse. Gouldner (1976: 23) writes, "The ideological mobilization of masses (like the use of ideology as a basis for social solidarities) premises a detraditionalization of society and of communication, of what is allowed to be brought into open discussion, to be sought and claimed." He differentiates ideology from religion by the kinds of claims each makes and by the greater rationality of the former's arguments. Thus "ideology is a very special sort of rational discourse by reason of its world-referring claims. It defends its policies neither by traditionalistic legitimation nor by invoking faith or revelation. As a historical object then, ideology differs from both religion and metaphysics in that it is concerned to make 'what is' in society a basis for action" (31).

The post-Enlightenment concern with the development of science and the growth of reason was helped by the creation of a class of intellectuals no longer dependent on patronage or inheritance of their livelihood. The liberal, middle-class backgrounds of the emergent intelligentsia determined the unreligious nature of the new ideologies, so that, for example, "the language, the symbolism, the costume of 1789 are purely non-Christian" (Hobsbawm, 1977: 26). Hobsbawm goes on to argue that if the intellectual leadership of the French Revolution had stemmed more from the masses who actually brought it about, then doubtless its ideology would have shown more signs of traditionalism. Tradition maintained the power of both church and monarchy, and confirmed people in their old communities. Ideology, however, conjured up abstract ideas and new solidarities, most obviously of nation or class, which lay beyond the ordinary experience of everyday life and the particularist ties of family, religion, and locality. Turning to Gouldner again: "Ideology serves to uproot people; to further uproot the uprooted, to extricate them from immediate and traditional social structure . . . thus enabling persons to pursue projects they have chosen. Ideologies thus clearly contribute, at least in these ways, both to rational discourse and rational politics" (1976: 25).

Political activity that does not fit into such a contemporary "ideological" mold has been called "pre-democratic" (Apter, 1965) or even "pre-political" (Hobsbawm, 1959). Yet all these arguments seem very Eurocentric, being based solely on the European experience and its particular set of relations between the political and economic spheres, the emergent bourgeoisie developing new forms of participatory politics. Bracketing the issue of how "rational" were and are politics in the West, it is clear that different conditions operate in the political spheres of the Third World. Specifically, Iran's autocratic monarchy, weak development of an independent bourgeoisie, and consequent lack of political development have meant the inadequate institutionalization of channels of participation and their lack of autonomy from the state (Zonis, 1971; Abrahamian, 1982). Even as late as the 1970s there was a poorly developed political-party structure and no public sphere for political debate, all such activities being completely circumscribed by the state. Secular ideologies, and a secular intelligentsia to articulate such ideologies, were weakly rooted in Iranian life, while religious tradition was well established and deeply valued, offering a long history of opposition to monarchical power (Akhavi, 1980; Fischer, 1980a). Rather than seeing religion and ideology as radically different forms of political discourse, in the Iranian case it is perhaps more useful to view them both as forms of politics within the actually existing Iranian environment and try to examine the various resources each could muster in their struggles against the state and against each other. The period from 1977 to 1979 is a moment of real political encounter in Iran, with a clashing of ideological claims about the nature of Iranian society, its history, and its future. The claimants weigh in with very unequal resources and borrow and steal from each other's discourses in the competition for leadership in the popular movement. Indeed, the comparative "lack of development" of the political sphere in Iran is typical of many Third World states supported by the West, in which economic modernization was always given a far higher priority than democratization or participation in political life. The "disjunctures" internally between these spheres are as significant as the international "disjunctures" of cultural values in explaining the actual dynamics of the Iranian revolution.

The media developed in politically consensual societies in the West, and thus have tended to support political legitimacy. In the Third World, however, where the legitimacy of regimes is still an issue and where institutions and mechanisms of participation are not established, the media as state organs may lack credibility and even in the diffusion of Western contents serve to delegitimize the regime. Although there was considerable attention to and investment in the national reach of mass media in Iran, it never created the legitimacy that the Shah aspired to and, despite Iran's ancient history, national identity as defined by the Pahlavis did not become the prime identification for most Iranians (Cottam, 1984).

Ayatollah Khomeini returned to Iran in a jumbo jet, having mobilized a popular movement using international telephone connections and portable cassette recorders. This movement was no simple return to medieval times as some detractors argue, but a contemporary revolution with a religious face.

Big Media's Role in Creating an Identity Crisis

Part of the process of dependency is the creation of mythology about the power of developed nations, about what constitutes development, about the "modernity" of other nations, about their higher level of economic well-being, social organization, and cultural taste. Radio and television are far more subtle carriers of ideology than a state propaganda unit, because they infiltrate private space with an illusion of being value-free, yet establish very powerful mythologies.

Electronic media brought the world into Iranian homes—the strange, skewed world represented in imported Western television programs, with their images of violence, sexual explicitness, and consumer durables. Soekarno once claimed that Hollywood was a revolutionary force because its films presented to the Third World the economic lifestyles of the developed world, precipitating "rising aspirations." In Iran, secular intellectuals also pointed to the legal and judicial systems, the educational system, and the health-care systems that were the backdrops to the narrative plots as the real structures of development that Iran badly lacked. "Relative deprivation" has frequently been proffered as an explanatory cause of revolutionary mobilization; that is, the idea that needs are not absolute but rather that economic and social well-being is based on some subjective/collective assessment and acceptance of one's own situation in comparison to others (Runciman, 1966). Such "comparison" has typically been thought of in single-nation terms, as comparisons between social classes within one society. The spread of television and film, however, with their colored pictures of life elsewhere, implies that if this model of comparative well-being has any validity, it is now being conducted on a global, not national, level. The global flow of peoples is predominantly into the advanced industrialized countries, producing severe brain-drain effects in many Third World nations, but not everyone either can or wants to leave home.

Some Iranians argued for a more coherent policy of development with the establishment of basic infrastructure like that enjoyed by the West, and they used the television images as political examples in popular debates. Others, namely the politicized clergy following Khomeini, argued that the media were pernicious and corrupting, eroding indigenous identity and part and parcel of the continuing dependency of Iran on the West. These themes are elaborated in chapter 6. There were many different reactions to media and its content in Iran. Perhaps most crucially, both orthodox and critical perspectives lack a theory of the relationship between modernizing and conservative tendencies; they lack accurate models of the political dynamic of identity politics and of how "tradition" is in itself altered. Each perspective underestimates the continuing role and enduring power of indigenous structures and institutions of culture and communication. The Iranian experience seems to show that traditional communications networks may remain embedded in the social life of the community, and traditional opinion leaders are likely to maintain if not increase their vitality and credibility. Also, the assumption that "traditional" and "modern" systems of communication each represent a completely autonomous communication system is shown to be wrong in Iran. New media technologies do not simply replace what has gone before; rather, older forms alter in relation to the new. In Iran complex and integrated communications structures have existed at various moments of contemporary history, as during the constitutional revolution at the turn of the century or under Mossadeq in the 1950s. The extremely bifurcated communications and cultural structures under the last Pahlavi shah were a regression from a more vibrant political culture. Thus, what is often referred to as Iran's "dualistic culture" (Tehranian, 1980; Keddie, 1983; Arjomand, 1978) was not the result of an "automatic" process but the consequence of a centralized and repressive modernizing strategy.

In the end, the dynamic of the Iranian revolution seems to prove both developmentalist and dependency models wrong. The media did not serve to support economic development and political participation, partly because the regime controlled the latter, but neither was the population overwhelmed by alien values and habits. Both models tended to see Third World audiences as homogenous and passive, absorbing foreign values and losing authentic identity, albeit one perspective saw this as the necessary costs of modernization and the other critiqued this negative process of dependency. Media scholars have only recently started serious research about the non-Western audience with empirical work on the impact of Western programs on other peoples (Liebes and Katz, 1990; Kottak, 1990; Straubhaar, 1981). In Iran, broadcasting linked outlying regions and their mass of tiny villages (estimated to be in the range of 69,000) to urban centers, specifically Tehran. Radio and television actually constructed a national audience, connecting people through information and images to the national project. It created a mass audience, though not quite a mass public, but it also, through the large amount of imported material, altered the spatial environment, linking Iranian villages to the "global village" with outcomes that no one had foreseen or intended. Thus the media contributed to the deep identity crisis Iran experienced in its process of rapid but dependent development, and precipitated a traditionalist backlash to "protect" older identities. A popular and powerful rhetoric of anti-imperialism railed against a cultural flow that Iranians perceived as motivated to further undermine their sense of self.

Yet although a return to tradition might satisfy some identity needs, it does not necessarily resolve any of the other issues involved in the Iranian crisis, such as economic inequality, political repression, and independent development. In fact, the experiences under the Islamic Republic suggest quite the opposite. Therefore we must also critique the rather simplistic demand for the preservation of indigenous culture that was promoted as the solution to imbalanced global flows of cultural products and that became one of the central precepts of the New International Information Order debate. Arguments for the preservation of cultural identity and maintenance of cultural autonomy have resounded through international debates and forums, often espoused by autocratic states. Herein lies the problem: by focusing so intensely on the potential impact of cultural products from outside, less emphasis is given to the promotion of political democracy and cultural diversity within Third World states. As the Iranian case shows, a collective need for cultural identity might be satisfied, but only at enormous cost to other, equally significant needs.

If we seem to have strayed very far from the Alborz Mountains, whose snowy peaks give us a good vantage point for surveying Iranian political and cultural life, to arrive in very abstract territory, it is not hard to return to Iran. What we want to do in this volume is to give a concrete, historically grounded account and analysis of one nation's insertion into the modern world system and explain how both its structural crisis and its identity crisis have to be understood within such a global framework. We will show how the two crises mutually provoke and produce each other. Part of this account is a socially grounded analysis of cultural power, which involves looking at various kinds of cultural resources, including the institutional power and media resources of different social formations. It also requires examining their discursive practices, which implies the social familiarity of their language, the mode of delivery, the collective historical memory and tropes that can be drawn upon, and the ideological space that can be claimed. We need to locate and root the rhetoric of the Iranian revolution in the "habitus" (Bourdieu, 1977) or the lived collective experience of Iranian social life as well as explore the scope of the spontaneous reinvention of political life that blossomed in 1977–79. We propose a political-economic analysis of cultural revolution.

Chapter 2
Small Media and Revolutionary Change:
A New Model

The particular dynamics of the Iranian revolution, and the many unexpected political experiences of the past few decades, suggest a need and give us the basis for a new model of contemporary revolutionary mobilization that is significantly different from previous dynamics of revolutionary upheaval. Mediated culture has become part of the causal sequence of revolutionary crisis, as well as central to revolutionary process.

All revolutionary movements are creative evolving processes that write their own scripts, even as they draw inspiration from older revolutionary movements. This is especially the case for the non-Western political movements that developed within repressive state structures since the 1970s. There was no precedent for such movements, no model that came close to the existing conditions in the Third World in the 1970s or Eastern Europe in the late 1980s. Indeed, the nature of such repressive systems—whether dominated by party, monarch, or self-proclaimed dictator—was such that most opportunities for typical formally organized political activity had been blocked, so that political transformation seemed next to impossible.

Yet suddenly, at the end of the 1970s, there was revolution in Iran and Nicaragua, popular mobilization in the Philippines, and then, a decade later, the collapse of the Soviet Union and the unprecedented upheavals in Eastern Europe. All revolutionary processes are political processes, whether or not there are underlying economic causes and/or demands. Thus all revolutions are also communicative processes, including the articulation of sometimes-competing ideologies and demands, the development of leaders and followers, the circulation of information, the exhortations to participation and mobilization. Popular mythology might think of the storming of the Bastille as the revolutionary act, but in fact much of the politicizing and argumentation, the reading and writing, the persuading and criticizing, that went before were as much if not more "political" than the final dramatic acts of violence. Revolution has rarely been thought of in communications terms. For example, only recently, with the flourish of publishing that not only celebrates but also rethinks the French Revolution of 1789, have media forms and communicative networks been set at the center of its analysis. Darnton and Roche (1989: xii) write that historians have generally "treated the printed word as a record of what happened instead of an ingredient in the happening. But the printing press helped shape the events it recorded. It was an active force in history . . . we have never attempted to understand how the dominant means of communication in the most powerful country of the West contributed to the first great revolution of modern times."

In the contemporary world, media are part of political problems and part of the solutions, essential elements of repressive political structures as well as vehicles for their overthrow. Media can be used by states to establish their definitions of the political, their versions of history; they are part of the ideological state apparatus, the forces of repression. At the same time, media can be the tools of popular mobilization, they can maintain alternative histories and promote oppositional culture—in short, they constitute the resources and forms of expression of popular movements. Especially within repressive regimes, when there appears to be no public space for "political" activity, media foster the politicization of the "cultural." Media can no longer (if they ever could) be left out of analysis of the process of political transformation known as revolution. Timothy Garton Ash (1990: 94) wrote of the revolutionary year of 1989 that "in Europe at the end of the twentieth century all revolutions are telerevolutions." At issue is how certain forms of media can function to support popular mobilization, particularly within repressive contexts.

The Problem of Defining "Small Media"

"Small media" has become a popular rubric for various kinds of mediated alternatives to state-run broadcasting systems, but the definition of non-mass media has never been very precise. From Schramm's (1972) attempts to define "big" and "little" media, to definitions of "group media" (*Media Development*, 1981), "community media" (Wade, 1981; Byram, 1981), or "radical" media (Downing, 1984), what has been crucial is a notion of these media as participatory, public phenomena, controlled neither by big states nor big corporations. Thus the distinction between "big" and "small" cannot depend on particular kinds of technologies or even on their putative audiences, but rather on the manner of use of all technologies. Even broadcast media could have a different shape, as suggested by Brecht (1930) over sixty years ago:

> Radio should be converted from a distribution system to a communication system. Radio could be the most wonderful public communication system imaginable, a gigantic system of channels—could be, that is, if it were capable not only of transmitting but of receiving, or making the listener not only hear but also speak, not of isolating him, but of connecting him. This means that radio would have to give up being a purveyor and organise the listener as purveyor.

This is an activist model for the "emancipatory use" of the media (Enzensberger, 1970), which focuses on popular involvement rather than on professional production, on horizontal rather than vertical communication, and on active participation in meaning-making rather than the passive absorption of mass-mediated culture and values. Of course, in Western democracies locally based and organized, nonprofit, participatory forms are many and various. They include local/free newspapers, community radio and television channels, citizens' video, community computers, and so on (Downing, 1984; Jankowski et al., 1992). Such media projects are developed by pressure groups, political organizations, counterculture aficionados, and local communities and minority groups.

These alternative, participatory media forms not only satisfy demands for different contents, catering to tastes, interests, and orientations not catered to by mass-media output and sometimes challenging that output, but are also vehicles for direct participation in the mediated communications process and for the extension of the voices of groups and ideas otherwise not heard. The very existence of this non-mass-media environment is a measure of the vibrancy of a democratic society. Downing (1984: 2) stresses the importance of self-managed dissonant media, which "have posed a genuine alternative to the media patterns of both West and East."

The kind of media use described might be covered under Fathi's (1979) rubric of "public communication." This shifts focus to an autonomous sphere of activity independent of the state, the popular production of messages, a public coming into being and voicing its own "opinion" in opposition to state-orchestrated voices; to the use of channels and technologies that are readily accessible and available; and to messages that are in the main produced and distributed freely as opposed to private/corporate production for profit or control by state organizations. Jankowski et al. (1992) call such media "the people's voice," although "people's voices" might be more apt. Throughout this volume the rubrics of "public communication" (as distinct from state or private communication) and "small media" (as a counter to the "big media" power of states or corporations) will be used interchangeably to cover the wide stock of mediated cultural resources in different settings that can be utilized to conscientize, politicize, and mobilize popular revolutionary movements.

Alternate Channels and Political Challenge

The acknowledgment of the power of small media in political movements has been slow to develop, but that does not mean that this is a new phenomenon. On the contrary, an enormous range of channels has been used in a variety of historic contexts to agitate, politicize, and mobilize.

The printing press has played a vital role as an agent of social change and democratic politics in the West (Eisenstein, 1979) as in the English civil war (Stone, 1972) and the American and French revolutions (Davidson, 1941; Darnton, 1979). As has been well documented (Speier, 1950; Habermas 1989; Gouldner, 1978), the emergence of a "public sphere" was heavily dependent on print materials and suggests a crucial relationship between literacy, political participation, and democracy. The Third World experience has been quite different, however, often because state support for electronic media has been greater than support for universal literacy.

In some twentieth-century revolutions, formal party organization has been the central carrier of revolutionary ideology, with strong emphasis on charismatic authority. Both the Soviet and Chinese revolutions utilized innovative forms to mobilize and indoctrinate; Trotsky's propaganda train and the rapid production of Soviet film, Mao's little red book and Madame Mao's operas, the use of political poetry and wall posters (*tatzepao*) are all well known.

In the contemporary development of popular movements against strong states we face a new model of revolutionary mobilization. Its mode of participation is extensive—mass— but low level; its ideology is populist and profoundly antistatist. Indeed, that ingredient provides the glue for the populist solidarity that is rapidly manifest. Most groups in the society become convinced that the first and necessary step in change is the removal or fundamental alteration of the existing state structure. In Iran, because the royalist despotism of the Shah was associated with Western neocolonialism and dependency, anti-Westernism was a key ideological notion.

The forms of organization are creative and spontaneous, based on a mix of small media and traditional networks rather than on formal parties or organized unions. The dynamic is predominantly urban. Recent events saw mass demonstrations in Beijing, East Berlin, Bucharest, Budapest, and Prague—not in the outlying countryside. Leading activists and major participants were students and intellectuals (as in Iran, the People's Republic of China, Czechoslovakia, and Romania), not the peasantry. In the cases of Iran, the Philippines, and Poland, religious organizations and religious leadership also were significant. Although members of the urban working class participated in the mass demonstrations and rallies, their organizations were not central to the process; it was really only in Poland that an older form of political organization, a trade union, evolved into the more encompassing structure of Solidarity and came to play the crucial role in a struggle that lasted much longer than many of the more precipitous events of 1989. These movements suggest new forms of populist solidarity to achieve major political change, at least temporarily, although many of these tenuous coalitions splinter as soon as the immediate shared goal is achieved.

In all these recent movements, the distribution of various kinds of small media and the ability to produce and disseminate messages, often through electronic means, was key. Thus, these movements reflect a certain level of economic development and spread of consumer durables, even within contexts of otherwise extreme economic dislocation and shortages, as in Poland and Romania. Often, this communications hardware has been smuggled in illegally, against existing state regulations. This process may also simply involve the shift in use of ordinary media from predominantly entertainment purposes to function as centers of political persuasion and mobilization. These situations reflected strong states with elaborate forces of coercion and persuasion, and powerful, centrally controlled mass media, with almost no possibilities for alternative political mobilization. The final dynamic of populist mobilization in these circumstances was comparatively brief yet immensely powerful, often fueled rather than quashed by regime violence against the participants.

Small Media and Revolutionary Mobilization

In this section we will suggest some problematics that a model of small media needs to address to help elucidate and explain their crucial role in political mobilization in repressive contexts.

Small Media as Political Public Space

> *The wall is the voice of a people shouting.*
> Omar Cabezas
> (quoted in Mattelart, 1986: 37)

The essence of repressive societies is that political activity is severely restricted, and as part of that restriction comes a control over public communication. Although there are important analytic differences between one-party systems and authoritarian systems, in practice the recent experience of living under each has been remarkably similar, particularly with the development of sophisticated information technologies of surveillance and large modern bureaucracies. In China and Eastern Europe, the single Communist party has dominated, defining the political sphere, operating the state-controlled mass media, and running super-efficient secret-police networks. In Iran, a royalist dictatorship created the single political party, the mass media were state-controlled, and the secret police, SAVAK, monitored all public activity. One-party systems have sometimes been thought of as highly "mobilized," yet a more accurate analysis reveals a cadre of highly mobilized and motivated people, the party members (who often constituted not more than 15 percent of the population), and the rest of the population. In Iran, the level of political mobilization was very low until the Shah changed strategy in the mid-1970s and developed a single party and attempted a popular mobilization, which backfired. In such big-state, big-media environments, the possibilities for the more familiar elements of democratic participatory political organization, such as political groups and parties, unions and interest groups with their regular and open meetings, and an independent political press or electronic media, were utterly circumscribed.

As Barrington Moore (1978: 482) argued, "for any social and moral transformation to get under way there appears to be one prerequisite that underlies all . . . *social and cultural space* within the prevailing order." In Iran, however, a public sphere of autonomous, citizen-directed, participatory debate functioning independently of the state appeared not to exist. This sphere is essentially a communicative environment in which people can freely voice opinion, gather to debate, and create politics. Yet political resistance developed, somewhere in the interstices and crevices of such systems. But where? Here the potential for small media to act as a resource of resistance, a tool of revolutionary mobilization, exists, in the carving out and occupation of such oppositional "space."

As potential sites of struggle, as carriers of already-familiar forms of communication and symbol systems, as structures that are embedded in everyday life and very hard to control, small media and cultural resistance offer fertile ground. Media function as a "virtual space" that temporarily connects people through the use of shared printed material, visual slogans, or electronic broadcasts. In situations where people are disallowed somatic solidarity—to physically assemble, demonstrate, march—small media can help to foster an imaginative social solidarity, often as the precursor for actual physical mobilization. Thus they are vitally important resources for mobilization (Tilly, 1978).

If the party was the means to political change in Russia in 1917 and in China in 1948, it was also the major means of political control and orthodoxy in communist regimes. Given the massive top-heavy bureaucratized structure of the party with enormous reach into ordinary life that evolved in both societies, opposition within such systems had to be particularly subtle and creative. In the comparatively silent world of state socialism, small media have been crucial in the reestablishment of "horizontal linkages" against the "Soviet pyramid" (Liehm, in Downing, 1984: 310). In Eastern Europe as in the Soviet Union, the counterpoint to state surveillance and state-run media was the powerful networks of samizdat and *magnetizdat*. Occasional, small circulation and clumsily produced materials were, in this highly censored context, of direct political significance in developing a public sphere. "Books, irregularly appearing periodicals, almost illegible newssheets, retyped lectures, 'public' gatherings of 80 people squashed inside a single apartment, 'public' lectures attended by 120 people: these are potent reconstructions of an oppositional public realm" (Downing, 1984: 308).

Sometimes the reclaiming of actual public space is more overt. As Rothschuh Villanueva and Cabezas show for Nicaragua (in Mattelart, 1986), various indigenous forms of cultural expression became part of the popular cultural opposition. Walls of city streets became the canvas of a political movement, the means of communication of the masses as well as ways for organized political groups to communicate with the masses, providing a voice for the people. There was danger if one was caught creating these public messages, but usually guards painted out slogans or poured black tar over them—and they would then be repainted. "The fundamental forms of communication of the FSLN with the masses were leaflets, flyers, 'pintas' [wall graffiti], the seizure of radio stations, its own propaganda linked to each of its battles, and the counterculture which grew throughout the war of liberation. On the walls in various cities in the country, one can still read the war slogans and the calls to insurrection. Flyers containing the denunciation of assassinations were covertly distributed on the buses, and the messages stuck to the lips of the people" (Rothschuh Villanueva in Mattelart, 1986: 34). Similarly, in Iran city walls revealed the ongoing struggle with tatters of posters, whitewash over old slogans, and ever-new slogans, a public dance of speaking and silencing. Public space potentially heralded a public sphere.

In Iran no public sphere existed. The royalist dictatorship controlled directly or indirectly all forms of expression while SAVAK, the security organization, surveilled all public life. No autonomous political parties, independent labor unions, or interest groups were allowed (this is expanded in chapter 5). Such control sounds like a state socialist or fascist regime, but even those regimes are typically far more politically mobilized than was Iran. The royalist dictatorship was a particularly repressive form of authoritarian system, and there appeared to be no space within which any kind of oppositional, popular movement could launch itself.

Yet the dynamics of recent movements and the role of small media suggest we have operated with a far too narrow definition of the "political public sphere," using this term in a very formalist and delimited manner and often obscuring the relationships between communication, culture, and politics. The apparent "lack" of formal organizations such as parties and unions, and the apparent "lack" of public opinion because little measurement of opinion existed are taken as the absence of politics. But politics in Iran has always been more fluid, more informal, and more invisible than the organized politics of the established democracies, revealing another blind spot of a narrowly Western optic. There have always been informal political circles (*dowreh*) and gatherings of known individuals based on familiarity and trust developed over time (Bill, 1972; Zonis, 1971), but there was little sense in the public arena that such political groups were growing, articulate, or effective. Chapter 5 elaborates on the renewal of *dowrehs* and other informal groupings in 1977, in the buildup to the revolution, as well as on the other social spaces that became sites for political discourse.

In Iran, as in Poland, the Philippines, and elsewhere, public "space" could also be found within the religious networks. The religious leadership often possessed far more extensive and far more culturally appropriate resources for mobilization than did the secular intelligentsia. The resources of the religious leadership in Iran included a nationwide network of physical spaces—the mosques—that were points of public assembly, the only such network not penetrated by the state. The extant traditional network and the repoliticization of popular culture is the subject of chapter 5.

Small Media: Technologies for Political Survival

In Iran, new technologies of communication also helped to open up a potential public sphere of dissent. Small media such as audiotapes became electronic extensions of the religious institutions and its political discourse, and photocopied leaflets were the preferred weapon of the secular groupings, giving voice to what was to become an enormous popular movement.

The argument that political mobilization depends on developing political resources, usually some form of public communication, is not new. What is significant is that at certain moments, and more and more with the spread of certain technologies, control is impossible, even within the most repressive, security-oriented states. This is so for two main reasons: the nature of new communications technologies, and the development of international communications systems and international reception of messages. It is increasingly difficult even for the most repressive regime to control political communications. Many strong states have tried at times to control directly the importation and circulation of certain media technologies (personal computers and satellite dishes in the former Soviet Union, for example) or to impose economic barriers (such as the severe tax on videocassette players in India) (Ganley and Ganley, 1987; Boyd et al., 1989). Yet borders are leaky, smugglers adaptive, and popular interest and demand for media technologies generally high.

Certain technologies carry within themselves the means for reproduction, making control an even more difficult task. Key to the success of some recent movements or to the longevity of others has been the technical fact that contemporary small media—particularly audio- and videocassettes, xerography, personal computers, and fax machines—are the source of multiple points of production and distribution. Audiocassette systems, video recording, and Polaroid photography, for example, require no independent processing techniques but contain within the hardware the possibility of instant production and reproduction of messages. Anyone can reproduce such messages, and indeed the dynamics of movements depend precisely on each participant's making additional copies and spreading them around. Thus, Soviet samizdat would be typed and retyped in multiple copies to the extent of carbon-copy legibility by anyone who could do so. In Poland the underground network was created by KOR (Committee for Workers' Self-Defense) with signed communiqués that publicized the struggles of workers and intellectuals, and carried the exhortation that "by disseminating this bulletin you are acting within your rights, and playing a part in their defense. Read it, copy it, and pass it on" (quoted in Downing, 1984: 326). Xerography not only makes light of such tedious work but also offers an advance over various printing processes because it produces instant and virtually untraceable copy (absent the most sophisticated forensic science) from potentially multiple sources so that the loss of one machine does not imply the demise of an entire movement. The good old days when smashing the printing press meant the end of radical agitation are long gone. The networking of personal computers and on-line information systems offers similar possibilities of uncontrollable multipoint production and dissemination of messages. Unfortunately the political right has jumped to use such channels, as the use of computer networks by racist groups in the United States and the circulation of anti-Semitic computer games in Austria attest.

In Poland, the opposition movement graduated from the classic samizdat method of reproduction based on typewriter and carbon copies to the recycling of antiquated duplicators, photocopiers, and offset lithography to create the technological tools of the underground network. Cassette tapes of the Gdansk negotiations circulated through factories. The political police spent a considerable part of its time trying to repress this growing underground small-media movement, and even a year after martial law had been imposed its squads seized over a million leaflets, silenced eleven radio transmitters, found 380 printing shops, and confiscated nearly 500 typewriters (C. Civic, quoted by Downing, 1984: 327). Independent media work still continued, however. Within the Polish context, these self-managed media created new spaces for public argument and debate, independent of the power structure, and proved to be important first steps in the giant movement that ensued. As Downing notes, "no alternative communication channel should be written off simply because it is small" (345).

The availability of certain of these technologies is in itself an indication of the level of technical modernity achieved in a society. Fax machines in Chinese cities, used to dramatic effect during the Tiananmen Square uprising, are a direct outcome of the modernization strategy adopted after the death of Mao in 1976. The wide spread of such electronic consumer durables as cassette players inside Iran is not without its irony. Technological diffusion has been at the heart of the dominant paradigm of development, and technological dependency is the lived experience for many Third World countries. The contradictions of a movement based on anti-imperialist slogans and nurturing a long-standing cultural identity that makes use of technologies delivered by Western and Japanese manufacturers further demonstrate the complexity of the problematic of development. The tension between admiration and hostility toward Western technology is frequently solved by the Third World nation's coming to consider the technology as neutral, as not in itself embodying values or altering mind-sets. The Iranian popular movement was delighted to have an array of sophisticated technologies available for its use, and even the Islamic Republic has reflected little on the real social impacts of technological diffusion.

In Iran it was interesting to see how the function of certain technologies shifted from one of bureaucratic control to one of political participation. Before the popular movement developed, the use of photocopy machines even for university teaching was heavily controlled. The simplest reproduction of a diagram or set of figures for classroom use was a major procedure in universities, requiring multiple signatures and often taking so long that the need had passed by the time permission was granted. Come the movement, and a sea change occurred! The photocopy machine at Iran Communications and Development Institute (ICDI), for example, where Annabelle worked, became the hub of activity; its operator was a key political actor in the evolving movement, and the different fellow travelers of various political factions would vie for access to the machine. Other researchers who worked at ICDI during the revolution have noted the same phenomenon (Green, 1982).

Small Media in the Global Context

Another factor that profoundly complicates the issue of "control" of the national political environment is the spread of international communications, which has collapsed global space, promoted an immense speedup of historical processes, and eroded the container effects of national boundaries (Giddens, 1990).

There are always lengthy debates about the "first moment" of revolutionary processes, but at the end of the twentieth century it seems that when the will exists, popular mobilization can be astonishingly spontaneous and rapid, given the number of strong states that cracked open at the end of the 1980s. The instant dissemination around the world of information and images about political change also fosters a possible "contagion effect" of popular political upheavals that is thus stronger than ever. One of the most notable elements of the 1989 events, as with the Iranian movement, was the comparatively open access that international television and press crews had to the sites of political activity. The main televisual news agencies, Visnews and UPITN, and the television networks such as CNN and others, sell their news footage to many other stations, so that the dramatic live coverage of the unfolding movements centering on Tianamen Square, around the Brandenburg Gate, in Wenceslas Square, in Budapest and in Bucharest, would be seen throughout the world. This truly was revolution while the whole world was watching. In regard to the revolutions in Eastern Europe, Ash (1990: 78, 126) had predicted that "in Poland it took ten years, in Hungary ten months, in East Germany ten weeks; perhaps in Czechoslovakia it will take ten days." The ten days turned out to be twenty-four, but the demonstration effects and the speedup of history appear to be real processes, partly explainable by the extensive media coverage of what had happened in the other countries.

By the 1980s, with much of the globe caught in a snare of underwater cables and fiber optics, satellite footprints and shortwave transmissions, telecommunications, fax, and mail, national boundaries are porous. Many people living within strong states are able to pick up foreign media messages at the turn of a dial. Estonians could regularly receive Finnish television, and southerners in Guangdong Province in the People's Republic of China can watch Hong Kong television. An international cacophony of nations broadcasts internationally in nonnative languages (Head, 1985), often using shortwave radio reception (Soley, 1987). There is an active international underground traffic in cassette tapes, videotapes, and all kinds of print media into situations where such media are restricted for political or moral reasons (Ganley and Ganley, 1982; Boyd et al., 1989; Sreberny-Mohammadi and Mohammadi, 1987); the underground may be driven by a mix of commercial and political reasons.

International communications can play complex roles in domestic political upheavals. First, it has profoundly altered the nature of political exile. Exiled political activists no longer wait for events to change so that they can return home, but instead can propagandize to change conditions from outside their country, a deterritorialization of politics (Shain, 1987; Sreberny-Mohammadi and Mohammadi, 1987). There is considerable international clandestine radio broadcasting (Soley, 1987), as well as the documented beginnings of exile videography: Polish exiles in Paris smuggled videotapes *into* Poland, and Czech activists smuggled tapes of illegal demonstrations and state-orchestrated violence *out* of the country. Members of the Iranian exile community, both before and after the revolution, produced an enormous amount of political literature and broadcasting, altering the new environment in which they sojourned as much as they attempted to alter conditions back "home."

Not only do exiles send materials home, but as political actors they can try to mobilize international public opinion to take up their case in international public forums such as the United Nations. A large part of the function of groups such as Amnesty International and Human Rights Watch is to alert international public opinion about rights violations within specific countries and to mobilize resources to effect change. As we will detail in chapter 6, the Iranian secular middle-class political groups tried hard to utilize various international channels to mobilize international public opinion in their favor, and achieved some modicum of success.

Occasionally, such international communication actually benefits or links political elements *within* a nation who otherwise cannot communicate or even know of each other's existence. Here, the international linkage becomes a necessary intermediate stage in what is really domestic political communication. A classic example is BBC news transmission about the activities of the anti-Hitler resistance inside Germany that was picked up by other resistance elements, a process documented by the White Rose group (Scholl, 1983). A more recent example would be the use of fax machines in the Chinese student movement in May and June 1989: because of the limited infrastructure of internal telecommunications and fear of surveillance, it was easier and faster for Chinese students in Beijing to fax messages out to their U.S. counterparts, who then faxed the message back to another city inside China, than to trust internal communication. The nightly news broadcasts of the BBC that reported demonstrations and deaths in various cities of Iran played a similar role, representing the movement back to itself as well as reinforcing the global importance of its actions.

Beyond the organization of exile communication for political purposes, international news carriers are crucial to the provision of information and imagery worldwide, made even faster with the use of satellites. Sometimes such channels provide information that is kept restricted within the society in question, and states attempt to block their penetration through jamming or preventing the purchase of shortwave receiving equipment. The detailed coverage of major stories by Western international broadcasters, such as the BBC and the Voice of America, Deutsche Welle, Radio Monte Carlo, and Israeli radio, has made them primary information sources in many political upheavals, often listened to on shortwave behind drawn curtains. In Iran, international media attention appeared to validate the "historical importance" of the events at hand. *Time* and *Newsweek* covers on the Iranian revolution produced significant public interest at Tehran newsstands. At ICDI, the Iranian tea-boys clamored for translations of articles in these news magazines and were impressed that even American publications were writing about the Iranian revolution. Such major international channels are also perceived to be highly professional and "objective" in their news coverage, thus adding a great sense of veracity to their broadcasts (Gauhar, 1979). Even political activists accepted international news reports and figures, especially in preference to those of the state-run broadcasting system, and frequently quoted the BBC or other such channels in their own communiqués. Among ordinary people, the reputation of international broadcasters was high, to the extent that a Tehrani electronics salesman in the north of the city told us in 1979 that people came to purchase "a radio BBC"! Revolutions are national political phenomena fought on specific pieces of real estate, but global communications flows allow, and even foster, the "deterritorialization" of politics in terms of the possible separation of political actors from their specific "sphere of influence" (see the special edition of *Third World Quarterly* on "The Politics of Exile," 1987).

Small Media as the Catalyst for Political Participation

The connection between communications and participation is poorly developed. The basic mass-media model of vertical message transference sees the audience only as a group of message consumers (accredited with varying degrees of selectivity, and so forth). Yet the proliferation of new media, the lowering of costs, the differentiation of the audience into taste cultures, and new models of the active audience offer opportunities for communications participation so that the erstwhile "passive" audience can actively produce not only meaning but messages. Much of this is not new in the West, where community radio, local publishing ventures, and a host of pressure groups using a variety of channels exist. What certain technological developments offer, however, is the potential for developing and renewing participation in societies with state surveillance and limited possibilities for independent political participation, even inside authoritarian states. In such contexts, to communicate is to act politically, with the implication that simple definitions of participation or its lack may well be outdated.

The relation between communications and politics is symbiotic, and it is impossible to separate the issue of participation in the political process from participation in the communications process. In fact, the practice of both Pahlavi shahs, particularly the last, was to discourage all forms of mass political participation, which they seemed to feel could as easily go against them as for them, a typical fear of authoritarian regimes (Perlmutter, 1981). Indeed, many theorists of political modernization, including Lerner and Huntington, have been fearful of the extremism of mass participation.

These outlooks appear to work within a narrow definition of the "political" that does not accord well with the Iranian experience, or with the Chinese, East European, and many other contexts. Under such repressive states, the ideological and cultural spheres cannot have any autonomous development but are orchestrated by the state, as is the process of economic development. Thus the "political" is not a neatly delimited sphere to which specifically political demands may be made. The very lack of development of institutions of participation encouraged the strengthening of preexisting collective identities and the politicization of cultural practices and rituals.

Political communication has been far too preoccupied with that most visible of participatory activities, voting. But not all systems have voting procedures, and all political systems have participation. Even passivity is meaningful. In Iran, the Shah promoted a strong self-deceptive tendency to believe that all was well (i.e., *qui tacit, consentit*) induced by the failure of those around him to provide the full facts about social discontent to his attention, partly because he made it clear that he did not like to hear bad news (Graham, 1978). The outward appearance of submission is no proof of the inward acceptance of oppression, however. That the Shah was psychologically affected by the depth of popular hostility that became evident in 1977–78 seems to be a factor in his irresolution about responses to the political opposition.

At the popular level, once the pervasive silence was shattered by the speaking out of intellectuals and professionals who were not immediately pounced on by SAVAK, and then by the first demonstrations, the collective fear of reprisals and feelings of powerlessness were rapidly dissolved. Fear was sometimes transformed into its opposite, a desire for martyrdom. The contagion effect spread and the surveillance structure of the once-absolute state fell asunder. Communication acts were in themselves political moments of involvement and daring, and the public process of communicating that such events had occurred required further involvement. We shall examine the welter of leaflets that were circulated, the calligraphic graffiti, the stencil images of urban guerrillas, and the posters. Each of these represented an individual or group become political participant. In a context that had allowed no autonomous political participation for decades, the exhilaration of involvement and the visible and audible breaches in the wall of public silence were critical initial steps in the formation of the mass popular movement. Indeed, one interesting aspect of the mobilization is the shift between intellectual initiation of the process and the subsequent mass takeover and leadership, that is, the extent to which the previously mass "spectators" became even more "gladiatorial" than the secular activists (Milbrath and Goel, 1977) and were ready to encounter and battle with the military forces of the state.

There is a tension between this claim we are making about the "spontaneity" of participation, and its orchestration by the clergy. The Iranian popular movement cannot be seen simply as a voluntaristic process of a developing public opinion, although there were sizable segments of the Iranian population who had been waiting for the chance to act and for whom the fracturing of state power suddenly offered undreamed-of opportunities. For most ordinary Iranians, involvement was provoked by the combination of the coercive power of primordial identity, the continued social status of the *ulema* and their political rhetoric. The Shah, on the few state occasions when it could be controlled, provoked participation through fear, fear of reprisal and of involvement with SAVAK. With the clergy and Khomeini, participation was orchestrated through the politicization of a deep-rooted cultural identity and the compulsion of religious duty—an ideology, leadership, and ethos accepted as compelling by a crowd of believers in the absence of alternatives, and a deeply coercive process.

The Iranian movement, much like the movements of Poland, the Philippines, and even Nicaragua, can be characterized by massive, low-level participation that cut across clear social-class divisions, evident in such actions as participation in mass demonstrations and the shouting of antiregime slogans from urban rooftops. The political culture of mistrust (Zonis, 1971) and private grumbling was rapidly transformed into an immensely powerful collective movement of strangers.

Small Media and Indigenous Culture

One way in which cross-class solidarity was effected in Iran was in the repoliticizing of familiar traditional popular culture. In authoritarian systems, with severe repression of the political sphere, popular culture almost inevitably becomes the locus of political opposition, the venting of oppositional sentiments, the developing of critiques, and the playing out of alternative visions. As we have already argued, even if the existence of some delimited formal sphere called the "political" is lacking, that does not mean that politics does not exist, but rather that it is not in actuality separated from the broader sociocultural milieu in which competition for symbolic meaning occurs. Separating culture from politics is difficult, and, in processes of political change, many indigenous cultural resources may be mobilized and developed to create a cultural resistance with political impact against would-be hegemonic regimes.

Obviously these processes can take many forms by utilizing traditional channels and by combining the use of modern small-media technologies with traditional cultural forms (music, poetry, and so on). The Afghan resistance to the Soviets very rapidly developed a clandestine communication system based on cassettes in a way that imitated the Iranian movement; perhaps uniquely, but culturally appropriate, Afghans have woven carpets that incorporate motifs of contemporary warfare, a highly unusual example of cultural resistance. Glasnost revealed not only deep ethnic cleavages in the USSR but also a lively underground of punk and heavy-metal music.

The themes of indigenous cultural identity and its erosion by external cultural elements, and the deleterious effects of Western culture may function as popular rhetorical tropes that help to build a mass movement against some external power. In Nicaragua, Somoza was seen as the local representative of imperialism, and resistance took the form not only of military and political resistance but of cultural resistance as well. A dynamic counterculture built on older, traditional cultural forms, substituting popular testimonial music for "disco," a poetry of revolutionary content, a revolutionary film industry, and revolutionary song. Thus "Guitarra armada" ("Armed Guitar") by the Gody brothers was said to have "organized the collective spirit of the people by extracting the themes and chords from the deepest of our roots and preparing this feeling for the struggle" and "the masks of Monimbo, the contact bombs, and the drums of Subtiava are indigenous forms of cultural expression whose origins go back to the colonial period. They are cultural forms which could not be destroyed by the implantation of a foreign culture that is alien to our character. The people not only learned to resist, but also to fight, to sing, and most important of all, to triumph" (Rothschuh Villanueva in Mattelart, 1986: 35–36).

The performing arts, puppeteers, and other traditional cultural forms have also been involved with political mobilization. These forms acted as vehicles of expression of protest, dissent, and reform in India, so that "these native media of 'sung communication' and 'enacted information' proved more than a match to the Government-controlled mass media during the many political and social campaigns launched by Gandhiji" (Ranganath, 1980). Bassets (in Mattelart and Seigelaub, 1983) describes the variety of clandestine communications developed under and against Franco's dictatorship, from typewritten letters to clandestine press agencies, from the underground political press to anonymous poetry or simply the symbolic painting of letters on walls (P for protest, A for amnesty, L for liberty). Although this particular underground movement did not develop into a successful social movement, as happened in Iran, and change accrued "naturally" with the death of Franco, it is interesting to note the reduction of Spanish society and communications practices into two separate, culturally and politically antagonistic realms, very similar to the reduction of Iranian life into a "dualistic culture" of state and oppositional culture. Bassets analyzes the relationship between the clandestine culture and the exile culture, the latter serving as a historical memory bank preserving radical cultural and political expression even with internal repression. He also describes the international broadcasting and humanitarian organizations that played a vital information role as part of international public opinion, elements we have already noted as significant in the Iranian experience too. As we will see in chapter 6, the themes of indigenous cultural identity and the harmful influences of external (notably Western) cultures had been articulated by Khomeini for many decades and were central political causes of the mobilization, not only its tools. This created a hypostatization of "indigenous culture" and its freezing into some regressive, never-to-be-recuperated image of a glorious past.

The repoliticization of popular culture as a mode of generating solidarity appears quite common, although in different contexts different media and different genres will be invoked. Popular culture takes many forms, and cultural resistance and opposition are not necessarily revolutionary. Popular culture can be highly politicized, and entertainment can be a powerful vehicle for political gathering and mobilization. The showing of an underground video in a private house in Poland or Czechoslovakia, the semipublic viewing of "critical" films, and the production and distribution of an opposition leaflet all create a symbolic space that serves to redefine the political. Participation in such events and the acceptance and reading of such material are forms of political action in and of themselves, carried out in defiance of and at possible risk from the state. Vaclav Havel, the president of the Czech Republic, was imprisoned for a number of years as a dissident playwright, and Charter 77 in that country was comprised of many creative artists and intellectuals. The poets Said Sultanpour and Golesorkhi were imprisoned by the Shah. Repressive states understand well the potential power of popular culture to undermine them, hence the widespread repression and censorship regularly reported in *Index to Censorship* (Article 19) and by Amnesty International.

Much of the power of the small media used in Iran was due to their integration of the culturally familiar, their embeddedness in the extant public (as opposed to regime-dominated) cultural frameworks of the society. Yet because of regime censorship no well-developed national-popular culture had emerged inside Iran other than a traditional religious culture. There was a limited reading public, so novels had limited circulation; film was popular, yet the cinema-going public was essentially young and male. Only perhaps in music did traditional forms and instrumentation blend with Westernized forms to create a truly new and popular cultural form, continued in exile in California (Naficy, 1993).

Small Media and Religious Networks: A Crucial Linkage

Various aspects of preexisting popular culture may be built upon, but the key element in many recent movements was religion. Religious networks functioned as a site for an oppositional public sphere, religious thematics were reconstituted as political rhetoric, and religious leaders emerged as political figures. In the Philippines, Nicaragua, and South Africa, religious perspectives, religious leaders, and religious space have constituted crucial elements of the popular mobilization. The Polish experience with the growth of Solidarity reflects perhaps the closest similarities to the Iranian situation. These include the importance of the church as an alternative public space and guarantor of culture and values in a centrally administered environment; the building of cross-class coalitions with a church base; the skepticism about the official media; and the initiation of an alternative media network (Liu, 1982). In Poland as in Iran, it was not just a random element of traditional, indigenous culture that served as the basis of popular mobilization but religious culture, which provided the nexus of authority, popular cultural practices, and experimental solidarity able to mobilize a previously nonparticipatory people. As Zubaida (1987: 145) notes, "religion is . . . the sphere of social solidarities based on common belonging, with specific institutions and rituals of worship, which identifies the believers and separates them from the practitioners of other faiths . . . in situations of communal competition or conflict, individuals respond according to communal solidarity, in which the religious component is essential." The comparative evidence suggests that this is not a phenomenon limited to Islam and Iran—see Tiryakian (1988) on Nicaragua and Poland, for example—but rather it is to be understood within the context of the weak political development of civil society in autocratic states. That this religious unity may be a temporary phenomenon, with deeper social rifts and ethnic antagonisms subsequently reexposed—as after the Islamic revolution—is not to dispute the temporary community-binding powers of religion.

Thus it is religion as habitus, the daily lived practices of a culture, that creates ties of affect, of meaning, of shared experience. And though the Iranian movement does not involve competition with other religious communities, it does involve competition with more modern ideologies of nationalism and class analysis, none of which had the rootedness or emotional resonance of Islam. Even the most skilled politician with a secular rhetoric began with enormous disadvantages in the emergent political culture of Iran in the 1970s.

Not only does religion function as community-binding, but religious leaders occupy a particular place in traditional political cultures. It is useful to think of the Iranian religious leaders as organic intellectuals, to use Gramsci's (1973) term. They possessed long and deep roots in the popular culture, were in command of the most powerful set of shared beliefs and values in the society, and were the sons (very occasionally daughters) of the popular, usually traditional, classes. These traditional classes in Iran (the bazaaris, small landowners, petite bourgeoisie) were the most upset by modernization and the new forms of economic organization, which undermined their traditional spheres of operation. There were strong antidevelopmental as well as anti-Western tendencies among these groups, and their own economic dislocation provided a major source of dissatisfaction.

For the clerisy, the secular intellectuals, the university was the central location for their social authority absent the free press and party formations that are the typical crucial linkages with mass followings (Gramsci in Forgacs, 1988). Higher education underwent considerable expansion under the Pahlavis, but university attendance was primarily an urban-middle-class phenomenon, although children of the traditional classes were beginning to attend. It was in the universities that many of the central "texts" of the revolution circulated, the writings of Shariati or the novels of Al-Ahmad; they were also the spaces where a different kind of open-ended, critical, rational discourse was developing. Yet this "modern" mode of discourse was still poorly rooted, limited in the social groups it included, and frustrated by the lack of other vehicles to translate these ideas and modes of debate into more popular, accessible forms.

In contexts where the political public sphere and civil society are poorly developed and secular debate highly circumscribed, religious identity provides a kind of latent political solidarity, taken for granted or dormant until called upon, then readily mobilized against alternate visions of the collectivity. But religion in the politicized discourse of the Iranian revolution offered even more potent dynamics of mobilization. Religious tradition provided a discourse of religious duty, of compulsion to act, that was readily adopted by the religious leadership. Thus, far from a simple voluntaristic choice to act, strong elements of social coercion were built into the relationship between religious leadership and its mass following in Iran. Furthermore, as in many religious traditions, the very repetitive interaction between religious leaders and followings enabled the former to develop an oral language honed on frequent interactions with a predominantly nonliterate audience that was accessible and familiar, and played on deeply valued identities and outlooks. This relationship and the dynamics of compulsion are developed further in chapter 7. In comparison, the would-be secular leaders in Iran were poorly equipped at every level, having to invent their political organizations, rhetoric, and practice almost from scratch in 1977.

Forms of Small Media and Social Authority

We want to avoid a narrow, deterministic technological logic that privileges the power of media or that would argue simply that small media make revolutions, but at the same time it is necessary to recognize that the form of media itself effects the nature of the communication and the response. This is particularly significant for political processes where the use of different forms of media can create different kinds of relations between sender and receiver, leader and followers.

Oral/aural culture was rooted in the constant interchange of communally possessed knowledge, unlike the individualized speculation more characteristic of writing. Oral culture is thus essentially authoritarian, not interested in the new but desirous of fostering and preserving the old, the traditional, by saying it repeatedly. Ong (1967) argues that oral culture has a penchant for citing authorities to claim contact with the communal heritage and for negotiating the complexities of everyday life, and often is marked by the daily relevance of prayer and religious ceremony. Religious knowledge possesses authority not only as the received "word of God" but because it is community-binding, a "tribal possession," and of necessity authoritarian. Cultural maintenance and group continuity are one and the same, and support an accepted pattern of authority.

The weak development of print forms and the severe control of them, coupled with state support for electronic broadcasting, created in Iran, as in other parts of the Third World, a powerful secondary orality (Ong, 1982). Like primary orality, secondary orality has a mystique of participation, fosters a communal sense, concentrates on the present moment, and uses formulas. As we have already argued, immediate oral communication plays on the ethos of the speaker, the rhetoric of the religious opposition implicitly invoking its already-considerable social authority. Secondary orality plays on and elaborates the already-established ethos of the now-mediated speaker. Thus cassettes of Khomeini's speeches carried not only the "word" of the political message (which argued that it was the duty of all believers to mobilize to defend their faith) but also the "voice" of the sender, an already-admired charismatic figure, and became an immensely powerful form of communication experienced in countless Iranian living rooms.

The Discursive Reconstruction of Collective Memory/Identity

In this chapter we have focused on the evolution or reconstitution of an oppositional public sphere comprised of small-media technologies and the extant religious network, re-creating the social space and structures for political work. We have suggested how religious identity in particular could be built on as a cultural identity that readily promoted solidarity, and how religious figures possessed a spoken language easily understandable by illiterate populations. Perhaps one of the final elements in the puzzle of political change is the actual discourse of revolution, how alternative identities and political goals were constructed in language to frame revolutionary ideology. The articulation of such discourse includes a sense of collective memory, a rewriting of collective identity, and the politicization of "tradition."

Revolution is made in the historical present, building on images of the past, thrusting toward the future, albeit often looking backward, as Benjamin (1970: 262–63) described the angel of history. All nations propound a collective history; authoritarian states advocate a single authorized version of the past, with a rewriting of names and dates (and a retouching of photos, like the erasure of Trotsky from Soviet photographic records), and an authorized version of events in which they are the progressive apogee, thus creating a certain kind of collective identity of which they are the final embodiment. The breaking up of the Soviet empire has unleashed a massive retrieval and "reinvention" of nations and ethnicities throughout Eastern Europe.

Such constructions of collective remembering not only (re-)create a past but perhaps more crucially (re-)create a collective identity that has a past. Opposition may consist of "refusing what we are," in Foucault's (1988) terms, and reconstituting a preferred collective identity that empowers actors. This is the shift from being subjects of/subject to a regime to becoming human subjects writing our own history. Competition over memory is also competition over how current collective identities should be conceived. Here Benjamin's (1970) idea that revolution is a "tiger's leap into the past" becomes more complex; there is no single past, but rather competing definitions of how the past is to be read.

In Iran, there were a number of competing versions of "collective memory" including that of the royalist state and also those of the opposition. The Shah actively promoted the notion of 2,500 years of Persian monarchy, of which he was the pinnacle, symbolized most ostentatiously by his own coronation at Persepolis in 1971. This was, of course, a quite discontinuous tradition with no single bloodline, his own father having established a new dynasty after an interregnum in the 1920s. This version of history skirted over questions of political legitimacy or possibilities for republican structures, and ignored the changing physical boundaries of the entity called Persia/Iran or the difference between the ancient empires of Persia and the modern state of Iran.

Secular opposition groups borrowed both national and international "spirits of the past" to reconstruct their tradition. Many articulated a line of political struggle from the constitutional movement at the turn of the century, the Jangali movement in the north that established the first revolutionary republic on Iranian soil, through Mossadeq and his nationalist-democratic movement, to the development and role of modern political groupings such as the *Tudeh, Fedai'i,* and *Moja-*

hedin. Some also called into play international proletarian struggles and global revolutions, orienting the Iranian movement toward a world revolutionary tradition. In Tehran in 1979 it was easier to buy cassettes of Cuban, Algerian, and Chinese revolutionary music than a dozen eggs. It is not surprising that in the brief period of secular-religious accommodation after the Iranian revolution, there was a symbolic gathering at Mossadeq's village in memory of his political struggle against the Pahlavis, as well as the organization of a major demonstration at Tehran University in honor of the young Fedayin who died at Siahkal and elsewhere (see figure 10.1). In a similar fashion, in postrevolutionary Czechoslovakia there were new commemorations of Jan Palach, and in Hungary, Imre Nagy was reburied with appropriate ceremony.

The religious elements could call upon a known and valued current communal identity, with a clearly demarcated past, heroes, and key events, to reconstitute a collective identity capable of challenging both the national identity of the royal despotism and the alternative identities proposed by the secular opposition. Although Shiism is not a monolithic unity, with both quietistic and radical interpretations and traditions, and deep internal lines of conflict, for popular consumption at a moment of political rupture a rather unified rhetoric was articulated, spearheaded by Khomeini. It was a time-binding, community-binding discourse of religious identity that, when coupled with the social spaces and social authority of its articulators, was a hard ideology to challenge or ignore.

This should be seen not as the "invention of tradition," a post hoc attempt to rewrite the past (Hobsbawm and Ranger, 1984). At the same time as collective memories are conjured up, the present intervenes to redefine past events and actors and functional symbols in current opposition. "Tradition" is not simply frozen memory but an active adaptation to the new, current time frame and sociopolitical context. In the politicization of memory and cultural tradition, both are changed. No longer can tradition be lived innocently and naively. In its active mobilization as a resource in an ideological struggle against an opposing cultural and political reality, tradition itself is irrevocably altered, undergoing the process of retraditionalization that has already been discussed.

Summary

This alternative model of popular communication for mobilization that focuses on small media or grass-roots media, on cultural resistance and popular empowerment, is enjoying quite a vogue. Communication as people's power (*Media Development*, 1988; Jankowski et al., 1992; Dowmunt, 1993) appeals to our optimism and our desire to know that change is possible, that people can take control of their own lives, that both the models of development and dependency underestimated the traditional cultural resources that the Third World and other peoples possess.

But we must be wary of creating a new "myth of small media" to replace the "myth of the mighty media," to use Shinar's (1980) label, as the new reigning model. What can be important and exciting about this new line of thinking is that it takes the existing cultural frames seriously, as well as acknowledging the complex set of reactions and interactions that develop between big media and small, between the state and the people, between the national and international contexts; it is often rather naive, however, about social structure and class differences, and operates with too-simple dichotomies such as state and people. Although for limited periods of time a situation may indeed take on that coloring, when the dust settles it is usually clear that certain interests win over others. Notions of solidarity, populism, even indigenous culture, may be useful rhetorical tropes in political struggle—and in academic analysis—but may come to cover over, rather than uncover, problematic questions.

The story of the Iranian revolution is presented here as a case study of one particular revolutionary situation in which regime hegemony utilizing big media was successfully confronted by political and cultural resistance based on small media. As will be presented in the following chapters, the specifics of the Iranian case and its particular conjunctions of forces must be acknowledged, as well as the operation of many other forces beyond the communicative and cultural.

Certainly the Islamic Republic inherits its own set of contradictions, particularly in the cultural sphere. It was one thing to rally under the known umbrella of Islamic identity to get rid of a dictator seen as an American puppet, but it was quite another to accept the imposition of new restrictions and controls by an Islamic government. Chapter 10 explores the institutionalization of the Islamic Republic and its cultural and broadcasting policies, the massive move into exile, and the attempt to use small media to oppose Khomeini from outside Iran, and the subtle and not-so-subtle cultural resistance that flourishes even inside the Islamic Republic. New forms of opposition developed against the Islamic Republic, and popular culture once again became the site of political struggle, the ironic dialectic of history.

II
The Political Economy of Media in Iran

Chapter 3
Media and the State in Iranian History

*One great difference between the progressive West and the
unprogressive East lies in the nature of their communications.*

Sykes (1915: 2:367)

*Apart from the telegraph, other forms of communication within
Persia were still, by the 1860s, mediaeval. There were no car-
riage roads, no railways and no post offices. Things were not
much better by 1921.*

Wright (1977: 135)

Outside Contacts and the Beginnings of Technological Development

By virtue of its location, Iran is, and always has been, a cultural crossroads
between East and West. Iran was opened up to external influences in many different forms, but the force of Western influence became especially pronounced from
the early Qajar period in the mideighteenth century on through the nineteenth century. Perhaps the essence of dependent development is that a nation has things
done to it rather than doing things itself. For much of the early period of modernization in Iran, indeed through the nineteenth century, that was the situation, as
rival foreign powers fought out their own struggles for control of resources,
strategic locations, and trade with Iran. In the process, certain modern technologies and developmental infrastructure were brought to Iran, but always in a manner that suited the needs of the foreign power before satisfying Iranian needs. The

early development of transportation and communication systems exactly reflects these dynamics.

The benefit of good communications to the development of empire, as well as the use of level of communications infrastructure as a yardstick of development, was already well appreciated at the turn of the twentieth century by Sir Percy Sykes, the British orientalist. Indeed, among the enduring legacies of imperialism are the systems of communication and transportation laid down by the British, French, and others that form the basis of many Third World communication systems even today. A historical perspective quickly reveals that the diffusion of modern communications technologies in the Third World was not a neutral, unmotivated process but a central strand of modernization, yet much of the time the initial purpose was to benefit imperial interests rather than the nation in which such developments occurred. Iran, though never directly colonized, lay on the path of many imperial interests and thus became a site of considerable interimperial rivalry for influence over and involvement in the building up of Iran's infrastructure in a manner more closely linked to great power needs than to those of Iranian society at large. Yet it remains too simplistic to remark that communications technologies—as most other technological forms—were first developed in the West. We must also note that members of the Iranian ruling class, specifically its shahs, were eager players in the technological modernization of their country; they were great admirers of Western gadgetry, quick to see its appeal and potential domestic use, especially as instruments of coercion and political control.

In Iran, the growth of point-to-point communication was closely linked to the growth of systems of transportation such as rail and road networks and was a central element in the broader development of a modern infrastructure. The advent of the telegraph, the telephone, and the postal service illustrate the interplay of imperial interest and regal power in the path to the modernization of Iran.

The Telegraph

Telegraph technology was brought to Iran from England in the 1850s during the reign of Nasser-iddin Shah, who liked it very much and ordered a line to be established between Golestan Palace and Lalehzar Garden. Between 1856 and 1876 (1274–96) telegraphic cable was laid to many towns; some rejoiced in the connection, while others showed public resistance (Ardekani, 1988–89: 2: 189–98).

The real spread of the telegraph occurred in the early 1860s, not because of internal need but to facilitate British control over India, the jewel in the crown of empire but the thorn in its flesh of political control (Sykes, 1915: 2:366–70; Issawi, 1971: 152–54). Britain had tried laying undersea cables from the Red Sea past Muscat to Karachi in 1859–61, but the operation failed. The alternative was an overland cable, and the British negotiated in turn with the Turks and the Persians for the right to lay cable. Initially, there was quite some hostility to the proposals for a number of reasons (no immediate benefit to Persia was envisaged, there was concern about the spread of newfangled foreign technologies and about British intentions), but in December 1862 Britain and Persia signed an agreement (formalized on October 20, 1863) for the construction of a single-wire line. By the end of 1864 the line linked Khaniqin-Tehran-Isfahan-Shiraz-Bushire and was 1,100 miles in length. Persia was to pay the cost, estimated at 100,000 toman, and purchase the materials in Britain, yet the line was to be under British supervision. Persia received an annual royalty and was paid for all local and foreign messages (Sykes, 1915: 2:369). By 1872 so much traffic was carried that three lines had been erected, and by 1875 the director of the Persian Telegraph estimated two million pounds sterling had been invested.

By the 1880s Iran was well equipped with telegraph lines that connected it with various parts of the world and linked up its towns. For the British, Wright (1977: 128) argues, "from the mid-1860s until the end of the Qajar period the Indo-European telegraph was Britain's most precious interest in Persia, outranking in importance both the Imperial bank, and the Anglo-Persian Oil Company." Indeed, the Indo-European Telegraph Department was actually a branch of the Government of India, although headquartered in London. It was mainly British and Armenians who worked in the telegraph stations across the country, which became well known as watering holes for intrepid nineteenth-century European travelers, including George Curzon (1892). As the system was developed, it also became a source of much hostility between the British and the Persians. There were acts of sabotage and robbery on the lines, and linesmen had to be employed to protect the property and repair the lines (Wright, 1977: 132–33).

For Iran, the development of the telegraph was of considerable importance. As Wright (1977: 133) suggests, "the telegraph not only provided valuable revenue for the Persian treasury but also greatly strengthened the hand of the Shah in dealing with his far-flung provinces. Additionally it brought Persia into contact with the outside world as never before and was probably more responsible than any other single factor in stimulating those reformist and nationalist movements which began to stir in the last quarter of the nineteenth century." Nasser-iddin Shah had quickly realized the potential for political control that the telegraph afforded him, requiring that the telegraph operators should, beyond their obvious duties, provide a daily report on what was going on in their areas (Ardekani, 1988–89: 2:220). By the end of his reign, the telegraph was an established channel for the court and the government, and fixed prices per word had been set. In 1896 Persia joined the International Telegraphic Union.

The telegraph also helped the establishment of newspapers in Iran. The first daily was founded in 1898 and tapped into the foreign news coming in over the wires from Reuters en route to the Indian press. By 1914–15 there were 9,730 kilometers of telegraphic links, but less than half were controlled by Iranians. Most belonged to foreign companies or governments (Jamalzadeh, 1983 [1362]:

180; Issawi, 1971: 153); lines were extended to strategic places, such as Jask on the Persian Gulf, not necessarily to those areas with the largest population concentrations, to service foreign interests rather than foster national communication.

An indication of the socially perceived power and influence of the telegraph—essentially, the notion that the lines ran straight to the Shah's palace—can be seen in the fact that telegraph offices were often used as places of asylum and refuge, as during the Shiraz bread riots of 1893, to the embarrassment of both British and Persian officials. The stations were not only the means of direct communication with the governor or the Shah, and thus a locale from which to make political demands, but also a means of access to the outside world, with messages sent out to London and Paris about internal political strife, requesting Western powers to exert pressure on domestic rulers. By the time of the First World War the Italians and Germans also wanted to install radio telegraphy, but their plan was opposed by the British, who wanted the service installed by the Indo-European Telegraph Department. Thus just within this one sphere, multiple standards and multiple authorities coexisted, and the British, Russians, Germans, and Italians all vied with each other to balance the political influence and economic benefits to be derived from Persia. For the British, at least, the desire was essentially to maintain the status quo in Iran unless a clear profit could be predicted from a project. India was to be protected above all, and nothing would be supported that would result in a loss of control or establish competition with Indian trade and development.

The Telephone

Other communications technologies were also eagerly received by the Persian elite, especially by certain shahs who were particularly intrigued by modern technologies. Nasser-iddin Shah was introduced to the telephone by his crown prince Kamran Mirza, who in 1888 set up a telephone link between his palace, Kamranieh in Shemiran, and the office of the Ministry of War, his ministerial responsibility, in the heart of Tehran. Later, links were made between Golestan Palace and Saltanatabad, the Shah's summer palace. Various ministries for the Shah readily perceived the telephone as a coercive instrument, providing him with better control over and access to his government officials.

The first telephonic system for public use seems to have been developed by an entrepreneur called Haji Seyyed Morteza Mortazavi, who was given government permission for fifty years to develop a system not to exceed 24 kilometers in Tabriz, with 10 percent of the profits to be paid to the government after ten years (Ardekani, 1988–89: 3:2). Later, entrepreneurs in Mashhad, Urumieh, and Tehran also established systems. As the system expanded, rivalry developed between the Italian Marconi Company, working with a German syndicate, and the British government, who wanted the services installed by the Indo-European Telegraph Department (Jamalzadeh, 1983 [1362]: 184). Telephone lines were installed just before the First World War, and by 1914 the Societé Anonyme des Telephones Persans had nearly one thousand subscribers in twelve towns (Issawi, 1971: 154). The British-Persia Oil Company had its own lines, and the fishing industry in Astara and Anzali had also developed its own telephone system. By 1923 Tehran had a major company that sold shares and made an agreement with Siemens (the German communication company) to develop the system, and the basis of a national public telephone system really took place in the 1920s.

The Postal Service

In a history somewhat parallel to that of the telegraph, the postal service developed in Iran through British involvement. Up to 1874 there was really no postal system for private individual use in Persia, and a limited system for government use. Internal private letters and parcels were carried by merchants or travelers. External contact was primarily responsible for the creation of the first formal postal systems. For example, British imperial need for communication between London and India meant the British Legation organized mounted messengers (*gholams*) who carried mail once a month to Constantinople and Shiraz, from where new couriers took it on to London and Bushire. From 1862, and with regular steamship sailings between Bombay and the Gulf, the Persian government was pressured to accept Indian-controlled post offices from where mail continued by boat to Bombay. By extension, the British provided a semipublic postal system from Bushire to the rest of Iran, whereby messengers of the Legation and Telegraph departments would deliver mail along their routes back to Tehran. This system was controlled by the Postmaster General in Bombay, letters were franked with Indian stamps carrying pictures of Queen Victoria, and Indian postal rates were charged. The Russians had an embassy postal service that took mail from Tehran to Tiflis and then to Saint Petersburg, and the French had a route from Tehran through Istanbul to Paris.

As international trade in imports and exports (particularly with Russia, Turkey, and Europe) developed strongly in midcentury, so too did a demand for improved communications. In 1874, Amir Kabir inaugurated Persia's own postal system, with a post office in Tehran, under the charge of Mr. Readerer, an Austrian consultant. He wrote a report on July 25, 1876, to the International Union of Postal Services that described the growing Iranian demand for sending parcels, especially gold and silver, abroad for commercial purposes. The growth of an internal postal service initially depended on riders and foot delivery, and the routes ran along the main road arteries in Iran. By 1890 the Persian government signed a postal-service exchange with the Ottoman Empire and later signed agreements with other countries. Reports about theft and insecurity of delivery encouraged the government to invite a Belgian expert to reorganize the system and train Persians to handle the service. In 1907 the postal service became independent of the

Customs Office and was made a ministry, quickly joining the International Postal Union (Ministry of Post, 1916).

By 1914–15 there were 158 postal offices, 15 branches, 263 post houses (manzel), 2,370 horses used for delivery, 632 coaches and carts, 260 horse riders and postmen (Jamalzadeh, 1983), and the yearly net income was substantial. Most of the main roads ran from Tehran to other cities such as Rasht, Mashhad, Tabriz, and Kermanshah. Delivery of a letter from Tehran to Berlin took about eleven days (Jamalzadeh, 1983). Foreign control of the postal system was hard to break, so that even when the Persians objected to the continuation of the foreign-run system and developed their own stamps, and despite national government pressures, the British-run offices remained until 1922 (Wright, 1977: 135–36).

As a brief aside, we might add that in media studies far less attention has been devoted to such point-to-point communications systems than to broadcast systems, although the former may create the infrastructure of participatory communication and growth of a public domain of free expression not controlled by the state. Media indicators stress mass communication, not interpersonal mediated communication, although the latter might be a far more potent measure of development. Even now, in the 1990s, the postal service in Iran is insufficient for the size of its territory and population.

By the time of the establishment of the Pahlavi dynasty, the elementary infrastructure of point-to-point communication had been started across Iran, and all these systems were consolidated in the Ministry of Post, Telegraph, and Telephone in 1931. These systems were to expand considerably over the next decades, but they ultimately took second place to the massive development and expansion of broadcast communication under the Pahlavis.

The British were tolerated to their face by Iranians, but behind the scenes the robbery and disruption of equipment showed hostility to the *farangi* (foreigner, i.e., Westerner), and general resentment simmered. There were more organized, political reactions to this early imperialism, such as the Tobacco Rebellion of 1891, which protested and managed to cancel the concessions given to the British. Early political awareness grew in relation to foreign-power penetration in Iran, setting the stage for an ongoing anti-imperialist thematic in oppositional Iranian politics, monarchical power seen as supported by imperial power. The supreme indignity was suffered in 1907 when Russian-British rivalry over Iran produced the Anglo-Russian Treaty, dividing Iran into zones of influence separated by a neutral area. Particularly under the Qajars, Iran lay open to Western penetration, to development projects designed with imperial strategies and needs in mind— from which Iran benefited when it suited the imperial powers and through which Iran was left stagnant when it did not suit them. Although some achievements in laying an infrastructure of communications and transportation (including the laying of some railway track and a limited amount of paved road) had already been achieved by the time of Reza Khan's coronation, nearly all such work was done by foreign powers, either in the prewar period as part of their policy of economic imperialism, or during the First World War for immediate strategic purposes.

This development of infrastructure (as with much of the banking and commercial system, the medical system, and even the educational system) was established mainly by interimperial rivalry rather than by any autonomous strategy or planning on Iran's part. Iran was the passive prize of imperial machinations. The relationships of power embedded in the transfer of such technologies from the West, and the relationships of superiority and inferiority that were implied, have proved to be lasting legacies, not only in Iran but in much of the Third World. Superiority was transformed into an often quite unreasonable sense of foreign, especially British, power and influence inside Iran; inferiority was translated into an unreasonable acceptance of anything that came from abroad (while resenting its appearance) and a consequent devaluing of Iranian culture and habits. This process was to become exacerbated after the Second World War as British influence gave way to American involvement.

Reza Shah, Nationalism, and "Modernization from Above"

Under Reza Shah, the first Pahlavi monarch, a process of "modernization from above" was started with a focus on Iranian national, not foreign, interests, although the mythology of foreign penetration was never absent from his period of rule. A cossack officer when he seized power in 1920, Reza Khan had the possibility of creating the first Iranian Republic, but instead, in December 1925, he established the Pahlavi dynasty and was supported by the British as an anticommunist, nationalist monarch. He set out to create the first modern, centralized state in Iran based on a Western model of industrial development. He rapidly created a political dictatorship, banning all political parties and relying instead on his own charismatic authority and his command of the army. A newly formed police force and gendarmerie helped the army enforce the king's plans. Tribal and regional revolt were suppressed, the power of the clergy was severely curtailed, and opposition leaders were exiled, jailed, or even executed.

The government was also the country's major entrepreneur, holding monopolies on the production of sugar, matches, glass, and textiles. In what is one of the classic patterns of Third World modernization, a strong state taking the initiative from a weak bourgeoisie to push the industrialization process along, Reza Shah launched Iran's industrialization program. His main aim was not only to introduce mechanical industry but to substitute the cohesive force of the central state for the old corporate bases of society, while concentrating on the development of light industry in order to decrease imports and increase exports. Cotton, wool, and silk textile factories were established; sugar refining and other projects to process and store agricultural produce were started; cement factories, an iron foundry, and a steel mill were built; and the hub of all economic activity in Iran, the exploration and mining of natural resources, expanded.

While developing a strong nationalist rhetoric that stressed the long history of a sovereign Iran and the need for a powerful, independent state in which each individual could play a useful and fulfilling role, the model in Reza Shah's mind's eye was of an imaginary West, for he had never traveled beyond Ataturk's Turkey to see for himself what modernization looked like. Two contradictory cultural tendencies were set in motion. One harked back to an ancient Persian cultural heritage. The Pahlavi dynasty was named after the ancient language dominant under the Sassanids. Architectural forms quoted the classic forms of Persepolis, with police headquarters, military command posts, and other government buildings adorned with columns and lions rampant. The *Shahnameh* of Ferdowsi was popularized, fostering the myth of 2,500 years of continuous monarchy that was to be used so liberally by Reza Shah's son.

The other tendency looked outward beyond Ataturk to the contemporary West, to its technologies, way of life, and aesthetic styles. Substantial developments were made in many basic spheres, such as education, medical care, transportation, and communications. There were campaigns to alter clothing styles: baggy *tomban* (wide-legged trousers) and felt hats were exchanged for Western suits and fedora for men, and the veil was banned for women. Education was revamped along French lines and the first batches of students were sent abroad to study. Even in town planning, the appearance of squares with statues (usually of the Shah) at the entrance to each city, and abundantly in Tehran, created an unfamiliar Europeanized atmosphere.

To propagate Reza Shah's simplistic ideology an extensive propaganda campaign was developed, centered on public lectures and a torrent of print materials—newspaper articles, magazine features, and pamphlets—that all tended to repeat the same general slogans: the need for a strong state, the duties of individuals within that state, and the great progress achieved. There were also more specific messages about the new duties of women, social morale, and principles of hygiene (Mowlana, 1963).

The press could have been a useful tool for Reza Shah, who quickly applied his regulative authority to control access to the medium. Only those who would cooperate with him were issued licenses, and even this privilege was subject to censorship. The Iranian press had started very much as a partisan press, papers and journals linked if not directly affiliated with particular political groupings. In times of political hegemony when party political activity was curtailed, the press also ceased to function. Under Reza Shah the press was enjoined not to "disturb the masses" or to try to interest them in matters they could not understand, nor was it to criticize Reza Shah's government or, above all, to try to topple him. Mowlana (1963: 479, 483) has summarized this period thus:

Under the rigorous censorship of Reza Shah's regime, freedom of thought, of speech, and of the press were suspended. Any discussion of political topics let alone criticism of the government was unthinkable, dangerous even in private conversation . . . Reza Shah followed an authoritarian theory of the press, something of an imitation of the fascist ministers of propaganda.

Reza Shah's main ideological opponent was the left, especially the *Tudeh*, the Communist party. In 1931 a law that specifically dealt with political and press offenses was passed, the main feature of which was the provision of jury trials for such offenses. The law was designed to deal with the spread of foreign ideology, meaning Marxism and collectivist orientations, and assigned prison terms for those who advocated forcible overthrow of the sociopolitical status quo, for those advocating the separation of national territory from the whole (an allusion to the Azerbaijan Republic declared by Pishevari), and for those trying to weaken patriotic feelings. This law was used extensively against socialist and communist intellectuals. In 1937 the members of the *Tudeh* group centered around Arani and the magazine *Donya* (World) were arrested and sentenced to lengthy prison terms. Arani died in jail, and it is widely believed that he was murdered (Alavi, 1978).

In January 1939 a new government office was opened called the Office for the Education and Guidance of Public Opinion. It consisted of a committee of representatives from Tehran University, adult education institutes, music centers, the scout organization, and the Press and Publications Department. Its mission was to encourage a nationalist spirit through the media of the press, books, public lectures, cinema, music, and national songs. The OEGPO sponsored lectures, published its own materials, and supplied articles for the press. Mohammad Hejazi, a prominent novelist, was appointed head of the press bureau and published a sixty-four-page magazine, *Iran-e Emruz* (Iran Today), devoted to descriptions of national progress. It is estimated that the free adult lecture program attracted over 1.5 million people during 1940–41 (Mowlana, 1963: 483), who listened to such subjects as "the duty of youth in the present age," "the war against superstition," and "loyalty to the Shah and patriotism." Mixed in with health care and advice on child rearing, diet, fashion, and exercise, the social components of modernization were directly political propaganda messages.

The Establishment of Radio

Radio was the first truly popular medium in Iran. It provided a means of potential ideological hegemony over the whole nation, fortifying Reza Shah's fundamental aim of creating a strong, centralized state, a unified Persian culture of the disparate ethnic elements. It was also a useful tool for disseminating modernizing values and political rhetoric as well as staving off the foreign influences penetrating Iran. It served Reza Shah's geopolitical interests well.

The beginnings of radio in Iran match the earlier dynamics of the telegraph, although this time the Germans rather than the British were the central foreign players. Wireless telegraphy, or long-wave radio, began in Iran for military purposes when the Germans in May 1915 established a connection between Isfahan and Noen in Germany. Because it raised army efficiency, expansion and development of the telegraphic system was accomplished soon after Reza Shah took power. The Ministry of War negotiated in 1924 with the Soviets to purchase a wireless telegraph set with twenty-kilowatt long-wave power (Pezhman, 1948: 507). Typical of the pomp and monarchical circumstance that was to attend most media developments, the inauguration of *Bi-Sim-e Pahlavi*, the Pahlavi wireless system, coincided with Reza Shah's coronation celebrations in April 1926; an opening message was sent out inviting any receiving station to communicate with Iran. Moscow responded with messages of congratulation (Kimiachi, 1978). A 120-meter antenna was erected in Tehran and set at its base was a cannon ball in which Reza Shah had placed an essay about his love for Iran, service to the country, and hopes for the future (Pezhman, 1948: 506). The ministry established the "Army School of Wireless" to train students in the use of this new equipment. In 1926 the Department of Wireless was transferred from the Ministry of War to the Ministry of Post, Telegraph, and Telephone. In 1928, with French help, a short-wave system was introduced with more powerful transmitting capacity; this was extended still further in 1935. Thus the telegraph had been expanded to the wireless telegraph, which in turn led the way for radio broadcasting, a typical pattern of development. The next stage was the establishment of a full-fledged radio broadcasting system.

By 1930 there were a few hundred radio sets among the multilingual Tehran elite, brought back from trips to Europe along with phonographs and records. Broadcasts from Berlin, Ankara, Moscow, and London could be received. From 1934 a law formally allowed the importation of radio receivers, and antenna could be erected after obtaining permission from the Ministry of Post, Telegraph, and Telephone. In 1937 this ministry submitted a proposal to Reza Shah that outlined the establishment of a national broadcasting system. As a government-initiated project, finance was provided from the public purse, with personnel from the OEGPO, because broadcasting was conceived as an extension of earlier propaganda efforts. Thus it appears that a combination of public pressures, or habits already spreading through the Tehran intelligentsia's contact with the West, and a recognition of the propaganda potential of radio as an instrument of modernization, prompted government support for its development.

The first equipment consisted of a two-kilowatt medium-wave transmitter to cover Iran and to broadcast to other countries. It could be received at quite a distance and newscasts were quickly developed in Arabic, French, Russian, English, and German to redress the former one-way flow of information into Iran. Ten one-kilowatt transmitters, purchased from the telephone company of Britain, were established in provincial cities such as Tabriz and Isfahan to relay programs from Tehran, where initially all production was based. The foundation for a centralized nationwide system of radio was thus created from its inception.

On April 24, 1940, with calculated symbolic significance as the date was the crown prince's twenty-first birthday, Radio Iran was inaugurated, and the first nationally broadcast message was the national anthem. The crown prince enacted the necessary formalities and the prime minister, Matin-e-Daftari, read a short message in which he promised that radio would be a source of news, information, and entertainment for the general public, and that listening centers would be established where people could listen for free (Kimiachi, 1978: 69). The press carried brief notices of this event, and *Etela'at* newspaper carried an editorial that pointed to the reasons behind the development of radio. Radio was described as "one of the most important human inventions . . . among the most valuable gifts of civilization and progress" and could be considered "the voice of a nation heard in different parts of the world . . . and can be used as an element in strengthening the unity of a nation" (*Etela'at*, April 24, 1940).

Initially programs ran from 7 to 11 P.M. with one and a half hours of Persian and Western music, two hours of news in various languages, and some drama and school programs. Pars news agency, which had been established in 1934 as a service of the Ministry of Foreign Affairs, subscribed to A.F.P., U.P., and Reuters, and became the single central supplier of news to press and radio, an important censorship mechanism for the system. Soon talks on economic, cultural, and industrial affairs were broadcast. One commentator has assessed early radio thus: "The radio programs followed very much the line of the newspapers. There was popular music, both Iranian and European, but propaganda and instruction were the keynote. From the beginning, broadcasting in Iran was not a medium of entertainment but an effective instrument of government propaganda" (Mowlana, 1963: 495). It is somewhat ironic to note that the first Persian announcer, Abul-Qasem Taheri, was later enticed by the BBC and helped to establish the Persian-language broadcasting of the BBC World Service during World War II.

Fifteen minutes each day were leased for spot commercials that were not to offend public morality. Foreign companies, however, were not entitled to make use of radio publicity nor were the commercials broadcast abroad. No license fees were charged for radio, but owners were supposed to declare themselves to the Ministry of Post, Telegraph, and Telephone as well as to the central gendarmerie. UNESCO (1950) reported twenty thousand radio sets in Iran in 1940 and about sixty thousand a decade later, roughly one set per three hundred people. Thus the basic pattern of Pahlavi development was lain down in Reza Shah's reign: a monarchical dictatorship that disallowed any autonomous political activity; a strong security machinery of police, army, and secret police for surveillance, control, and enforcement of the royal will; and the beginnings of an ideological system used to propagate nationalist feeling, develop "modern" sentiments and attitudes, and legitimize the system. Radio broadcasting was from the beginning state-run and centrally organized with various censorship and control mechanisms well in place. But it was developed too late for Reza Shah to utilize it fully. On August 25, 1941, angered by the Shah's refusal to allow Allied supplies to be transported through Iran to German-occupied Russia, fearful of his increasingly sympathetic tendencies toward Hitler, and needing considerable amounts of oil for their war effort, Allied forces entered Iran and cut short Reza Shah's rule. Iran was divided once again into British and Soviet zones. Reza Shah was made to abdicate and sent into exile, carried by a British vessel to Mauritius, and later taken to Johannesburg, where he died.

If the origins of Iranian radio lie initially in military control and later as an instrument of political hegemony, television began as private entrepreneurship, a classic multiplier of consumerist modernity, and was only later taken over by the state as an instrument of its modernization project. To discuss the development of television in Iran adequately, it is necessary to describe in more detail the advent of Mohammad Reza Shah to power and the developmentalist orientation that his state would pursue. But first came a hiatus in the strong state, which allowed an opposition to develop.

Interregnum: Weak Government and Free Press

The typical pattern of Iranian political life has been that when the central authority is at its weakest, a dynamic political public sphere emerges with a variety of political groupings and communicative channels. When central authority is strong, an atmosphere of repression exists, with central control over political activity and expression.

The Allied invasion almost destroyed the Pahlavi state, which was politically discredited by its inability to prevent foreign occupation and politically undermined by the opposition political groups that sprang up. Liberties not enjoyed since 1921 were restored: trade unions, a free press, and rival political parties all flourished (Halliday, 1979: 24). Yet the discontinuity in political life since 1921 had almost wiped out any experiences gained before then. Politics had to be reinvented. As Mehrdad (1979: 195) has argued, "political parties which suddenly sprang onto the scene had practically no past and no tradition upon which they could rely; only the *Tudeh* party was an exception . . . in 1941, political life had to begin anew." This discontinuity of political activity was an important factor in the 1978 mobilization too, and partly accounts for the "spontaneity," lack of experience, and lack of formal political organization that the 1977–78 movement reflected.

By 1941, about fifteen political parties had been declared, some with *Tudeh* affiliations and some liberal and religious nationalists who later joined forces to create the National Front. A lively press developed, both general informational and sectarian, repeating the pattern of the constitutional period and that of the early 1920s. By August 1942 there were 50 newspapers; 120 by the winter; and 200 by the next summer. By 1945 more than 4,000 newspapers, magazines, and other publications existed (Taheri, 1980: 13).

Foreign powers sponsored their own publications, in foreign languages as well as Persian, and even the radio was compelled to allot a certain amount of broadcast time for Allied war propaganda of the British and Russians, which often tended toward criticism of the host government. By the Tripartite Treaty of January 1942, a veto by any one of the three powers (Iran, Britain, or the USSR) could prevent a piece of news from being broadcast or published. This tended to work in favor of the Soviets for a complicated set of reasons, and certainly did not help the maintenance of an independent press. Foreign publications continued until the summer of 1947, when some embassies began printing material highly critical of other embassies' political policies. Iran, anxious to avoid international squabbles breaking out in her territory, banned all embassies from publishing anything whatsoever. Although strict legal controls on the press still existed on paper, they had become unenforceable. In spite of stiff licensing procedures, the authorities were so weak that they could not stipulate any serious conditions and virtually anyone who had anything to say or, more accurately, believed that he or she had something worth saying, could have his or her own mouthpiece. Attempts to stop newspapers on grounds of "incitement to sedition" were still made occasionally but in practice this only meant that a paper ordered to cease publication appeared under a different license the same day. Renting newspaper licenses, in fact, became a business in its own right, with individuals securing licenses to print and then renting them out to publishers of banned titles (Taheri, 1980: 13). Taheri evaluates this period of press freedom in a very negative manner, arguing that much of the press power was used solely for personal vendettas and pecuniary ends, and papers were full of slander and innuendo.

Figures about newspaper circulation and readership during this period are guesstimates. Most newspapers were cheap to purchase, the average price of a daily paper being less than a penny. It appears that in the early 1950s some of the political dailies achieved circulations of fifty thousand, no mean feat given the population was around fifteen million, with 80 percent illiteracy. Certainly, press influence was far greater than circulation figures alone would suggest. Newspapers would be read in teahouses, mosques, and other public places, a widespread practice even now, so that the "informed public" might well have been ten times the actual circulation figures. A rather novel process developed around the more expensive weekly publications. The newsvendor had one week in which to rent the magazine to many people as possible, on an hourly or daily basis, and then the "unsold" copies could be returned to the publisher. Taheri (1980: 15) says this practice continued until the 1960s and reflected the prevailing low incomes, as magazines could be rented at a fraction of their cover price.

This period also saw the revival of the press as party organs, in much the same way as had occurred during 1912–25. The most extensive publishing operation was that of *Tudeh*, which published a number of papers including *Besuye Ayandeh* (Toward the future), but all shades of opinion and party orientations flourished. The National Front published *Bakhtar Emrouz* (The West today), and the Toilers party published *Shahed*, (The witness). The political-party publishing ventures went through many transmutations with frequent suspensions, particularly when press criticism of the cabinet became too virulent, as in December 1942 when all the daily papers in Tehran were suspended. One way around this was for a paper to appear the next day under a new name. Some of the journalistic ventures were one-man affairs, the publisher, editor, and journalist being one and the same. These were often unstable publications and sometimes ended abruptly, as with the murder of Mohammad Massoud in 1948.

During this period, the regime faced a number of serious internal crises. From 1941 to 1946 the two central problems were the issue of oil concessions for the Russians, and the question of autonomy for Azerbaijan and Kurdestan, both declared autonomous republics with Soviet support. The Majles, headed by Qavam, and the press resisted Soviet inroads to protect national unity. The early years of peace from 1946 to 1953 were dominated by one major political figure, Dr. Mohammad Mossadeq, who struggled to nationalize the Anglo-Iranian Oil Company and to curb the powers of the Shah to those specified by the written constitution. Mossadeq wished to break the British stranglehold over Iran's greatest national asset, oil, which was inscribed in the 1933 Oil Treaty that Reza Shah had signed with the Anglo-Iranian Oil Company. This treaty had meant that the country, its freedom of action, and its capacity for development were actually sold for money that the people never enjoyed and practically never saw. As Nirumand has argued, "It was not Iran that profited by the oil deal, but Britain (and a few Iranians), into whose pockets and foreign bank accounts the money flowed. It is natural, therefore, that most of the protests against the 1933 contract came from the people, rather than from politicians, and were aimed against British domination rather than the Anglo-Iranian Oil Company" (1969: 46–47).

In 1947, as leader of a minority group of deputies in Parliament, Mossadeq formed the National Front, which in October 1950 called for the nationalization of the oil industry. A series of political crises finally brought Mossadeq the premiership on April 29, 1951, and four days later he signed the oil nationalization bill. This move took Mossadeq into direct conflict with the Western powers at the height of their cold-war tension with the Soviet Union and its Eastern Allies. Britain took the oil issue into the international arena and gained U.S. support, initially for a boycott of Iran's exports and a cut in economic aid, and Iran's national treasury was emptied rapidly. Foreign troubles did not remain separate from domestic concerns for long.

Mossadeq and Mohammad Reza Pahlavi were set for a pitched battle about the appropriate role of a twentieth-century monarch. Mossadeq favored a reigning king like the British system, and the Shah, like his father, expected to rule with an iron fist. Mossadeq requested control of the war ministry from the monarch, and in July 1952 a series of violent demonstrations pressed his claim. The king refused, Mossadeq resigned, and another elder statesman was appointed. Martial law was declared in Tehran, members of the Parliament spoke against the monarch's usurpation of the people's power, and the clergy urged resistance. The bazaar closed, clashes between demonstrators and security forces occurred, and a general strike was called. On July 21, 1952 (30th Tir), military forces occupied key areas in Tehran, but despite the threat of their presence, demonstrators poured into the streets demanding the resignation of Qavam-o-Saltaneh and the return of Mossadeq. The popular slogan shouted was "Ya marg Ya Mossadeq" ("Either death or Mossadeq"), which was transmuted into "Either death or Khomeini" in 1979. The demand was achieved at the cost of several hundred dead and injured. After the success of the Islamic revolution in February 1979, the first commemoration ceremonies were held for those who died on 30th Tir. But from his reappointment, Mossadeq began to lose grip on the political situation. He managed to exile the monarch's twin sister, Ashraf, and the Queen Mother, thought to be the main culprits behind such anti-Mossadeq actions, and Qavam fled into exile.

Mossadeq became the first politician to use radio to master public opinion, and developed a chatty manner of speaking to the whole nation over the air. He would mobilize public support for his policies and inform people about government actions once they were accomplished. A famous example of this is his decision to subsidize the price of Caspian Sea fish as a good source of protein, which was announced over the radio. The next day many people were delighted to find that it had indeed happened, with fish very cheaply on sale in major cities. Massively popular, Mossadeq would undoubtedly have continued to enjoy strong public support if certain opposition forces from within and without had not intervened simultaneously. The Shah rejected attempts to curb his power and the compulsion to return lands illegally seized by his father. Large estate owners were worried by Mossadeq's plans for land reform, and army generals were angry at their loss of privileges when Mossadeq took over the Ministry of Defense. Ayatollah Kashani, once an ardent clerical supporter, had also turned against him and began to mobilize the populace against the premier. The British were desperate to maintain economic benefits and political ties with Iran. The United States was terrified by the growth of Soviet influence in the Third World and saw the *Tudeh* party growing increasingly powerful in the face of Mossadeq's declining influence. The two Western powers began to concoct a secret plan. A parliamentary crisis culminated in a referendum that voted to dissolve Parliament on August 2, 1953. The United

States found its opportunity to voice alarm that Mossadeq had become a victim of communist agitation and was abandoning constitutional procedures (Roosevelt, 1979). President Eisenhower spoke in a press conference on August 6 about the growth of communist influence in Asia and asserted administration readiness to prevent Soviet expansion, especially in Iran. On the 20th Mordad, 1953, General Zahedi orchestrated the coup against Mossadeq, who was arrested. The Shah, who had fled into exile in Rome, was returned to Tehran, the second Pahlavi monarch to be set in place by foreign help (Zabih, 1982). What is most significant about this period is that it marks the elimination of Britain's preferential position in Iran and the incorporation of Iran into the U.S. sphere of influence in the Middle East. The subsequent promotion of Mohammad Reza Pahlavi into a subimperial role in the Middle East, and the profound sociocultural effects of this incorporation, became both cause and object of political mobilization in the 1970s, when the anti-British slogans of the 1950s turned into "yankee, go home" and later "America, the great Satan."

What is also of significance for our argument is that the period 1941–53 had witnessed the embryonic development of a public sphere, with its multiplicity of political groupings, avalanche of published materials, growth of trade-union activity, and other manifestations of popular democracy. Central state weakness and ironically foreign-power intervention in Iran allowed for this occurrence, which was not to be repeated until the massive popular mobilization of 1977–79. Indeed, it could be argued that the 1978 movement was really a reconstruction of the democratization process cut short in 1953, and which took such a religious coloring because of the total elimination of autonomous secular political communication and activity from that year on. Because the 1953 coup and its aftermath eclipsed the secular nationalists and democrats who were indigenous forces for change and ideologically closest to the West, it almost prefigured the efflorescence of conservative elements to take up the oppositional role. As Cottam (1984) has powerfully argued, "the rhythm [of change] was deeply influenced and in startlingly contradictory ways by encounters with those people who were far ahead of Iran in terms of change—especially British, Americans, and Russians . . . the Khomeini phenomenon is a product of the alteration of natural change patterns in Iran by the interference of external powers . . . the conclusion is defensible that had Mossadeq not been overturned by a foreign-sponsored coup, the Khomeini regime would never have appeared." It was the erosion of the emergent public sphere of 1945–53 that *reduced* Iran to a "dualistic culture" of the dictatorial state and religious opposition. The eclipse of orthodox political organizations and the co-optation of secular political language drove politics into new forms of mediated communication, and made the remaining available channels of communication, the traditional social networks, so important. Thus, in some way U.S. intervention against the popular movement of 1953 received its popular reply, somewhat belatedly, in the anti-American flavor of the 1978 mobilization.

Chapter 4
Dependent Development and the Rise of Television

This chapter analyzes the growth of dependent development and monarchical dictatorship in Iran from 1953 to 1977, and the role played by media, especially television, in those processes. Oil rent (Mahdavy, 1970) financed the massive and rapid transformation of Iranian society under Mohammad Reza Pahlavi, particularly from 1963 to 1975, based on the same dynamic established by the first Pahlavi shah: monarchical dictatorship using a highly centralized and bureaucratized state for rapid capitalist development and mimetic Westernization. Political considerations and the consolidation of power dominated the period after the coup.

The Reestablishment of Royal Dictatorship

Despite the reinstatement of the Shah through the CIA-sponsored coup, martial law continued through the year 1953, strict controls over the press were established, and all political opposition was squashed. In September 1953, after a *Tudeh* caucus had been discovered inside the army, even stricter measures of political control were taken. A bill was passed that carried stiff penalties for members of any organizations that were "collectivist" in nature, that were against Islam, or that attacked the constitutional monarchy. Zahedi remained prime minister until April 1955, presiding over the 18th Majles in which all the deputies asserted their loyaly to the Shah.

By 1957 the Shah felt secure enough to sponsor the formation of two new political parties, *Melliyun*, or Nationalist Party, and *Mardom*, or People's Party, indications of the political euphemisms that were to become the hallmarks of this period. *Melliyun*, headed by the prime minister, Manouchehr Eqbal, was to be the majority party in the Majles, supporting the government. *Mardom*, led by Assadollah Alam, a school friend of the Shah, was to be the loyal opposition, supposedly free to criticize internal but not foreign affairs. Thus, the state began to orchestrate political life, creating political parties by royal fiat with no grass-roots support from any particular class or interest.

Entrepreneurship and Dependent Development

The late 1950s was a very poor time for independent political expression in Iran, but an excellent time for entrepreneurship. The abrupt end to a period of political instability provided the psychological context favorable to a new bout of capital investment. The period 1953–59 was one of distinct economic growth (Bharier, 1971; Katouzian, 1981). Gross national product grew approximately 7 to 8 percent and gross domestic capital formation grew rapidly. Government monies began to flow again with the resumption of oil revenues, and an expansionary atmosphere promoted competition among budding capitalists. The amount of revenue spent on imported capital goods rose significantly in the 1950s. The structure of imports reflected the demands of members of the landowning group, the commercial bourgeoisie, the tiny industrial sector, and the growing middle class, all of whom could afford the purchase of imported or montage-made manufactured goods. In a manner typical of much of the dependent Third World, a low-income market was being supplied with consumer goods and machinery manufacture on the basis of industrial technique designed for high-income countries. The intensive industrialization that began in the late 1950s and continued throughout the 1960s had a twofold purpose. The first was to reduce Iran's dependence on the export of primary products, and the second was to increase the rate of economic growth. This latter aim was pursued mainly through a policy of import substitution in order to satisfy the existing demand for manufactured products. Oil revenues were a mere 34 million dollars in 1953, but they had risen to 555 million dollars in 1963 and to a colossal 19 billion dollars by 1975 with the rise in world oil prices. By 1977 oil rent accounted for 77 percent of government earnings and 87 percent of foreign currency earnings, and was the basis for the projected 69 billion dollars required by the Fifth Development Plan of 1973–78. This revenue, coupled with foreign investment, was used to create a more differentiated industrial base, including energy, steel, petrochemicals, machine tools, and rubber, as well as production for consumer demand at home in the areas of clothing, canned foods, beverages, radio/television/telephone, and motor cars. Much of this production was "montage" assembly of foreign technologies based on franchise agreements.

Thus the 1950s saw the beginnings of full-fledged capitalist development in

Iran, in a "dependent" form, with the seeds of a new capitalist class, a comprador bourgeoisie. Jazani (1973) has divided this class into two groups, the first of which he designates "the imperialist partners in industry, trade, and finance" and the second of which includes army generals, government ministers, and the royal circle. This class maintains both dependency and dictatorship, and Jazani argues that the roots of this class formation were lain immediately after the coup of 1953, although some argue that this class really only grew after the White Revolution and the state capitalist policies of the 1960s. The essential elements of this class are clear: it was initially dependent on foreign, mostly American, capital, and it brought in imported manufactured goods, or acquired patents and franchises for the establishment of montage industries in Iran, bringing in prefabricated parts, cutting transportation costs and insurance, and using cheaper Iranian labor to assemble the final product. Such montage industries maintained their dependence on the foreign mother industry for parts and design, and made autonomous industrial development hard to acheive because of a continuing lack of adequate industrial experience and insufficient investment in technological research and development.

From the early 1960s a few major entrepreneurs dominated the economic scene and acquired the franchises on various manufactured consumer durables (Vaghefi, 1975; Graham, 1978). Family Chosroshahi held the monopoly on pharmaceuticals, glass, and shoes; Lajevardi controlled textiles and computer technology; Elghanian held 1,079 different patents, established a plastics industry using Iranian raw materials to effect American designs, and built the Plasco building on Istanbul Avenue in Tehran, the first Western-style covered shopping arcade, which rented space to small storekeepers. This arcade housed the only instant photo machine in Tehran in the summer of 1979.

Each of these families helped to revolutionize Iranian everyday life, as well as the visual appearance of the city and the home. But perhaps no one did more than Habibollah Sabet Pasal, who literally created the Iranian Pepsi Generation, importing soft drinks, cars, and television. Sabet, through his Firuz Trading Company, virtually controlled the domestic consumer durable market, holding the franchises for Electrolux, Kelvinator, Westinghouse, General Electric, Volkswagen, General Tyres, and Pepsi-Cola. Such goods appealed to a particular middle-class and upper-class elite, initally centered in Tehran, who already had some taste for a Westernized lifestyle and who had the disposable income to purchase these new items. Even so, however, the market was limited, although the manufacture of consumer durable goods such as household equipment, furniture, and television sets benefited from a quite income-elastic market in which a small rise in income meant a far greater rise in quantity of demand.

The family's entrepreneurial talent was no doubt sharpened by the business acumen that Sabet's son, Firuz, had acquired at the Harvard Business School. Upon Firuz's return from the United States, father and son acquired state permission to establish the first television station in Iran, which was to operate tax-free for five years. It is fascinating to note that this event was considered important enough for Mohammad Reza Pahlavi to write about it in one of his volumes of memoirs; the entry reads, "one young man, the son of a prominent businessman, studied at Harvard . . . wrote a thesis on the possibility of adopting modern television broadcasting to Persia's particular needs. When he returned, he became a pioneer in establishing Iran's new television industry" (1961: 138).

Sabet was also the RCA representative in Iran, and therefore sold the household television receivers needed to pick up the messages he was organizing and producing. He also immediately sold advertising airtime to local entrepreneurs, thus establishing a highly integrated money-making system with its own built-in modernizing potential, the ability to awaken consumer demand. Thus, unlike telegraph, wireless, and radio, which were established, owned, and operated by the Iranian government, television was first introduced, established, owned, and operated by a private entrepreneur, part and parcel of the burgeoning, albeit dependent, development of Iran in the 1950s.

The Sabet plan met favorable acceptance from the Shah, especially after Sabet had broadcast the wedding of the Shah and Farah to the Queen Mother, who was recuperating from a broken leg and had been physically unable to attend the ceremony (Kimiachi, 1978: 112). A parliamentary bill in June 1958 gave the private company permission to establish a television broadcast center in Tehran, and the system was inaugurated in October 1958 with the mandatory speech of the Shah, who said he was very happy to have television broadcasting in Iran to help "the training of youth and improve social knowledge" (*Kayhan*, October 4, 1958). What kind of training or what kind of social knowledge was never spelled out.

Television of Iran was the first commercial station in the Middle East. It was run by an American, Vance Hallack, and other Americans trained an Iranian staff, although it was continually dogged by a shortage of skilled domestic personnel. The U.S. broadcasting standard of 525 lines (NTSC) was adopted, which Sabet's RCA imports received well.

Initially, the programming of the station consisted of imported serials and film from the United States (which made up about half the broadcasting time) and domestic production. The latter was heavily influenced by American formats; for example, quiz programs sponsored by advertizers with consumer durables as prizes for the winners. Domestic news was compiled from Pars News Agency feed, and foriegn news was taken from the United States Information Service (USIS) and was sponsored by Pan American Airlines. By the end of the first year, programming had reached six hours every night of the week (Kimiachi, 1978).

In 1960 the first regional station was opened, in Abadan, with a relay station in Ahwaz, also in oil-rich Khusestan Province. These sites could only have been chosen for their economic potential. Although not the most populous regional city (Isfahan and Shiraz had larger populations), Abadan was the center of the oil industry and contained both a sizable foreign community as well as a growing cadre of skilled and well-paid industrial workers. Because the expansion of television helped through advertising to promote the interests of the comprador bourgeoisie that owned the montage industries and controlled consumer durable imports, this expansion south was a clever business move. Nothing could have spread consumerism as rapidly and tellingly as television. Radio, although available to a larger population, lacked the visual stimulus of actually seeing inside a "modern" home to appreciate the new mood of a consumption-oriented environment. The cinema was already carrying some advertising, but its viewing audiences were almost totally young and male, and mainly cigarettes and cars were advertised there. Television receivers were owned only by a small and upwardly mobile class, the exact audience who might be persuaded to purchase a refrigerator and a washing machine after purchasing their television. Even in the late 1970s, television advertising was dominated by household consumer durables, and then by cosmetics, the advertising message oriented mainly toward capturing the imagination of status-conscious housewives.

Thus, though radio was from the beginning a government monopoly, television began in the hands of a private entrepreneur who realized its potential as a multiplier of modern consumption values that were overtly displayed in advertising and more subtley revealed in the depiction of Western lifestyles in the imported films and serials. By the early 1960s, the Sabets were millionaires, and had played a key role in the transformation of urban—and, soon to follow, rural—Iranian social and cultural life.

Changes in the control and organization of television were imminent, however. The tax-free concession to Sabet was renewed for another five years in 1963, but the Iranian government was beginning to shape its own plans for the future of television in Iran.

The State and Capitalist Development

The rationale behind the government's takeover of Sabet's television network has never been fully explained. One possible reason might be that the Shah was always fearful of the development of any potential autonomous base of social power that might threaten his own position, such as the excessive growth of a private sector with great wealth. Most large businesses were able to function only through building relationships with members of the royal family, usually by giving them honorary shares in the venture; this still did not make these businesses immune to shifts in monarchical mood, as the campaigns against profiteering and the arrest of various entrepreneurs in the 1970s demonstrate. If this were the primary reason for the television takeover, however, it could have been solved by Sabet's making a royal a part-owner of television. The Shah craved not only power but wealth, which indeed was used to support his control, and he had established a vast royal empire of business holdings, the Pahlavi Foundation (Graham, 1978: 152 and appendix). One of the most influential leaflets of the revolutionary movement, known as *Octopus*, purported to detail the immense wealth of the Pahlavi family and its cronies, and appropriately provoked public anger and resentment.

Another possible reason for the takeover was the growing criticism against Bahaii influence in the court. The Bahaii circle in Iran to which Sabet belonged has tended to be elite and well educated, and had attached itself with considerable success to the royal family. The Bahaii group possessed many technical skills that the Shah could use; had influence abroad, especially in the United States; and maintained no unified political position in Iran, their "internationalism" supposedly taking them beyond the realm of domestic politics. This made them individually good political tools, and the list of Bahaii in the court circle and directly involved in domestic politics is extensive, having included Parviz Sabeti, once head of SAVAK's elite control section; Ayadi, the king's physician; Rouhani, Minister for Agriculture; Malek Abhari, Vice-Minister of Post, Telegraph, and Telephone, and others (Najafi, 1978 [1357]). Fear of the development of a separate power base by the Bahaii, especially with the control of television, which provided significant employment opportunities, a dynamic economic enterprise, and a unique channel of influence, could have prompted the takeover.

A third possible factor, which is probably the most crucial to a long-run analysis of the role of television in Iranian life, was the broader shift in political mood and economic activity of the period 1960–63 that signaled a turning point in the development of the bureaucratic state in Iran. In the early 1960s, with the Kennedy administration ensconced in Washington, pressure was applied not only to the Iranian regime but to other Third World systems to undertake reform programs, particularly land reform. The logic behind this pressure was twofold: to support the modernization of certain Third World client states to preempt the rise of revolutionary movements and opportunities for Soviet influence, and to remove obstacles to the full development of capitalist relations of production in the Third World. The exact extent of American advice or pressure on the Shah to carry out reforms remains unclear, but, as a producing nation that stood to gain tremendously by the capitalist impetus of the Shah's policy and that wanted a stable Western ally to represent its interests in the Middle East, the "White Revolution" obviously did not hurt U.S. interests.

The Shah put forward a six-point program that he claimed amounted to a "White Revolution"; the program was overwhelmingly passed through a plebiscite in January 1963. Land reform had already been proclaimed under Amini's administration in 1962 but was now incorporated into this more wide-ranging "revolutionary" project that included the sale of state-owned factories to finance land reform, the nationalization of forests, an amendment of the election law to include female suffrage, and the establishment of a Literacy Corps (Touran, 1978).

The hostility of both secular and religious groups to the content and implementation of these plans was strong but manifested diverse political reactions: concern about the increasing power of the Pahlavi state, which was also consolidating SAVAK and the military; concern about the state capitalist road to development; and Khomeini's antipathy to the enfranchisement of women. Toward the end of 1963 a mass roundup of opposition politicians throughout Iran took place with imprisonment and exile (including Khomeini's) meted out as punishment (Zonis, 1971). Thus the different political forces that had resisted the Shah's consolidation of power and the general strengthening of the Pahlavi state were forced on the defensive. As Halliday (1979: 27) argued, the events of this period "marked the end of any hope that the forces released during the 1941–1953 period could soon reverse the verdict of the 1953 coup. Until the late 1970s the initiative lay with the regime, and the rises in oil revenue from 1971 onwards, by multiplying government revenues, gave an additional dynamism to the state's policies." Let us just note briefly the "language of color" that permeated Iranian politics, so that the Shah's "white" revolution was fought out against some secular forces of "red" revolution as well as the clerical forces of "black" reaction; it was perhaps the Shah's worst nightmare that the black and the red joined forces against him in 1977–79. It might also be wryly noted that white is the color of the shroud of the dead in Shiite Islam, proudly worn by demonstrators during the popular movement, so that even the Shah's own color was turned against him.

From 1963 and the "White Revolution," the major concern of the state was rapid modernization and intensive capitalist development based on oil revenues. Despite the focus on land reform, the central and most disputed element of policy (Lambton, 1969; Hoogland, 1982), agriculture and rural development had a low development priority, and the main demographic impact was to create a landless peasant migration to urban areas. That moves were made for the takeover of Sabet's private television station fits well into this pattern of the assertion of state hegemony through the quelling of opposition political activity once and for all, and the concerted development of a "revolutionary" developmentalist ideology to legitimize regime activity. Despite renewing the concession to Sabet in 1963 for five years, the government drew up its own proposals. In May 1964 the French group ORTF was commissioned through Reza Ghotbi—a cousin of Shahbanou Farah and a French-trained engineer—as a consultant to undertake a research project for the development of a government-financed and government-operated television station.

Television as an Instrument of Monarchist Dictatorship, 1969–78

The project to establish a government television station moved fast. In the summer of 1966, the Plan and Budget Organization allocated a budget for the project, and the Ministry of Economics donated land. A temporary structure was built, and on October 26, 1966, National Iranian Television sent its first broadcast meesage, a statement by the Shah, of course. Test programs were run, and complete programming commenced at *Noruz*, the Iranian New Year, in March 1967. The first week's programs included the broadcasting of the Shah's birthday celebrations from Amjadieh Stadium.

In June 1967, the Parliament approved a proposal for the economic and administrative independence of NITV, National Iranian Television, to be separated from the control of the PTT in terms of hardware, and from the Department of Publications and Broadcasting in terms of production and programming. In 1970, the Industrial Management Institute in Tehran was asked to plan a merger of NITV with the thirty-five-year-old radio network, and to plan for the rapid expansion of broadcasting services throughout Iran by establishing new production and transmission centers. In 1971 National Iranian Radio and Television (NIRT) was incorporated as a public broadcasting monopoly run as an independent government corporation. The Shah appointed Ghotbi as the first director-general; neither of them thought he would also be the last.

Sabet's television was taken over in July 1969. Sabet had been nothing if not generous to the Shah. During the Shah's brief "exile" in 1953, Sabet had presented him with a blank check to ease his sojourn in Italy. Having received permission to establish Pepsi-Cola plants in 1952 with privileges in regard to customs, Sabet naturally presented substantial shares in the company to members of the royal family. However, once it was decided that Sabet's television captured large audiences from the new government station (he continued to offer rather low-grade, American-type entertainment without political propaganda), he was forcibly bought out for a reputed sum of 20 million toman, against his initial capital investment of 70 million. His building was taken over and became the home of the new Educational Television. Subsequently, in the mid-1970s, with a supposed government move against the excessive profits of large entrepreneurs, a notion embodied in the nineteenth point of the "White Revolution," Sabet was severely penalized for ostensibly distributing Pepsi in dirty bottles. He began to transfer his wealth abroad, and left before the revolution. In July 1979, his holdings were taken over by the Revolutionary Committee of the Islamic Republic.

Prior to 1967 television had covered about 2.1 million people. When NIRT began regular transmissions that year, coverage rose to 4.8 million, and by 1974 had risen to over 15 million, roughly half the total population. That NIRT was accorded a very high priority in the state development strategy is evidenced by the large budget allocations that were provided to the organization. This allowed the use of the latest technologies, including microwave delivery systems to overcome problems of mountainous terrain. By 1975–76 radio covered almost the entire country, and 70 percent of the population had television reception. One indication of the prime importance attached to owning a television was the fact that people in villages without electricity, who had survived with oil lamps and iceboxes,

Figure 4.1. The original logo of NIRT, two lions rampant.

bought generators in order to be able to run a television. Television became extremely popular across all ages and social groups; the little audience research that was undertaken recorded roughly six hours of viewing a day with an average of seven viewers per set by 1974 (NIRT Commercial Affairs, 1974). Despite overall budget cuts in 1975–76, NIRT's total budget rose about 20 percent, and by 1975 NIRT was second only to Japan in Asia in terms of the development of its broadcasting capabilities. The big state had developed its big media.

Regime Ideology and Media Content

No regime survives only with the carrot of development and the stick of repression. Control must also be exercised ideologically, through the manipulation of symbols and values. Yet, as in the period of Reza Shah's rule, there was a curious and deep contradiction between the rhetoric of the regime and its attempt to resurrect old Persian symbols of national continuity and monarchical splendor, and the widespread celebration of Western popular culture that dependent development implied. Thus the new national broadcasting structure was a powerful weapon that was poorly used, which rather than mustering popular support for the Shah's modernization served rather to delegitimize the regime further. We will examine the structure and content of television programming, and then look at how regime ideology was elaborated in the media.

From the start there were two programs: the First Program was general content, the Second aimed to be educational and cultural. But research shows that about 33 percent of First Program content and 60 percent of Second Program content was imported (Katz and Shinar, 1974; Motamed-Nejad, 1977) and consisted of old films, serials, and musical shows, with *Tarzan, Days of Our Lives,* and *Marcus Welby, M.D.* being special audience favorites. The predominance of imported programming has been shown throughout the Third World (Varis, 1984). In Iran, such programs were cheaply available on the open market, there was an initial lack of trained domestic personnel in both the creative and technical sides of broadcasting, and the constraints of royal dictatorship and censorship meant that imported programming was less controversial than home-made materials that might be seen as critical. In addition to the two main channels, an entire channel of television and one of radio were devoted to English-only broadcasts aimed at the growing battalion of foreign workers living in Iran, which relied on even heavier amounts of imported programming and Western music.

Home-produced content was modeled on foreign formats, like consumer-oriented quiz shows. Occasionally, a well-made domestic serial appeared, such as *Morad Barqi* (Morad the electrician), which was based on the wisdom of folk characters and quickly became a favorite. People responded eagerly to content they could identify with and that reflected Iranian culture and identity, but not much was provided along these lines. The same situation has been documented in Latin America, where home-made *telenovelas* became far more popular than once-popular imported soap operas (Straubhaar, 1981).

National Iranian Radio and Television helped to spread a single national language throughout Iran (with limited broadcasting in local languages—although, since the revolution, there has been debate about "Persian chauvinism"). The other central contribution to indigenous Iranian culture was the support for and broadcasting of traditional Iranian music. In general, there was little on television to support the grandiloquent verbiage of NIRT documents about the purposes and goals of broadcasting in contributing to national integration and preservation of cultural identity (NIRT, 1974; Tehranian, 1977). From quite early in its establishment, NIRT was involved with international broadcasting. In October 1969, it started to utilize satellite broadcasting via the Assadabad earth station in Western Iran. Many international events could be broadcast in to Iranian audiences, such as the *Apollo* moon landing, World Cup football from Mexico, the Shah's visit to President Nixon, and the historic heavyweight-title fight between Muhammad Ali and Joe Frazier. Also, Iran was able to broadcast internationally the lavish spectacle of the 2,500th anniversary of the Persian Empire in October 1971.

That spectacle, celebrating the glory of pre-Islamic Iran and the continuity of a royal tradition, was typical of the central elements of the regime's mythology and manipulation of historical consciousness. This ideological outlook had been first elaborated by Reza Shah, but was taken to new heights by his son. Made-for-media pageants were staged, such as the belated coronation in 1967 when the Shah crowned himself not only *Shahanshah*, King of Kings, but also *Aryamehr*, Light of the Aryans; the elaborate multimillion dollar celebration of 2,500 years of the monarchy in 1971; the fiftieth anniversary celebrations of the Pahlavi dynasty in 1976; and, most ostentatious, the replacement from 1976 of the Islamic calendar with a monarchical one based on the coronation of Cyrus the Great. The ideological project motivating such claims was the necessity of the monarchy for a strong Iran, but this devolved into a personality cult with the obligatory picture of the Shah in every office, calendar, and textbook. Royal speeches at orchestrated rallies in January and February (6th Bahman, the date of the "White

Revolution") or October (4th Aban, the Shah's birthday) and royal "salaam" cere-monies where the Shah gave audience were broadcast at length. Royal ceremonies were media events whose purpose was to impress and awe the viewing public. Royal news was a standard front-page item in the newspapers and a high priority item in broadcast news; other domestic news stories received a low profile because of censorship difficulties, while foreign news received extensive cover-age instead (Sreberny-Mohammadi and Mahloudji, 1978). Ironically, it is possi-ble that the aura and mystery surrounding the King of Kings, Light of the Aryans, was actually diminished—rather than embellished—by this widespread everyday contact, as the emperor was revealed to be wearing no clothes.

The formulas of the "White Revolution," extended to seventeen principles and renamed the "Shah-People Revolution" in 1967, were elaborated as symbols of national integration and progress. Displayed on town lampposts, memorized by schoolchildren, incorporated into rural literacy programs, these principles re-mained little more than slogans rather than any coherently integrated ideological outlook. With important opinion leaders such as Khomeini refuting regime rhetoric and proffering Islamic identity and populist Iranian nationalism, regime attempts at legitimation were blocked. When the issue of dependency was added to opposition criticism, the regime's nationalist credentials were further under-mined. Although NIRT enjoyed some measure of independence from direct gov-ernment and security-force intervention, partly because of its head's close alliance with the court, there were still the occasional SAVAK-sponsored programs that had to be aired. In the early 1970s, at the height of the urban guerrilla movement, long lectures by Parviz Sabeti, a Mossad-trained top SAVAK agent in charge of ideological matters and the control of intellectuals, were presented on television, discussing the sinister designs of subversive groups. Later, "confessions" by cap-tured guerrillas were also aired. Such government interventions tainted the early independent reputation of NIRT and lost it considerable credibility. It is also worth mentioning here that a study of news comprehension revealed that a large percentage of the population simply did not understand the language of broad-casting, particularly news programming (Arbabzadeh, 1977). This suggests that an information gap, if not a wider perceptual divergence, was actually created (not solved) by broadcasting, which produced messages accessible and acceptable to an educated, cosmopolitan elite rather than addressing the information needs of the bulk of the population.

In 1975 the Shah suddenly made an abrupt switch of political management, amalgamating all political activity into one party, *Hezbe-Rastakhiz-e Melli* (National Resurgence Party) and ushering in a new mood of political mobiliza-tion. Again he appeared to be trying to preempt demands for political participa-tion and to provide greater political leadership. This was to prove quite counter-productive (demonstrating that the fears about mobilization turning against the regime were probably well founded) and heralded the collapse of the regime. The

Shah became the *Farmandar*, the Great Commander, guiding his people to the Great Civilization. The extent of development was said to have eliminated class and class conflict, and thus *Rastakhiz* was to be a party of national unity that everyone was supposed to join (Mehrdad, 1979). The party was to have two "wings" that essentially stage-managed internal "debate" and promoted the illusion of differences of opinion. Those who did not participate were to be considered *"Tudeh* sympathizers" and could be "slung out of Iran by their tails" like rats (*Kayhan International*, March 8, 1975).

Suddenly from political quiescence the media were plunged into the center of political debate, albeit under even stricter government control. A number of *Rastakhiz*-based papers were established to publicize party activities. To legitimize the new system, the Shah, in a nationally televised address, called for elections. Broadcast time was provided in a program called *Dar Rah* (On the way) for prospective candidates, all carefully vetted, to present themselves. The media, which had attempted to remain neutral within the political process, were now invoked as active mobilizers and began to show a real interest in debate. A series of programs hosted regime intellectuals arguing about the process of development, comparing traffic congestion with travel by camel, or evaluating the benefits of the traditional *qanat* water system over mechanized agriculture. Such programs were heavily stage-managed and the polarized terms in which debate was couched omitted any in-depth exploration of the failures of regime policy, yet they began to render such themes discussable. When the Imperial Inspection Committee was established in November 1976 to deal with waste and corruption in state bureaucracies, its deliberations were broadcast. A brief nightly satire called *Mr. Marbute* depicted corruption, people's confrontations with inefficient bureaucracy, and other social issues. Gradually, as the "wings" of *Rastakhiz* engaged in more radical debate about pressing social issues and how to solve them, and as the politicians themselves seemed to be demanding more freedom to criticize and to create policy, so the contents of press and radio-television reflected this sudden change of political mood. What had been intended as an astute political move to guarantee national unity only succeeded in putting political issues at the top of the public agenda and revealed that even within the political elite there was deep dissatisfaction both with the policy-making process and with the policies enacted.

The main set of symbols besides nationalism utilized by the regime was that of modernization. The nightly newscast on the main television channel began with a brief filmstrip in which various images of the Shah, in military uniform, being crowned, were intercut with images of a steel plant, dam, oil refinery, and the ornamental architecture of Azadi Square. It was presented as an "end of ideology" position, as though the evidence of rapid development was so overwhelming that no public discussion was necessary. Only patience was required until Iran arrived at the gates of the "Great Civilization," the golden future that the Shah promised in his book of the same name (Pahlavi, 1978).

But as in so much of the Third World, modernization came to be synonymous with Westernization, and broadcasting reflected the increasing foreignness of the general environment. Westernized housing styles, interior design, clothing, cuisine, and food habits were all evident. The modernization process always implies rupture with the past, but the internal culture shock in Iran was particularly rapid, brutal, and alienating, something the West really did not comprehend (Beeman, 1983). It also had important class dimensions, for the cosmopolitan lifestyle held up as the model of modern life and espoused by so much media content was only affordable by a small urban elite. It could be argued that one of the central dynamics of media in this period was to carry the economic and sociocultural gaps of Iranian society—indeed, the international class differences—into everyone's living room, so that instant comparisons could be made between the viewer's own situation and the situation of the players in the television programs. If, as Cottam (1979) says, one of the major shifts in Iranian society over the last two decades of Mohammad Reza Pahlavi was the development of a "mass public," television clearly played a significant role in this process and ultimately boomeranged against the regime. Much of the cultural programming and advertising served to heighten the gulf of wealth, lifestyle, and attitudes between a limited, cosmopolitan upper class and the rest of Iran. Mixed sentiments, of envy and outrage, of cultural inferiority and of cultural pollution, grew among this transitional population unclear of exactly where the "transition" was leading. This cultural content also contradicted the putative "nationalism" of the regime, or implied that nationalism was merely a formal, political identity while the internal culture became a hybrid internationalized phenomenon—a process that many in both secular and religious camps saw as undermining any sense of Iranian identity. These contradictions were raised not only as social scientific analysis; rather, these issues became part and parcel of the internal debate within Iran about the impact of modernization and explicitly began to challenge the claims of the regime. Like so many other development projects, including dams, high-rise apartments, art museums, and monuments, radio-television was both functional and flamboyant, a prestige symbol of development in itself as well as a potential carrier of development. As in other areas of Iranian development, such as defense and nuclear power, the high-tech focus was not matched by adequate supplies of trained personnel, with consequent wasted capacity and frustrated employees. Numerous contacts working within NIRT would frequently complain of the difficulties in getting a production team together.

That the emphasis was more on centralized control of communication than on the fostering of interpersonal communications is evident from the continuing primitiveness of travel across Iran and the poor postal and telecommunications systems. The wait for telephone installation was many years and the cost was prohibitive to many. The heavy focus on electronic media also tended to cover up the weak development of the press, and of reading habits in general. Despite the hosting of UNESCO conferences on illiteracy and an ostentatious concern with the issue, there was (and is) a continuing problem of illiteracy: not only did the rates of adult illiteracy remain high, but less than 40 percent of schoolchildren completed primary school (Abrahamian, 1982; Mohammadi, 1975). As argued earlier, literacy was at the heart of, though no guarantee of, the development of Western democracy. The absence of a significant reading public and the continued power of oral culture in itself supported the traditional authority of the *mullahs* and made it very difficult for a secular opposition to argue its perspectives. Although privately owned, the press operated under state surveillance in the classic authoritarian model, and there was little to choose among the dull dailies of Tehran. Indeed, while many of the UNESCO indicators of media development (including the numbers of radio receivers, television sets, and cinema seats) had been reached or surpassed in Iran, one critical indicator lagged badly: the provision of daily newspapers. Thus Iran appears to have leapt over one of Lerner's stages of media development, a critical stage for political development: the growth of a popular press combined with universal literacy. One media analyst commenting on the anemic state of the daily and weekly press suggested in the late 1970s that "if Iran continues on its present path it will be the first nation in the world to have nationally spread television before a nationally spread press" (Tunstall, 1977: 247). In general the parameters of Iranian cultural life, including publishing, cinema, theater, and the mass media, were negatively defined through censorship and control by the Ministry of Information and the Ministry of Culture and Art. Cinema relied heavily on imported American and Indian films and though the Iranian film industry was growing, much of what was shown was commercial and banal. Concerned filmmakers were frustrated; the film *Dayere-ye Mina* (The cycle), for example, which portrayed a real commercial enterprise that bought the blood of drug addicts and sold it to hospitals, took years to be released and finally enjoyed only a very brief run in Tehran.

Until 1975 there was a rather weak attempt at developing the political framework and ideological supports for the regime, with widespread fear of political mobilization because crowds orchestrated in support of the monarchy could as easily turn against the monarchy. Even the belated attempt to mobilize using *Rastakhiz* (Resurgence) backfired, and many of the palace cronies scarpered as soon as the going got tough, few being ready to die for the weak slogans of Pahlavism once their oil share was threatened. Thus from 1953 the Shah had ruled with a combination of rapid development and severe political repression, but the pell-mell rush toward Westernization created profound social dislocation and cultural confusion that the mass media appeared to exacerbate rather than alleviate. Until the creation of *Rastakhiz*, political participation and debate had a very low profile, and political communication centered on the reinforcement of key symbols and images rather than on the promotion of any coherent ideological framework or intensive political socialization. Basically the Iranian people had been offered bread and circuses and it was entertainment rather than indoctrination, economic consumption rather than political participation, that the mass media proffered. But because so much of the content was imported and so many of the social changes promoted Westernization, even the weak elaboration of nationalist symbols was belied by the images and the reality of daily life.

Demographic Changes

The oil-based development strategy had a considerable impact on the demographic shape of Iran, and on its social structure. Rapid urbanization was the major demographic change, especially from the 1960s on. In the 1930s, only 21 percent of the population lived in towns (population centers over 5,000 people); in 1966 the figure was 38 percent; and by 1977 nearly 48 percent of the population lived in towns (Abrahamian, 1982). In 1966, 21 percent of the population lived in cities with populations over 100,000 and by 1976 this figure was 29 percent. All the major cities experienced growth, but it was most pronounced in Tehran, where in the southern area a considerable shantytown expansion grew with areas known as *halabi-abad* (tin-can city), and the South City Pits (Kazemi, 1980). Little government support was provided for these urban migrants, and the clergy took on the task of financial and moral support of these dislocated "transitionals." If modernization always produces social upheaval, there is little doubt that the rapidity of the social mobilization in Iran increased the social and psychological turmoil, and, in a situation where so much was changing, these migrants particularly looked to the mosque and religion as points of familiarity and identity. Investments and improvements in health care and availability of facilities lowered the infant mortality rate and produced a rapid population rise, from 25 million people in 1966 to 33.5 million a decade later. Perhaps more significant than general population growth was the severe skewing of the age structure, so that by the mid-1970s half the Iranian population was under sixteen years of age and two-thirds were under thirty years. Children of the "White Revolution" with little independent political education and even less memory of political participation, but who were products of the television era and of economic boom, were to be an active element of the revolution under an Islamic banner once the boom faltered.

These demographic patterns were indicative of a shifting social structure. Industrial expansion and educational investment particularly promoted the development of the two modern classes, the salaried middle class and the urban working class. It should be noted that the peculiar effects of oil rent (Mahdavy, 1970) and rapid economic development on class structure, and the lack of theoretical debate, all mean that there is still no agreed-upon social scientific vocabulary to describe class structure in Iran. The descriptors used here are similar to those adopted by Abrahamian (1982).

The modern middle class, made up of salaried employees, civil servants, professionals, engineers, managers, teachers, and the rest of the intelligentsia, almost doubled in size from 1953 to 1977. In addition, there was a sizable body of students, both at home and abroad. Highly educated yet often unable to practice at efficient professional standards because of excessive bureaucratization, corruption, deployment of foreign experts in preference to Iranians, and living on taxed salaries while the private sector enjoyed huge tax-free profits, this class was poorly accommodated to the regime. It provided the technocrats that staffed the innumerable sectors of the government bureaucracy and who were co-opted with good salaries into a "sullen acquiescence" (Cottam, 1979) to the regime. The center of support for the democratic and independent nationalist policies of Mossadeq, this class lacked any real means of participation in decision-making nor did it possess its own channels with which to articulate grievances and make demands; its favored channels, professional associations and independent political parties, were banned and the press was weak and censored. Thus the dramatic speaking out through open letters in 1977 played such an important symbolic role in the breaking of the silence.

The urban working class employed in modern industry, oil, transportation, mining, urban construction, and services comprised 17 percent of the workforce in 1977. When agricultural laborers and other handicraft and bazaar wage-earners are included, the wage-earning class approached 3 million people and 25 percent of the workforce. Yet it has been estimated that 70 percent of all those in manufacturing employment worked in units of under ten people, so this was an extremely fragmented class. Structurally difficult to mobilize and lacking channels of organization since the banning of autonomous unions, this social sector did not display any evident consciousness of "class identity" but was amenable to the populist appeals of politicized Islamic identity. The ranks of this class were swollen by numbers of rural migrant laborers who sought seasonal employment, especially in the booming private-sector construction industry.

This group was important, for it linked remote rural areas with the modern lifestyle of the cities. As well as bringing money to the rural areas it also carried back social fashions and political ideas, particularly in the form of cassette tapes of Shariati and Khomeini. Instead of broadening its social base, these new social classes were developing with almost no links to the regime. With the drastic actions of *Rastakhiz* in the mid-1970s, the regime severed even the tenuous ties that had linked it to the traditional middle class.

Thus Iranian development was dominated by state disbursement of oil revenues, which rose dramatically from 1973, fueling the Shah's plans for a more rapid march to modernization, for making Iran the world's fifth most industrialized state and taking it to the gates of the "Great Civilization" that the Shah had promised. The massive social mobilization was absorbed in a highly "uncivilized" way, hardly producing the civilized urban environment that Lerner described as the modernization process. Ostentatious prestige projects, conspicuous consumption, and corruption were the reverse side of urban squalor and dislocation. Most important, the social forces unleashed by Westernized development found no way of channeling grievances and discontents into the system. Social mobilization was not matched by political participation, and the gulf between the government and the social structure widened.

Uneven Development Falters

The unevenness of the social improvements was marked by a severe urban-rural divide, and by a top-heavy concentration in Tehran. Urban income was about six times higher than rural, and the gap was increasing, hence the massive migration to urban areas. The lack of resources in rural areas meant that within a decade Iran had turned from being a net exporter of food to spending up to 1 billion dollars per year on imported agricultural products. Tehran, with 13 percent of the total population and 28 percent of Iran's urban population, absorbed half or more of all licensed physicians, dentists, university students, newspapers and periodicals, telephones, and companies (Kazemi, 1980: 25). Tehran itself was deeply divided by social class, progressing north by status to the extravagant residences of the upper class clustered on the slopes of the Alborz. Many basic social needs, including adequate housing, medical facilities, nutrition, and power supplies, still remained unattended. Despite a significant growth in higher education and a large body of state-supported students studying abroad, many rural areas still lacked basic primary educational provision and 68 percent of adults remained illiterate. The general quality of urban life deteriorated. The shantytowns grew, air pollution thickened, and traffic jammed. The percentage of families living in one room increased so that by 1977 an estimated 42 percent of Tehran inhabitants had inadequate housing. Profound social injustice and inequality were visible every day in Tehran, as Mercedes-Benz automobiles drove past women "washing" cooking pots in the filthy water of the *jubes*, the streams that flow by the roadside through the city, and as the urban laborers ate bread and onion on the ground at the base of the luxury apartment complexes they worked to build. If "relative deprivation" (Runciman, 1966) depends upon comparison, the contrasts were vividly displayed, but this only became a mobilizing factor, in a classic revolutionary pattern, when the period of economic development was reversed. Much of the negative side of rapid development might have been tolerated longer, if the economy had not been seen to falter dramatically in the mid-1970s. Bottlenecks in the ports and on the roads, severe energy shortages in Tehran, rampant inflation, spiraling housing costs, evidence of waste and corruption, and even a budget deficit threatened the entire foundation of the Shah's development strategy: the notion that wealth would eventually "trickle down" to all. The regime tried to blame the business community, pointing first at some big entrepreneurs who precipitated a huge flight of capital, and then at the bazaar community, doling out prison sentences and fines. The bazaaris, angered at being singled out for punishment, resenting the lack of attention to internal regime corruption and incompetence, began to pour more money into the coffers of its traditional leadership, the clergy.

From the beginning of his rule, Mohammad Reza Pahlavi was considered among a core sector of Iranians to be "dependent" upon the United States, and the reality of the relationship became less important in its consequences than the myths that developed. The Shah never truly acquired nationalist legitimacy, particularly within the politically concerned middle class, and despite the symbolic manipulation of the mass media they were mainly seen as carriers of Western culture, further reinforcing the real and the perceived problems of dependency. Thus, a mix of long-term features, such as lack of regime legitimacy and widespread cultural malaise, together with a series of events in the 1970s (the economic downturn, the establishment of *Rastakhiz* and a changed internal political environment, and a focus on human rights in the international arena) was to provide a new moment for Iranian political activity. It was not the clergy who began the process; rather, the kindling was lit by the secular intellectuals, many of whom were themselves engulfed by the revolutionary flames.

III
The Culture and Weapons of Opposition

Chapter 5
Oppositions: Secular and Religious

Having examined the state communications network and ideology, in this chapter we focus on the growing oppositional forces to the regime. We have argued that Iran had regressed to a dualistic communications structure, and now concentrate on the traditional social network of communication that centered on the bazaar and the mosque. Because of the repression of organized secular political groups and the censorships of publishing, this traditional network remained the only autonomous sphere of social life outside control of the state. We will examine the continued embeddedness and importance of religious rituals and locations within the daily life of the popular classes, and discuss the practiced ability of religious leaders to address the masses in a language they readily understood and to manipulate traditional symbols and statuses to which they responded. The chapter will present the continued power of religion within popular culture and the manner in which a politicized version of religious tradition was communicated to the masses.

This is essentially a sociological and cultural analysis in which the traditional classes are seen as possessing the necessary resources to translate a myriad of desperate discontents into a coherent political force against the regime. These resources include autonomous social spaces, a mobilizing ideology that called up a key social and individual identity (Islam), and the status, credibility, and rhetoric to forge an active movement in a population with almost no experience of political mobilization or participation. It was a prepolitical movement in which traditional leaders used available cultural symbols as a means of coercive persuasion, as opposed to secular politicians trying to build parties, create images, and convert followings. The forceful dynamic of the movement was made all the more piquant as it signified the last-ditch stand by declining traditional forces trying to preserve their influence and social standing. Thus, it was not so much a spiritual but a political/cultural revival against the particular forms of rapid Westernized development and dependency followed by the regime.

The Traditional Connection: Bazaar and Mosque

The traditional propertied middle class is still a key social force in Iran, indeed one that has benefited financially from the process of modernization. The bazaars, the core of this class, continued to control as much as half of the country's handicraft productions, two-thirds of its retail trade, and three-quarters of its wholesale trade (Abrahamian, 1982; Ashraf, 1983). It comprised nearly half a million merchants, shopkeepers, traders, and workshop owners, and had extensive relations with a bevy of peddlers, small retailers, and petty brokers. Many wealthy urban entrepreneurs extended their investments outside the bazaar to small factories and workshops, rural craft production such as carpet weaving, and commercial farming. The bazaar had managed to retain control of its independent craft and trade guilds, although almost all other professional and working groups had lost their associations and unions. Through these guilds, the bazaar retained a network of communication and influence over thousands of shop assistants, workshop employees, peddlers, and craftsworkers.

Many bazaaris had benefited greatly from the prosperous 1960s, building ostentatious new houses in north Tehran, traveling beyond the Hajj to Europe and the United States, and financing the expansion of seminaries (Akhavi, 1980). This financial support also allowed the religious establishment "to send preachers regularly into shanty towns and distant villages, probably for the first time in Iranian history. Paradoxically, prosperity helped strengthen a traditional group" (Abrahamian, 1982: 433). Some areas of bazaar influence declined, however, through attrition and the development of newer institutions such as modern banking and state-run credit institutions, multinational corporate power, and growing preferences for foreign goods. State economic policies also tended to favor the big bourgeoisie with foreign connections rather than the small-business owner.

Far beyond its economic role the bazaar has always been an important social center in Iranian urban life, the "cradle of traditional urban culture," as Ashraf (1983) calls it. The bazaar provides an informal meeting-place where news, rumor, and gossip can be created and disseminated with remarkable speed. It is a locus of information as well as commodity exchange. The bazaar has historically acted together with other traditional social groups in political opposition to shahs and foreign encroachments, as in the struggle against tobacco concessions to the British in the 1890s, the constitutional movement, the nationalization of oil under Mossadeq, and the campaign against the "White Revolution" in 1963. It could close its doors in protest and bring the economic and social life of the nation to a standstill. The bazaar is deeply interconnected through extensive familial (Fischer, 1983), financial, and ideological ties to the other core segment of the traditional middle class, the religious establishment. In terms of location, every bazaar has its own mosque, and the two institutions are socially, economically, and politically mutually supportive.

The religious establishment consisted in the mid-1970s of an estimated ninety thousand clergymen, composed of fifty *Ayatollah*, five thousand *Hojjat-al-Islam*, thirteen thousand theology students, and numbers of low-ranking *mullah*, traditional *maktab* teachers, *madraseh* lecturers, prayer leaders, and procession organizers.[1] Although a decentralized system, as will be explained in the next section, the religious establishment maintained the only autonomous national network, comprising 5,600 town mosques (9,015 in toto), a considerable amount of *waqf* (endowed property), a number of meeting halls called *Hosseinieh*, and six major seminaries (Akhavi, 1980: 208; Abrahamian, 1982: 433).

But the religious establishment was losing economic power and influence by the gradual incorporation of many of its traditional functions into modern specialist institutions such as education, the legal system, and modern bureaucracies, as well as through direct state penetration. Historically the sources of revenue of the *ulema* had consisted of income from legal and clerical duties such as the registration of titles, notarization of documents, court fees, and so on; of annual revenues from endowed properties; and from contributions by the faithful in the form of religious taxes, *khoms*. From the time of Reza Shah and with increasing institutional differentiation and legal reform, much of the first kind of income had dried up as state institutions took over such roles. There was increasing state intervention in the administration of endowments, often on the grounds of economic efficiency, and a trend against new endowments.

With the establishment of *Rastakhiz*, a major new state offensive against these loci of traditional power began. The state began to involve itself with religious education, to control endowments, and even to develop a Religious Corps (*Sepah-e-Din*) and to co-opt and utilize mass-media *mullahs*. The seminary buildings around Mashhad were bulldozed, ostensibly to increase open space around the popular tomb of Imam Reza. The Feyzieyeh seminary was attacked in 1975 (while students were commemorating the events of 1963 that had led to Khomeini's exile), and deaths, imprisonment, and extensive damage to property ensued. Clerical leaders were threatened, imprisoned, and sentenced to internal exile. These accumulating activities helped to develop feelings among the clergy "of being encroached upon, being made redundant, and having traditional moral leadership challenged" (Fischer, 1983); they felt that a noose was being tightened around their necks.

The *ulema* were left heavily dependent upon public largesse yet still independent of the state, a unique situation in the Middle East, in most of whose states the clergy had been co-opted through its subsidization. The public supported religious institutions, students, and cultural activities through their religious contributions (*sahm-e Imam*), which would be collected within the patch of each *marja 'i-taqlid*.[2]

The bazaar played a big role in maintaining the religious budget. Every bazaar has its own mosque, and bazaaris were prominent in organizing and financing community rituals. Again, the position of the bazaar was greatly altered by the creation of *Rastakhiz* and a more intrusive state policy. Branches of the party were opened up in the bazaar and forced donations from small businesses. The old guilds were dissolved and new ones created under non-bazaari supervision. Legal requirements for a minimum wage, registration of employees, and medical contributions were introduced. Beyond that, the government also proposed to set up state corporations to import and control basic foodstuffs such as wheat, sugar, and meat, taking over central economic roles. In addition, there was talk of bulldozing some of the old bazaar areas to replace them with supermarkets and modern shopping centers.

The major invasion of the bazaar came through the government's campaign against inflation, which was running wild by 1975–76. The government tried to clamp down on profiteering by arresting several big businessmen, precipitating a flight of capital out of the country and revealing the instability of even this class because it was, like everyone else, dependent on the whims of one man. But then the regime turned on the small businessmen and shopkeepers of the bazaar. Setting price controls and aiming to curb profiteers, cheaters, and hoarders, thousands of students were organized to bring offenders to guild courts organized by SAVAK, where fines, banishment, and prison sentences were given out to hundreds of traders. The bazaar felt it was being made the scapegoat for government economic mistakes and was being used as a smoke screen to hide the real and rampant corruption in government circles and among the royal family.

The increasingly totalitarian quality of the regime had pushed it into areas that the state had never dared penetrate before, and the anger and dismay of the bazaar was acute as it turned once again to its old ally, the *ulema*, for help and leadership. Perhaps the bazaar had been lucky until then, in that the threat of growing big entrepreneurship and foreign capital had not been as strongly felt as the economy boomed in the early 1970s, and the lack of unions and the difficulties of organizing its employees had meant the avoidance of pressures to modernize and improve working conditions. Suddenly the brutal attacks by *Rastakhiz* revealed a traditional class under pressure.

Thus not only did the secular forces of modernization and Westernization undermine the influence and status of this class, but the radical moves by the state threatened its very existence. These various pressures on the clergy and the bazaar meant they were increasingly on the defensive. This was a declining class under pressure (Germani, 1981), being forced to defend itself, which helps to explain the importance of the popular mobilization as the political project of the clergy, involved in a last-chance struggle against the further encroachment of modernizing social and economic forces.

A Brief Comment on Shiism

Shiism lacks a formal clerical hierarchy and centralized institutionalization like the Catholic church (the term "clergy" is used for ease rather than as a formal referent). An *ayatollah* is neither elected nor selected by an individual or body but draws his eminence, popularity, and recognition from competitive scholarship. The *ayatollahs* are the highest-ranking scholars of Islamic knowledge and jurisprudence, whose reputations have grown over time as the most popularly accepted interpreters of the Qoran and traditions, and who therefore have the right to *ijtehad*, the making of new interpretations. The *ayatollahs* thus enjoy considerable authority, for they have their title through scholarship, peer judgment, and popular acclaim. The *howzeh-e elmieh* (centers of learning) are operated independently of the state, located in the holy cities of Qom and Mashhad, and in Isfahan and elsewhere. In them, religious students (*tallabeh*) attend a religious school (*madraseh*) supervised by an *ayatollah*. They receive a traditional, predominantly tutorial-based, education (Fischer, 1983). On completion of their studies, many of these *mullah* (trained clerics) would return to their towns and villages.

Each believer must choose one *ayatollah* as his or her *marja 'i-taqlid* (source of guidance and role model), whose book of conduct and interpretations are to be followed, indeed imitated, for the *ayatollah* possesses esoteric knowledge unavailable to the ordinary person. This process of emulation lends ritual validity to the religious practices of the layperson, and the notion of a supreme source of emulation introduces the possibility of strong, centralized leadership (Cole, 1983). Clearly, access to such knowledge is a powerful basis for social status and endows the grand *ayatollah* in particular with great social influence. Such patterns of authoritative relations between the *ulema* and their followers are thus deeply rooted within Iranian Shiite culture, and were readily called upon in 1977.

Shiism does not have a single head; instead there are several respected *ayatollah al ozma* (grand ayatollah), whose reputations have grown over the years. Thus the period of Ayatollah Borujerdi's dominance, until his death in the mid-1960s, was quite unusual. Often there is a regional identification with an *ayatollah*, as with the popular support Ayatollah Shariat-Madari enjoyed in Azarbaijan; but there can also be close competition and conflict, as existed between Ayatollahs Khademi and Taheri in Isfahan. This high clergy has earned the respected leadership of the Shiite community and enjoys a considerable degree of autonomy and power in Iranian society as guardians of the traditions and protectors of the resources of the community. Even though there is no necessary single leader of this entire structure, the ability to coalesce at moments of crisis did exist. Obviously, the rise of Khomeini as symbolic and actual leader of the revolutionary mobilization was key to its contemporary success. This was a cohesive network, and the quickest way to pass information or to coordinate demonstrations was by a message or telephone call between trusted contacts and key clerical figures in different cities.

This network of religious communication has at various junctures of Iranian history been used effectively to challenge the political regime, by mobilizing the religious establishment and the popular classes and often making uneasy pragmatic alliances with the secular opposition. The political dynamic of the religious structure has also mirrored that of the secular groups, such that when the centralized state was at its weakest the religious leadership most confidently conducted its activities. The Tobacco Rebellion (Keddie, 1966), the constitutional movement, and the 1963 events were all important periods of religio-political activity (Algar, 1969).[3] For the popular classes in Iran in 1977–79 the radical pedigree of the *ulema* or the implications of competing doctrinal outlooks were hardly central issues. What was relevant to them was that a radical Islamic discourse was available that voiced their grievances, opposed a much-despised regime, politicized their identity in a manner that compelled participation, and offered a sense of power that had been long denied. This indicated that the political rhetoric of many of the radical clergy reverberated feelings and discontents latent in the broad population (or indeed already explicit for some) and set them within a comprehensible framework.

More than this occurred, however. The clergy constituted a religious sodality whose public authority had never really been undermined. On the basis of their traditional authority, indeed, to use the Aristotelian term, their ethos, they were able compellingly to persuade the population to act, even in the face of a highly armed regime (Aristotle, 1991). In a predominantly oral culture, communications processes are still intimately linked to traditional social practices. As Pye (1963) has argued, the acts of evaluating, interpreting, and responding to all communications were usually strongly colored by considerations directly related to the status relationships between communicators and recipient. Not only were the ayatollahs the intercessors between ordinary people and God; the religious establishment also used their status as possessors of esoteric knowledge, as guardians of the faith, as valued figures in the community, to compel the movement into being and to maintain its militancy. These were the legitimate, credible, authoritative leaders of the community who demanded allegiance and who expected a following. It was they who constructed the mobilization as a movement for God and Islam and who made it religious duty to participate in this holy struggle. People could not but become involved. In chapter 7 we examine the precise language and manner in which such authoritative demands were made.

The Religious Network: Formal and Informal

The traditional socioreligious network not only consisted of the formal religious institutions we have already discussed but also included an intricate layer of religiously based rituals and ceremonies that *mullahs* would attend, as well as a variety of popular cultural forms that still comprise the core of Iranian social life. For many Iranians this was their "public sphere," an arena of social life free of state encroachment and determination. This section maps out this varied system of popular cultural expression.

The extensive network of mosques and holy places under the supervision of the clergy provides ample opportunities for political communication. The mosque (*masjid*), often located in or close to the bazaar, is the central assembly point for the locality. It is a civic center with meetings, educational facilities, and library, as well as a specifically religious institution. Preaching is conducted from the pulpit (*minbar*), which has been used throughout Islamic history to inform, guide, and agitate (Fathi, 1979; Borthwick, 1965). Like clerical garb, the pulpit confers status on the user and provides a direct and authoritative platform for religious oratory and politicization. Yet, as Fischer (1983) notes, the *marja 'i-taqlid* did not in the main use the pulpit to preach, and a different set of names is associated with this activity, including Bazargan, Shariati, Falsafi, Hejazi. The important exception here is Khomeini, who actively encouraged more clerical figures to take up the role of preacher and to put the pulpit to better politico-religious use. Emotive sermons preached in local mosques precipitated many of the demonstrations of the revolutionary mobilization.

The seminaries, or *howzeh-e-elmieh*, are also important locations where the grand ayatollahs and scholars hold audiences. Feizieyeh Seminary in Qom was central to the revolt against the "White Revolution" in 1963 and played an important communications and coordinating role during the revolution when Khomeini was still abroad, Qom operating like an unofficial capital city. A great variety of social activities are religiously based but do not necessarily require the presence of a formally trained *akhund* (cleric). Religious and sociopolitical communication takes place in a *hey'at mazhabi*, a religious group gathering. These are small religious meetings usually held in private houses and often organized by local wealthy bazaar merchants. They are local phenomena, open to the public but usually drawing upon the neighborhood for attendance. They flourished particularly in the poorer city quarters and attracted workers, artisans, shopkeepers, and bazaar employees. They met weekly or monthly throughout the year, but more often during the religious months of *Ramadan* and *Moharram*. A *wa'ez* (preacher-orator) usually led the proceedings, and guests were served fruit and tea. It has been estimated that there were over twelve thousand of these "religious associations" in Tehran alone, mostly formed after 1965, some with titles to suggest their connection to a guild or profession, or to a town or region of origin (Najafi, 1976).

Among these *hey'at* there were the religious associations of shoemakers, fruit-juicers (street-corner vendors), public-bath employees, tailors, as well as those of the natives of Natanz resident in Tehran and the natives of Semnan. Other groups took on explicitly religious titles such as the Association of the Desperates (*bicharehha*) of Imam Hossein, or the Abjects (*zalilha*) of Imam Musa ibn Ja'far (Arjomand, 1988). At these *hey'at* interpersonal, political, and social networks were formed and consolidated, and then extended to wider channels like the bazaar or mosque. They served a similar function for the traditional middle class that the London coffeehouse or Parisian salon did for the emergent bourgeoisie, an autonomous arena wherein Iranian religious practice overflowed into political debate and the development of social solidarity. There are also innumerable *imamzadeh* (shrines of the imams), which are popular places of pilgrimages. Such *ziyarat* or internal pilgrimages would be organized through the *hey'at* as a community outing. Thus this bazaar-neighborhood organization is the skeleton of urban life and popular religion (Fischer, 1983: 134–35). During the revolutionary mobilization, it played an important role in raising money and passing information as well as promoting general debate and consciousness-raising.

Rowzeh are other gatherings that occur mainly for mourning ceremonies, especially during the important month of *Moharram*. This is the month in which the Shiite leader Imam Hossein was martyred by the tyrant Yazid at Karbala some thirteen centuries ago. At a *rowzeh* the theme of the martyrdom of the central Shiite figures such as Ali, Hossein, and other imams would be dramatically recounted by a *rowzeh-khan*, a reader of homilies, perhaps using a picture curtain or other props. It is interesting to note that the Greek root of the word homily means "the crowd," reverberating our stress on these gatherings as contexts of public communication as well as opportunities for moral preaching.

In the first ten days of *Moharram* a series of passion plays, or *ta'ziyeh*, is performed to present dramatically the themes of martyrdom. While such plays may be the outlet for a variety of personal and collective feelings, in periods of sociopolitical discontent the theme of just struggle against unjust tyrants can take on an explicitly political resonance (Fischer, 1983: 171–78). Once patronized by Qajar shahs and notables, *ta'ziyeh* performances were banned under Reza Shah, making a limited comeback under Mohammad Reza when they increasingly became a phenomenon of small towns and rural areas. The court also patronized them as interesting examples of folklore, another demonstration of the growing class polarization of culture under the Pahlavis. Another popular form of participation in mourning ceremonies, especially during *Moharram*, was the formation of a *dasteh* (procession) that would consist of lines of bare-chested young men who would flagellate themselves with chain and even cut their foreheads with a dagger, an exercise in pietistic forbearance and a dramatic reminder of the sufferings of Shiism. Much of traditional social life still revolved around these religious gatherings at which the drama of Karbala would be recited, acted out, and symbolically related to contemporary political events. Chapter 6 describes further the use of these themes of martyrdom and the polarity of Hossein and Yazid to mobilize the popular movement of 1977–79.

Occasionally religious lectures and large gatherings would be held in *Hosseinieh* (community centers), of which there were over three hundred in Tehran by the mid-1970s. The most important was *Hosseinieh Ershad* in north Tehran. This center developed a reputation in the mid-1960s as a forum for modernist Islamic debate and was used by such Islamic reformers as Mehdi Bazargan and his Movement for the Liberation of Iran, which wished to synthesize Islam with contemporary social reform. It was the main base of Ali Shariati, too, who also proposed a synthesis of anticlerical Islam with Fanonist liberation ideas. Shariati (1979) developed a binary class polarization between the *mostazzafin*, the disinherited, and the *mostakbarin*, the dominators. The relationship between the two classes is not simply economic but also cultural and can be extended to include the role of Western imperialism that wants to assimilate Third World cultures and swallow up their heritage and identity. The bulwark to this is to maintain faith and develop an activist Islam as a protection against cultural alienation. Shariati is highly critical of the traditionalist clerics who are removed from political life and thus allow despotism and imperialism to triumph. He connects faith with struggle, a unity of theory and practice, which is the principle of *towhid*, oneness of God but also a unified worldview. Some parallels with Khomeini's activist, populist rhetoric are evident, yet in the main the relationship between the religious leaders and Shariati was ambiguous, if not hostile, and his polarized tropes of class antagonism were appropriated and popularized by the clergy.

As anti-imperialists, antimonarchists, and anti-Marxists, as transitional ideologues against tradition and for progressive Islam and social reform, the group at *Hosseinieh Ershad* played an important role in educating and politicizing, particularly among lower-middle-class university students. The Hosseinieh was closed by the Pahlavi regime, and Shariati died in exile in London in 1977. Many, like Enayat (1982), consider him to have been the most important ideologue for the contemporary Iranian movement, whose radical Islam prevented the loss of many young educated Iranians to the ranks of radical secular groups.[4]

Yet other social gatherings have an underlying religious tone. The *sofre*, or ritual feast, is attended mainly by women "for vows, cures, sociability and homiletics" (Fischer, 1983: 137); during these meetings female preachers might read *rowzeh* (Keddie, 1980). Then there are the critical life-cycle events such as marriages and death, where a *pish-namaz* (prayer leader) or a *mullah* would probably be present to supervise the contract or to lead the funeral *rowzeh*. As civil ceremonies did not exist in Iran under the Pahlavi regime, even the staunchest secularist would be born, married, and buried within the folds of Islam (apart from those minorities of other religions, of course).

Religious imagery even undergirds athletic prowess. The *zur-khaneh* is a traditional gymnasium attended by craftsmen and laborers in which the virtues of Islamic chivalry were acted out in order to develop the true *Luti* character, a believer who combined physical strength with moral steadfastness (Bateson et al., 1977).

There is no clear dividing line between religious ritual and popular culture, between the activities of trained *ulema* and the social practices of ordinary people. All the rituals, practices, and ceremonies that have been mentioned here are religiously based and satisfy a wide variety of spiritual functions, mundane social needs, and community interactions. Much of Iran had remained deeply moral, religious, and traditionalist, despite the thin veneer of modernism. For example, in a survey of social attitudes conducted in 1975 across the country not only were high levels of daily praying (83 percent of respondents) and observance of fasts (79 percent) reported, but the practice of offering religious vows (47 percent), belief in predestination (67 percent), and belief in spirits (*gen*) (33 percent) were also strong. Education was the major determining factor; the higher the level of education attained, the lower the support for such traditional attitudes (Assadi and Vidale, 1977).

The available evidence suggests an expansion of much of this traditional religious activity in the 1970s. There was a rising circulation in religious periodicals, and religious books enjoyed a new popularity; there were numerous publishers of religious materials (Najafi, 1976). It appears that interest grew in the most basic of religious texts such as the Qoran and in interpretive texts on law and rituals, which sold hundreds of thousands of copies (Arjomand, 1984: 216). Najafi's figures relating to numbers of visits to religious shrines, pilgrimages to Mecca, various types of religious donations, mosque building, and other religious activities also indicate rising trends.

Fischer (1983) has noted the differences in "religious styles" between the ulema, the popular classes (who were more communal, activity-oriented, less intellectual), and the upper classes (who were particularly attracted to Sufism and were more individualistic, internalized, and privatized). But Fischer also suggests ways in which styles overlapped, stating that "if *rawda (rowzeh)* served to articulate the learning of the ulema with popular belief, the efforts of modernizers such as Shariati served a similar function in articulating the discourse of the *ulema* with that of the modern middle and upper classes" (179). He points to the multilevel appeals of Islam as the activist, politicized rhetoric of both Shariati and Khomeini began to percolate the society.

There is also evidence that in the 1970s what has been referred to as the modern middle class turned back increasingly to Islam. Their attendance at prayer-group meetings rose; Islamic associations grew in universities and colleges, and among highly qualified professional groups such as engineers and physicians (Arjomand, 1984: 219). Islamic associations also developed among students and professionals abroad, and it was among such groups that the triumvirate of Bani-

Sadr, Yazdi, and Ghotbzadeh who returned with Khomeini first became known. Women who had not worn it before turned to the *chadoor*, the veil, both as a symbol of collective identity and belonging, and as a symbol of resistance to the regime. *Sofre* of urban, educated women spread. I (Annabelle) attended some of these meetings in Tehran in 1977, where a *mullah* would preach and then answer extensive questions. As Fanon (1965) has analyzed for Algeria, so in Iran the veil has taken on powerful political symbolism at various historic moments, not least in women's resistance to wearing it under the dictates of the Islamic Republic.

It does not appear that this social activity was motivated by a great interest in religious reform and rethinking. Rather these activities were, as Arjomand (1984: 218) has described, "gatherings by newcomers to an alienating modern world to consolidate, at regular intervals, their attachment to the Islamic tradition and to reaffirm their collective sociocultural identity . . . in the 1960s and 1970s, the religiously inclined intelligentsia increasingly found this nativism consonant with their rejection of Western culture. These celebrants of Islamic collective identity who gathered in the middle-class Religious Societies . . . remained attached to primordial ties and traditional ways, and . . . resented certain aspects of the imported modern pattern of life." It is notable that the mass media, and the regime, had thus failed to make Iranian national identity a sufficiently strong collective identity, but were carriers of a threatening alien culture rather than bastions of an authentic indigenous one.

Khomeini: Politics, Preaching, and Publicity

Despite differences over key political and juridical issues, the *ulema* could act together when necessary, something the secular opposition never managed to achieve. The emergence of Khomeini as the central symbolic figure and charismatic leader provided unity to the entire national movement. Not only did he come to represent asceticism against the conspicuous consumption and moral laxity of the Pahlavis, and manifested a political stubbornness and refusal to compromise that appealed to the Iranian appreciation of authoritarian leadership, but his charisma also compelled a following. Khomeini had developed and maintained a radical critique of the Pahlavis and their development orientation from the 1940s. He also used an accessible rhetoric through which many of the central themes of the revolutionary mobilization were established. As Fischer (1983) has distinguished, unlike the other high *ulema*, Khomeini "cultivates a populist language of confrontation and a propaganda-style of comic-book-like hyperbole . . . Khomeini speaks the language of the ordinary man, attacking the intellectuals and eggheads, the rich and the elite. He plays a politics of trusting the masses."

Increasingly from the 1970s, Khomeini was the reference point for militant religious opposition to the Shah. He placed a great stress on the need for the religious leadership to involve itself in politics, arguing that imperialism had promoted a remote and pedantic religion obsessed by specific points of legal interpretation. He urged the *ulema* to publicize and to preach, arguing that "God had praised speech and expression, as well as writing and the use of the pen . . . Speech and expression are necessary for promulgating the ordinances of God and the teachings and doctrines of Islam" (Khomeini, 1970: 141).

Time and again he stressed the potential political power of the religious establishment; for example, he argued that "there are more than 150,000 students and scholars of the religious sciences in Iran. If all these scholars, authorities, proofs of Islam, and ayatollahs were to break the seal of silence from the list of crimes committed by the regime, would they not achieve their aims? Would the authorities arrest them all, imprison and banish them, destroy them?" (Khomeini, 1970: 205). One of the specific functions of the *Dar-al-Tabligh*, the Centre of Propaganda/Conversion, in Qom was the publication of journals about Islam in Persian and in Arabic, of which the most important, *Maktab-e-Islam* (School of Islam), had a circulation of around fifty thousand. From the mid-1970s Khomeini tirelessly argued for the need for the preaching of sermons, for the clergy to become involved in protecting the future of Islam. Extensive resources were amassed and religious figures began to work and distribute alms among the migrant poor in the shantytown areas of south Tehran (Kazemi, 1980: 81–86). *Mullahs* were sent to preach in the countryside, where only 12 percent of all villages had a resident *mullah*.

Of course, as religious figures became more political they were subject to regime repression. Many of Khomeini's followers were arrested from 1965 on and sentenced to internal exile (which only facilitated the spread of their ideas to remote areas) and to prison. The politicizing impact of many of the middle-ranking clergy in towns across the country was immense, and their sermons were frequently the catalysts for the demonstrations and activities of the revolutionary movement. These clerics included Ayatollah Sadduqi in Yazd, Ayatollah Montazeri in Isfahan, Khamenei in Iranshar, Ali Tehrani in Saqqez, and Taheri in Isfahan.

Despite regime attempts to control the religious network, the movement and the publicity continued. From the time of Khomeini's exile, religious figures around the country, including his brother Ayatollah Pasandideh, collected charitable dues in his name, which were used to support students, cultural activities, and political opposition activity. Bazaari merchants also mobilized considerable resources for the movement. Sanche (1979) has suggested that an annual contribution of 320 million dollars was given from the bazaar to the *ulema*. But not only did preaching, publishing, and other activities increase. Vividly colored posters, many centering on images of Khomeini, circulated from 1977 on. There was also a stream of tape-recorded messages, short missives and longer tracts that trickled and then flowed into Iran from Khomeini, and then burgeoned inside Iran, until an avalanche of these small media helped to push the Shah away. As we already dis-

Figure 5.1. Khomeini urges the people on to victory as his fist crushes the regime's tanks; in the center, a flag which reads "there is only one god" is hoist while in the background a statue of the Shah is toppled. The blood of martyrs spilled in the foreground rises to heaven in the form of red arrows toward the top of the poster.

Figure 5.2. Khomeini appears to orchestrate the revolutionary mobilization from afar, as suggested by the misty cloud and by the images in the upper right-hand corner of the Eiffel Tower (Paris as his place of exile), a mosque, and an airplane. All across (the map of) Iran, mass demonstrations and dismantling of the monarchical system (toppling statues) continue despite the regime violence. The Shah slinks away, his American and British moneybags overflowing, with only the devil and a black dog (signifying foreignness/uncleanliness) for company

Figure 5.3. Here Khomeini appears in a Christ-like pose, "suffer the little children to come unto me" as they do from far and wide on a pilgrimage, signifying the true imami status of Khomeini. The vine signifies paradise where the fallen marytrs (the tulips) will go, as Khomeini blesses their offspring. A pathetic little Shah clambers on his knees over spent bullets—himself asking for blessing/forgiveness?

cussed in chapters 2 and 4, bewildered by the meaning of such development for their own lives, the popular classes were ready to follow the commands of a traditional leadership in a movement of retraditionalization of the culture and the reinstatement of a core identity, Islam, which provided meaning and direction in an alien environment. The religious leaders (particularly Khomeini) possessed a language honed on direct contact with the Iranian masses, and were highly effective and credible communicators, speaking to popular discontents and transforming a passive population into active militants.

Chapter 6
Cultural Criticism, Secular and Religious

While there were many reasons for discontent inside Iran, from the lack of political rights and freedoms to the gross economic inequalities, one basic issue that was raised, by secular and religious figures alike, was the undermining of Iranian or indigenous culture, and the substitution of a superficial, commercial Western product instead of a thriving, dynamic cultural sphere.

The clergy had long spoken out against the dissolution of religious culture and attacked dancing, music, and the cinema as sinful. Khomeini also popularized the argument that the threat of indigenous culture was part of imperialist plots against Iran. As early as the 1940s he had expressed his rage at the moral and political effects of Western cultural penetration, in the context of Reza Shah's attempt to modernize the dress code and unveil women:

> Throughout these stages [of modernizing reforms], the foreigners who wanted to execute their plans and swindle you by putting the hat over your heads, were looking at you with deriding eyes and were laughing at your infantile acts. You were strolling up and down the streets with a chamber-pot-shaped hat, were occupied with naked girls, being proud of this state of affairs, not realising that they took your historical honours from one end of the country to another; that your sources of wealth throughout the country were being appropriated, and you were being trampled on from sea to sea. (Khomeini, *Kashf al-Asrar*, 1941; quoted in Arjomand, 1984: 206; see also Algar, 1981: 169–73)

> They have put chamber-pot-shaped hats over your heads and gladdened

your hearts with naked women in the middle of the streets and swimming pools. (Ibid.)

Music rouses the spirit of love-making, of unlawful sexuality, and of giving free reign to passion while it removes audacity, courage and manly valour. It is forbidden by the sacred Law, and should not be included in the school programmes. (Ibid.)

The loss of religious morality and indigenous identity, cultural pollution, and the negative effects of the mass media were well-rehearsed motifs in Khomeini's populist repertoire. Thus in 1971 he berates "the poisonous culture of imperialism . . . which corrupts youth day by day with some new tune, some deceptive formula" (quoted in Algar, 1980: 195). The media of the Pahlavi state were used to "drug people into acquiescence" and were filled with "bombastic propaganda" to "promote the regime" (Algar, 1980: 120). Thus the negative cultural effects of the mass media were an explicit theme in Khomeini's speeches and were echoed by other preachers in their sermons. A survey of the sociocultural elite of Iran in 1974 found that the *ulema* who were interviewed felt extremely negatively toward broadcasting, arguing that it was frivolous and immoral, and that even its religious broadcasts were devoid of authentic content (Tehranian, 1981).

The suffocation of indigenous Iranian culture and the undermining of identity became pervasive themes in Iranian literature and in the secular counterculture that grew under the Pahlavi regime. A leftist political underground developed from the 1960s, specifically with the formation of the two major guerrilla factions of the Marxist *Fedai'i* and the Islamic *Mojahedin*. Their activities through the 1970s included intermittent guerrilla attacks on government installations, attempts to carve out liberated territories in the north of Iran, organizations of university strikes, and the production of a steady trickle of political analyses of the dependent Pahlavi state, Western imperialism, and Islam as popular culture (Halliday, 1979; Abrahamian, 1989). A different political strategy was taken by many intellectuals (novelists, playwrights, poets) who created an extensive literary scene that in its core thematics was a powerful challenge to the regime, which censored or ignored most of its products.

At the same time that the state-run media began to play a more active role of political communication, the regime was acting severely to further limit alternative forms of communication. A renewed campaign of state control over the salaried middle class developed. Surveillance and censorship increased. Book publishing dried up. Toward the end of 1975 alone, over twenty prominent poets, writers, filmmakers, novelists, and professors had been jailed for criticizing the regime, and television had aired at least two "confessions" of ideological mistakes by writers; the press published others.[1]

Among the core themes articulated by this clerisy were not only the economic dislocation and inequality, and the repressive political environment, but also the claustrophobic cultural environment in which Iranian national identity was silenced in favor of a shallow and commercialized Western cultural invasion. Perhaps most well known is Jalal al-Ahmad's notion of *Gharbzadegi* (1982), Westoxification or occidentitis, as the prevailing Iranian disease against which religious identity was the only resistance. The theme is also present in the stories and writings of Samad Behrangi, a socialist (Hanson, 1983). Parviz Kimiavi presented it through film in *The Mongols*, where an invading force leaves television sets behind its conquest and undermines village life, and in *O.K. Mister*, which explores the historical exchange of oil rent for Western lifestyle in southern Iran. It is a central issue for the Islamic modernist Ali Shariati, one of the most influential thinkers behind the popular mobilization. Preponderantly university-educated, well read in European social theory and literature as well as Persian, these cultural literati reveal all the contradictions of displaced, deracinated Third World intellectuals (Laroui, 1976). They are often angry but politically voiceless, schooled in Western thought yet deeply disturbed about Western cultural penetration, often secular in orientation yet aware of the deep resonance of religion in popular culture, populist yet adopting writing styles and genres not readily accessible to the people they wish to address (and the subject of a burgeoning analytic literature; see Dorraj, 1990; Hillman, 1990; Ghanoonparvar, 1984; Fischer and Abedi, 1990). While often identifying with the masses, and supporting populist political orientations, these groups lacked both the public space beyond the universities and the modes of delivery to reach the broad nonnovel reading "public" they wished to summon.

Perhaps even more importantly, the themes of loss of indigenous identity, cultural malaise and alienation, reverberated among regime-supported intellectuals also, signifying their own concern about the erosion of Iranian culture and way of life in the face of the invited onslaught of the West. The problem of cultural identity was debated at international conferences such as the Aspen Institute/Persepolis Symposium in 1975. There Ehsan Naraghi, the head of the Centre for Research and Planning for Higher Education and a mediator between SAVAK and the intellectual community, described the "deep-seated malaise of the West" and urged the need for the preservation of the "cultural personality of Iran" and the tradition of "mystical-poetic experiences" as an antidote to the impact of Westernization (Naraghi, 1976). In 1977 the Shahbanou Farah Foundation and the Institute of Cultural Studies headed by Darioush Shayegan hosted a symposium entitled "Given the Domination by the West, Can There Be Dialogue between Cultures?" Invited guests included Roger Garaudy and the *Nouvelle Vague* group of French philosophers. At Iran Communications and Development Institute, I (Annabelle) edited an English-language quarterly journal called *Communications and Development Review*, which focused on issues such as "Inappropriate Technology—Appropriate Solutions" and "Science as Western Hegemony." The journal published articles by Denis Goulet and others on the dilemmas, especially cultural, of the development process. The ironies of this process are multiple: it was often conducted in English or French, and published proceedings in a European language; it used Western "experts" to criticize the West; it promoted regime-palat-able "debate" on the one hand while acquiescing to silence about other, equally if not more crucial, issues on the other. Yet at the same time it is interesting that the same deep-seated sense of malaise, of discomfort with the effects of moderniza-tion on a well-known and well-loved Iranian "way of life," was palpable among all strata of the intelligentsia, oppositional and regime-connected, religious and secular. This brought about some confluence of political analysis, the mixed oppositions jointly blaming the Shah for Iran's dependency as well as the West for its cultural imperialism. It was a radicalized Islam that was able both to devel-op a critique of, and an alternate identity to pit against, the twin processes of dic-tatorship and dependency.

The Resurrection of a Secular Opposition

The vacillation of the regime and its sudden change of tactics in creating *Ras-takhiz*, its increased use of censorship and then relaxation, indicated regime inde-cision and suggested that certain political and cultural issues could perhaps be voiced anew.

Iranian exiles had long been trying to publicize the violations of the Shah's regime, not only through Persian networks but through links with concerned intel-lectuals in the West, trying to mobilize international public opinion about Iran. These groups included the Committee against Repression in Iran, Campaign for Artistic and Intellectual Freedom in Iran, and P.E.N. International. Amnesty International, the International Commission of Jurists, and the International League of Human Rights all pointed out the lack of basic human rights in Iran in the mid-1970s. At the same time, U.S. President Carter was promoting his cam-paign about human rights and specifically mentioned Iran as a nation where civil and political rights were threatened. The Shah was concerned about American opinion and did not want to lose his image as an enlightened monarch, nor did he want to risk the special relationship and arms trade that he enjoyed with Washing-ton. Thus he felt pressured to "liberalize." By early 1977 there was an evident eas-ing of regime political control, with an amnesty granted to 265 political prisoners; foreign lawyers allowed to sit in on the trials of dissidents; and Red Cross repre-sentatives permitted to check prison conditions. Even the *Rastakhiz* party began to talk of the need for free discussion and to welcome "constructive criticism."

Initially it was the secular democratic opposition that began to test the extent of the liberalization, intellectuals breaking out of the alienated accommodation they had effected with the regime. The two main tactics were the drafting of "open let-ters," probably the first of the "small media" to be used in the contemporary movement, and the establishment of professional associations of writers, lawyers, academics, bazaar merchants, and pressure groups, such as the Campaign for the Defense of Human Rights and Freedoms, which included well-respected political figures like Mehdi Bazargan and Karim Sanjabi. The "open letters" were sent to the Shah and his ministers, and to the mass media, where they rarely received mention. They were also sent abroad and circulated clandestinely. These activists were in the main secular intellectuals identifying themselves within Iran and speaking directly to the Shah and his ministers (as well as addressing international public opinion) for the most elemental rights to free speech and association, and for a return to the laws of the 1906 Constitution. In retrospect these demands are mild in comparison with the radical clamor that was to come, but in the prevailing political conditions even this was a brave and significant breakthrough. Little did these democrats suspect that the crack they helped make in the dam of repression would have such powerful, radical, and ultimately antidemocratic repercussions.

By the summer of 1977 these intermittent communiqués were being supplemented by the organization of professional associations and pressure groups, as well as the reconstitution of formal political groups. Their very existence implied an enormous change in the political environment, and they provided important foci for the articulation of grievances and the beginnings of expression of public opinion. The Iranian Writers' Association was revived. An Association of Iranian Jurists was established. The Iranian Committee for the Defense of Liberty and Human Rights, comprised of prominent opposition writers, intellectuals, and political figures, declared its formation in a manifesto in December 1977. It contacted the international human rights agencies, maintained an office, and played a key role in linking and coordinating activities of the various groups. It was supported by a donation of 2 million toman from the Tehran bazaar, an indication of how modern and traditional, religious and lay sectors of the opposition cooperated (interview with Rahmatollah Moghadam Maragheh, a founding member, in March 1985; at that time, seven toman equaled one dollar). The Committee for the Defense of the Rights of Political Prisoners in Iran campaigned around freeing all political prisoners, the return home of political exiles, and an end to mental and physical repressions. It published fourteen bulletins between April 1978 and January 1979 (*Iranian Bulletins*, 1979). In July 1977 a group of writers and publishers formed the Group for Free Books and Free Thought to publicize incidents of censorship and torture of writers. The National Organization of Iranian Academics campaigned for academic freedom and for democratic procedures in education and beyond. It produced numerous flyers during the movement and important news bulletins called *Solidarity* (*Hambastegy*). Merchants in the Tehran bazaar established a Society of Merchants, Traders, and Craftsmen to limit the activities of *Rastakhiz* in the bazaar.

Old and new political groupings began to emerge. The National Front, renamed the Union of National Front Forces, began to publish *Khabarnameh*, a newsletter that demanded the dissolution of SAVAK, the release of political prisoners and return of all exiles, the end of censorship, freedom for all political parties, and the end of restrictions on unions and guilds. Karim Sanjabi, a key leader, stressed the Front's commitment to the course set by Mossadeq to make Iran independent in foreign affairs and to establish genuine democracy through recognition of individual rights, social freedoms, and constitutional laws. Mehdi Bazargan revived the Liberation Movement, and Moghadam Maragheh revived the Radical Movement. The *Tudeh* party reemerged to publish *Navid* (The harbinger) and *Donya* (World).

Thus, most of this initial activity was secular and middle class, the Westernized intelligentsia using the rhetoric of human rights and Western democratic practices. The Marxist and Islamic Lefts, the *Fedai'i* and *Mojahedin,* were still underground although their materials circulated. Specific critiques and demands were made of the regime through this "indoor" activity that was essentially moderate and democratic.

The First "Speaking Out": The Rise of the "Open Letter"

This first speaking out was conducted by secular middle-class intellectuals who singly or in groups signed "open letters," beginning an intense protest campaign through public communiqués (Phillipe, 1978; *Iranian Bulletins*, 1979). Only a few months earlier this activity would have almost definitely resulted in arrest.

One of the earliest of such letters was a lengthy epistle by a well-known journalist, Haj Seyyed Javadi (1978 [1357]), addressed directly to the Shah, in which he outlined his criticisms of the current state of the nation and focused particularly on the negative role of *Rastakhiz* on Iranian life. Another letter was addressed to the Shah in June 1977 by two former ministers of the Mossadeq period and the leader of the banned Pan-Iranist party, the National Front triumvirate of Sanjabi, Bakhtiar, and Foruhar. They complained that personal despotism had endangered human rights while inflation was threatening the livelihood of citizens and government neglect of agriculture was causing food shortages. They wrote that respect for the Constitution and the Universal Declaration of Human Rights was vital, and that the single-party system and political abuses had to end.

The two most important groups that engaged in this writing of "open letters" were lawyers and writers. In May 1977 a group of fifty-three lawyers sent a telegram directly to Moinian, the chief of staff of the Special Imperial Office, accusing the government of interfering in the judicial process. This was followed by a manifesto signed by sixty-four names on July 11, 1977 (Phillipe, 1978). The trigger for this action was new regime-proposed legislation about judicial procedures that was being passed without discussion. The lawyers based their arguments squarely on the Iranian Constitution, which they called "the declaration of our people's victory over despotism and self-interest," and its principle of the separation of powers and its safeguarding of political freedoms. They criticized the breakdown of the basic separation of powers, the monopoly of the executive by one man, and the subservience of the legislature. Behind their arguments lay a

Figure 6.1. A poster of assorted popular nonclerical figures who inspired the revolution. From top left, across: Golesorkhi, radical nationalist, poet, blinded and executed by the regime; Mossadeq; Sharif Vaghefi, one of the founders of the *Mojahedin*, executed by the Shah. Second row, left to right: Chosro Ruzbe, member of *Tudeh* party, executed by the Shah; Sardar Kuchek Khan Jangali, leader of the Jangali Movement; Samad Behrangi, writer; Bijan Jazani, one of the founders of the *Fedai'i*. Bottom line, left to right: Ali Shariati; Dr. Arani, one of the founders of the *Tudeh* party; Jalal-al-e Ahmad, writer.

belief in the importance law should have in protecting human rights and individual liberties, a role it had never been allowed to play in Iran; thus, they argued that "the independence and prestige of the judicial power is an objective necessity for social advance toward freedom." They demanded a commission to supervise legal reform. Most significantly, they stressed their professional status and their exclusive possession of the specialist knowledge to evaluate legal issues. An open letter in September 1977 to the Head of the High Court by fifty-four judges of Tehran elaborated on the executive's weakening of judicial power, political interference in the training of judges, and the general demise of the Constitution. They stressed their professional commitment and put forward specific proposals for reform, demanding that "the rights and liberties of the Iranian people, particularly those of expression, of the written word and association, must be truly respected" (*Iranian Bulletins*, 1979).

In October 1977 the Association of Iranian Jurists was formed. The manifesto signed by 141 lawyers announced their intention to campaign for the reestablishment of the rule of law and an independent judiciary. Writers were the other professional group that began to speak out. The Iranian Writers' Association had been formed in 1968 in response to government repression and based its charter on the Universal Declaration of Human Rights. During the 1970s, its journal *Arash* was banned and many of its most prominent writers and critics were harassed and even jailed (Saedi, Beh-Azin, Baraheni, Tonokaboni). The resurrection of this important group came in June 1977 when forty signatories in an open letter to Hoveyda, the prime minister, criticized the prevailing cultural atmosphere and poverty of intellectual life in Iran. Starting with Hoveyda's professed concern about book production, these writers criticized the concentration on physical problems of printing and distribution as well as the economic problems of expensive primary materials and high wages, while the regime totally ignored the wider political issues and the problem of "national culture." The basic issue was that "culture and intellectual and artistic creativity are at a standstill and stagnate," primarily because of the limitations on intellectual and artistic creativity and the controls over students and other potential cultural consumers. The writers of this organization made far more powerfully and eloquently the analytic argument of this book, that internal censorship and massive flow of cultural products from outside were undermining Iranian cultural identity. They bemoaned the fact that "we have become the consumers of their [foreign] material and intellectual products as a result of the suspension of freedom and the consequent intellectual stagnation, and have thus been afflicted by a total cultural sterility." Only with the removal of censorship and other controls could the national and cultural heritage be adequately preserved and developed, they argued. They demanded that the Iranian Writers' Association be allowed to function as a center for the exchange of ideas and be allowed to publish a journal. When no reply was heard from Hoveyda, another letter signed by ninety-eight intellectuals was written on July 19,

1977, elaborating the arguments and demands and requesting that the text be published in a newspaper. The regime did not respond.

From the summer of 1977 these intermittent communications were supplemented by the organization of professional associations and pressure groups, and the reconstitution of political groupings with the systematic development of manifestos outlining political critiques and making specific demands of the regime. It was the reemergence of participatory, autonomous, intermediary organizations such as had not been seen in Iran since the early 1950s.

There had always been a trickle of underground samizdat-type literature in Iran, but what was new in this revival was that these letters were being written by people *inside* Iran who signed with their *own names*, putting themselves in some considerable danger. These "letters" circulated widely, with photocopies of photocopies reaching the provinces. What is also important to note is that at this point this middle-class protest addressed itself directly to the court, petitioning it to change, perhaps in hindsight naively thinking that they had sufficient social clout to be worth listening to, and indeed that the regime was ready to listen and to change. Specific critiques of regime abuse were made and specific recommendations for reform were presented. The inability to practice adequately as professionals was an essential part of the argument. These "open letters" show little attempt to address a wider internal audience or interest in developing a popular movement. Instead, these groups tried to enlist the support of international public opinion through the United Nations, international agencies dealing with human rights, and other pressure groups abroad. One letter restated all the specific demands of a number of these groups, and their desire to be heard outside of Iran. What is notable about this document is that as late as November 1978 these groups were still petitioning the regime and formulating demands, while even the National Front leadership appeared by then to have abandoned the possibility of any compromise solution with the regime. The political muddle within this secular opposition was acute. This was a movement to open up a "public sphere" within Iranian society by members of the ascendant middle class. The essential aims of these groupings were the revival of the laws of 1906–9, which had created constitutional monarchy, and the removal of the obstacles to free speech and association, which had been imposed by monarchical despotism. As Mortimer has noted, "In retrospect, these demands appear to be relatively mild compared with the later loud clamours of 'death to the Shah' and 'down with the lackeys of imperialism.' But their articulation and expression in the form of openly-signed letters and declarations set against the then prevailing political conditions, was a significant and daring break-through" (Mortimer, 1979: 5).

But the regime was unable to assimilate these requests or open up channels of dialogue with these groups. It appeared to feel that the so-called liberalization would in and of itself bring credit to the regime and that the enthusiasm of the opposition would die away. The Shah himself noted that "the first signs of organised opposition" came from "liberals, left-wingers and people of wealth and power inside my country" (Pahlavi, 1980: 149). Even with the benefit of hindsight his mistrust is acute: "Their demands for 'authentic parliamentary democracy' were in reality nothing more than demagoguery that would result in a caricature of democracy such as has been seen so often in discredited multi-party systems. I wanted a true democracy designed to foster my country's real interests. But my opponents were not interested in that approach. As a result, the more I liberalised, the worse the situation inside Iran became. Every initiative I took was seen as proof of my own weakness and that of my government" (Pahlavi, 1980: 149). This comment echoes the perspicacious insight of a famous commentator on the demise of the ancient regime in France: "It is not always when things are going from bad to worse that revolutions break out. On the contrary, it often happens that when a people which has put up with an oppressive rule over a long period without protest suddenly finds the government relaxing its pressure, it takes up arms against it . . . the most perilous moment for a bad government is one when it seeks to mend its ways. Only consummate statecraft can enable a king to save his throne when after a long spell of oppressive rule he sets to improving the lot of his subjects. Patiently endured so long as it seemed beyond redress, a grievance comes to appear intolerable once the possibility of removing it crosses men's minds" (Tocqueville, 1955).

Lacking consummate statecraft, the regime blundered on and did not take seriously the limited and moderate demands of this initial movement, thus opening the way for a far more radical and demagogic force. The regime's reaction was confused, vacillating between further liberalization and back to repression. In August 1977 Amir-Abbas Hoveyda, prime minister for the past thirteen years, was removed in favor of Amouzegar, the general secretary of *Rastakhiz*. The press began to report the arguments and debates within *Rastakhiz*. More political prisoners were released and promises were made for legal reform.

The regime overreacted to certain events with violence, however, helping to precipitate the popular outdoor demonstrations. In November 1977 the Writers' Association organized a series of poetry readings at the Goethe Institute of the West German embassy, which provided a measure of security. Said Sultanpour, a well-known poet who had just been released from prison, read his work. Later he was to be arrested and executed by the Islamic Republic. These immensely popular readings were published and distributed as audiocassettes. A number of these events passed peacefully, but one night the police attempted to close the proceedings, provoking an angry demonstration in which a student was killed. Strikes and meetings spread through the university system. Thus the secular groupings, nationalist, democratic, and gradually also leftist, began the opening up of the political environment, and activities in universities grew, but it took the involvement of the religious forces to turn the movement into a truly popular, outdoor revolution.

Chapter 7
Language, Authority, and Ideology

However inventive the network of "small media" was in creating a political space, all the channels of communication in the world are no substitute for a language, a political discourse that is accessible to the people and articulates their sense of self and already-felt grievances and concerns. "Ideological space" operates in and through language, and in that sphere Khomeini and the clergy totally outmaneuvered the secular intellectuals. In many ways, the clergy must be seen as ultimately far more "political" than the secular groups, more practiced in talking to ordinary Iranians with a rhetoric honed over time, as well as being extremely adept in appropriating tropes from other perspectives to make them their own. Thus, the focus of this chapter is a more detailed examination of the content of competing ideologies, beginning with how questions of identity were articulated and going on to an exploration of the question of authority of competing leaderships and the modes of communication they used.

One central function of ideologies is to elaborate a worldview, but also, and perhaps more fundamentally, to construct or call up a collective identity, an "imagined community" (Anderson, 1983). Anderson's notion of an "imagined community" hinges on the dissemination of language, specifically vernacular languages spread through the medium of print, which undermined imperial Latin in Europe and laid the basis for the linguistic "nation" as an "imagined community." As we have already argued, a crucial element in the dynamic of the Iranian revolution was an identity crisis brought about in the explosive clash between a Westernized process of modernization and indigenous traditions and values, with their competing definitions of the community. Without answers to such questions, society cannot function, and the role of imaginary significations is to provide such answers. Moments of social crisis thus reflect contestation and redefinition of the "community," and the power of a real challenge is its ability to push a social crisis into revolution through the mobilization of some alternate collective identity (or identities). Yet this Althusserian structuralist notion of ideologies "interpolating" identities cannot simply mean that such interpolations are accepted by the "target" populations; indeed, the analysis of political rhetoric must investigate precisely whether there is any popular acceptance of the interpolative invitation.

Summoning Identities

The regime of Mohammad Reza Pahlavi had from the 1960s co-opted and reconstructed key notions in the secular political vocabulary; the Shah promoted his own, white "revolution," claimed to be a "nationalist," promised "democracy." He purported to be a "modernizer," actively promoting the "development" of his country. Already, key tropes of a critical, progressive language were "contaminated" by this royalist spin, and although such terms could of course be deconstructed and reused by a secular movement, such a process takes time and public space for its articulation.

Khomeini and his reconstructed religious rhetoric also appropriated and developed positions close to many secular radical critiques—arguments about imperialism, the satellite status of Iran, the regime's dependency on the United States; about inequality and class division; about national solidarity. His rhetoric left secular groupings literally speechless. Khomeini had long elaborated a powerful conspiracy concept of imperialism, a populist rhetoric about the underclass and the disinherited, and an idea of freedom promoted through cultural authenticity.

In addition, clerical language laid claim to two of the most inclusive and powerful collective identities, those of nation and of Islam. For example, Khomeini in his communiqués frequently addressed the people as *mellat-e agah va mobarez va shoja-ye Iran*, "the aware, radical, and courageous people of Iran," or as *mellat sharif va shoja*, "the dear and courageous nation," or *mazlum Iran*, "the oppressed of Iran" (Communiqué: On the Fortieth Day of the Martyrs of Tehran, Mehr 24, 1357). Here *mazlum* (the oppressed) connotes the opposite of *zolm* (cruel/despotic), a notion frequently used to describe the Shah's regime.

The dominant identity that was called on was that of the Islamic faithful, the community of believers, the best-known and most intensely experienced "imagined community" in Iran. The phrases found throughout Khomeini's speeches and those of the other religious leaders include *mobarezan . . . ummate musalman*, "the radical Islamic community," and *mardom musalman-e Iran*, "the Moslem people of Iran." Of course, the Islamic community is far larger than Iran, and analysts have pointed out the expansionary, quasi-imperialistic vision that lurks within these interpolations. One popular slogan, *esteghlal, azadi, hokumat-e Islami,* "independence, freedom, Islamic government," brought together notions of anti-imperialism, opposition to royal dictatorship, and desire for religious community transmuted into desire for an Islamic state, prefiguring a future. This was an inclusive language that reverberated basic, known, and valued identities that were widely shared, as Islamic beliefs and rituals provided the collective framework for the daily life of most Iranians.

This was a populist rhetoric, building on Shariati's binary paradigm of the oppressed, *mostazafin*, and the oppressors, *mostakbarin*. Not a complex and analytic formula, it was clear for most people who belonged in the relatively small latter group—the thousand families and cronies of the Shah—to identify with the former. Such a binary division was far simpler to understand than elaborate analyses of class formations and fractions (notions like comprador bourgeoisie, petty bourgeoisie, and peasantry, for example) and interclass alliances that some secular political groups offered, and it was experientially easier to identify imaginatively with one side of this binary structure. Such rhetoric could easily build unity, all the oppressed against the oppressors, and build on preexisting bonds of solidarity, the Islamic "community."

The identities that the secular forces tried to call upon were very different. When secular democratic and leftist groups began to produce leaflets through which to address the popular classes, language differences reflected the great variety of ideological perspectives on offer but in such a subtle way that they probably meant more to these groups as indications of political leanings than to the popular masses. For example, there were many ways to address the developing public. The broad secular opposition, including both the National Front and the left, tended to use *mardom*, a general term for people, and *mellat*, the nation—broadly inclusive terms but ones that made important distinctions. *Mellat* implied all Iranian nationals, but signified difference and distance from *dowlat*, the state; for the left, it also implied a national politics as opposed to dependency and neocolonialism, and thus signified a progressive popular identification against imperialism. Another term used by the left was *vahtan/vahtanparast*, which played on the idea of homeland/patriotism (although Iran is mainly considered the "motherland" and is sometimes given as a name to girls) against the antinationalist policies of the regime. The left thus trod an uneasy path between a nationalism that mobilized against dependency and an anticapitalist internationalism.[1]

Although this was simple and direct terminology for addressing the nation, these ideas were also often used by the religious leaders. Indeed, rhetorically, all participants—regime and opposition, secular and religious—were "nationalists," all claiming the same "imagined community" yet all imagining it differently. The effect of this terminological overlap was to blur the distinctions between the various political projects, especially between the left and the Islamic forces, to the detriment of the former and the benefit of the latter (Moghadam, 1988).

Leftist groups such as the *Tudeh* party, the *Fedai'i*, and even the Islamic *Moja-*

hedin also used the international class-based language of Marxism, invoking such socioeconomic identities as *kargaran* (workers), *zahmatkeshan* (toilers), *tudeh* (the masses), and *khalgh* (people). It can be debated as to what extent class-based politics had ever developed in Iran, and certainly it has lacked continuity. The period of *Tudeh* party activity in the 1940s and 1950s was perhaps its apogee, and certainly for the subsequent twenty-five years it had been exiled, or underground, and for all popular purposes nonexistent. Given the age structure of Iran, with 50 percent of the population under twenty-five years of age, it is reasonable to suggest that these kind of class-bound languages (not to mention the political theories and scenarios that lay behind them) were quite unfamiliar and irrelevant for most Iranians beyond a highly activist intelligentsia educated in the West. The leftist political groups thus attempted to assert class identities as the central organizing principle of political analysis and action, yet it seems clear that such "appellations" reverberated poorly in the Iranian context. Social analysts of Iran (both Iranian and Western) are hardly agreed on the terminology with which to express Iran's class structure, with its complex interrelationships of oil rent, dependency, and royal dictatorship. The lack of class politics over a considerable period of time rendered such language highly abstract and unevocative in the Iranian context. Also, some Islamic radicals, including the *Mojahedin*, inspired by Ali Shariati, proposed a synthetic analysis of class struggle and Islamic community, arguing for broad class unity under the leadership of the revolutionary clergy, simply subsuming the difficulties of analyzing class and different class interests.

There was also conflict between the regime and parts of the secular opposition as to the meaning and nature of modernization, which both claimed to support. Much left analysis refused to acknowledge the extent of Pahlavi economic development, however skewed or incomplete a project that was, and the extent of diffusion of capitalist orientations and consumerism in Iran, nor could it acknowledge the left's own social deracination as Western-educated intelligentsia. The secular groupings were ready targets of charges of Westernization by the clergy because their rhetoric often made references to democratic practices and human rights, to Montesquieu and the International Court of Justice, to freedom of speech and assembly as enjoyed in the West. Frequently, indeed, the secular middle-class groups appeared to be more concerned to mobilize international public opinion rather than their own internal followings as an important force able to pressure for changes in the regime. This is evident in many of the early "open letters" by the Committee for Human Rights and the leaflets of the National Front and the burgeoning professional groups of jurists, university professors, and so on. This attitude is highly revealing, for it signifies a disbelief that internal forces are sufficient to produce change and a belief that external pressure can affect the regime. Comparatively little attention is paid to developing a political rhetoric with which to address the Iranian masses. Of course, this all reinforces our central argument that contemporary revolutions are "international" phenomena, interacting in a global environment determined by imperialism, within flows of ideas and images of other "worlds" and modes of behavior, and with multiple sites for possible conflict. Our point is not that it was "wrong" for the secular leadership to try to mobilize international public opinion, but that as part of an "international middle class" (Gouldner, 1979) it was actually easier for educated Iranians to speak to their global contemporaries than develop a language and conceptual framework intelligible to and sharable by their more traditional fellow Iranians. It is also an ironic counterpoint to the frequent Iranian recourse to conspiracy theories that in the middle of a popular movement so much attention is given to mobilizing the outside.

In the debates in February and March 1979 about what to call the new state that the popular movement had precipitated, the winning argument was that "Islamic Republic" needed no qualifying terms (such as democratic) because it implied them all. Khomeini paid little attention to his ideological competitors in the sense of actually taking up and arguing with their positions; rather, he used generalized ad hominem slurs. One of the most telling slurs that the religious opposition employed against the secular groups was the name *fokul-cravati*, tie-wearers, thus labeling these groups as "infected" with non-Islamic, nonindigenous values. The secular democrats were further mocked as "xenomanics, people infatuated with the West, empty people, people with no content" (June 5, 1979; Algar, 1981: 270). Marxist analysis did not have to be enjoined, for Marxists were simply atheists, *kafer*. Islam was proffered as an answer to all these issues: Islam was progressive, supported democracy, valued freedom. Talk of democracy was not necessary, because "Islam is superior to all forms of democracy" and justice is "the very substance of Islam" (January 2, 1980; in Algar, 1981: 338). Discussion about human rights was given equally short shrift. Khomeini argued that it was the major imperial powers who promoted this idea and, in a brilliant appropriation of Marx's critique of religion, said, "The Declaration of Human Rights existed only to deceive the nations; it is the opium of the masses" (July 10, 1972; in Algar, 1981: 214). Secular leaders only talked; the working people of Iran constituted "the real Society for the Defense of Human Rights" (June 5, 1979; Algar, 1981: 270).

Khomeini's repetitive demand for unity, *vahdat*, and the subsumption of specific demands and arguments under the promise of Islam, deflected debate. In the spirit of solidarity, the communiqués of most political groups proclaimed support for Khomeini as symbolic leader of the mass mobilization. This achieved a movement in opposition to the Shah's regime but one in which the future was never clearly defined. That there were many competing visions of the collective future became instantly apparent once the Shah had left, when the unity of the movement fractured and the latent hostilities and conflicts erupted into the bitter and bloody battles of the postrevolutionary period. In terms of Therborn's (1980) notion of clashing, competing, and contaminating ideological struggle, the real losers were the secular political groups. Their analytic language was claimed by forces more powerful than they were, which either possessed the repressive powers of the state or the coercive powers of religious tradition, clerical status, and the compulsion of charismatic authority.

Language, Authority, and Forms of Communication

Identity and authority are deeply interconnected. As Holzner and Robertson (1980: 5) argue, "No conception of authority makes sense unless we speak also of the ways in which units are identified and identify themselves. By the same token, identity implies authority in that identification of self and others involves problems of authorship and authorisation." Thus we have to probe further as to who claims or "writes" identities, and how such identities are authorized or validated. Lurking in these very sentences are further issues of the form of communication used in these processes (see also Norton, 1988). Authority's roots appear to lie in writing. Yet the authority of writing is not absolute, but has become privileged through complex processes of social transformation in the European experience, processes that have not necessarily been duplicated in the Third World. The earlier, primordial oral authority may remain far stronger than the relatively modern authority of print.

For example, Walter Ong (1967) proposes that oral/aural culture was rooted in the constant interchange of communally possessed knowledge, unlike the individualized speculation that writing fosters. Oral culture is thus essentially authoritarian, not interested in the new but desirous of preserving the old, the traditional, by saying it repeatedly. Hence, Ong argues, oral culture has a penchant for citing authorities to claim contact with the communal heritage and for negotiating the complexities of everyday life, and is often marked by the daily relevance of prayer and religious ceremony. Religious knowledge possesses authority not only as the received word of God but because it is community-binding, a "tribal possession," and of necessity authoritarian. Cultural maintenance and group continuity are one and the same, and support an accepted pattern of authority.

In Europe, the printing press was the preeminent mechanism through which to challenge the established orthodoxies of the church. Gouldner (1976) goes so far as to argue that the emergence of print is synonymous with the emergence of ideology. Although in traditional, religious societies only relatively fixed and limited claims could be made, and the justification typically was authorized by the authority or social position of the speaker, ideology conjures up abstract ideas and new solidarities beyond the experience of everyday life and the preexisting particularist ties of family and locality. Gouldner (1976: 25) argues that "ideology serves to uproot people, to further uproot the uprooter, to extricate them from immediate and traditional social structure . . . thus enabling persons to pursue projects they have chosen. Ideologies thus clearly contribute, at least in these ways, both to rational discourse and rational politics." Print fostered vernacular Bibles, scientific classification of the natural world as well as scientific speculation, playing cards, and the early serialization of the novel in the new newspapers. Anderson (1983) notes the novel and the newspaper as major reinforcers of national identity. Print was the vehicle for scientific and rationalist challenge to received wisdoms and church superstition, and gave voice to the growing secular bourgeoisie, the new intellectuals, and their assertion of new claims to social authority. Thus Gouldner gives what is in essence the Weberian analysis of the shift from traditional legitimacy to ratio-legal legitimacy in the West, a very specific grounding in a theory of communicative competency. He argues that in the West the shift from traditional culture to modern, rational culture meant the rise of new forms of discourse, substantively manifested in ideology and later in social science. The method of institutionalization is what specifically concerns us, however. Gouldner (1976: 17) argues that "public discourse could no longer ground or justify itself on *authority* per se, as it once had done . . . the correctness of world-referencing assertions had become *problematic*, and . . . these could not be justified by invoking the public authority of the speaker . . . definitions of social reality advanced by any of the elites, old or new, could now be subject to systematic questioning, to examination, to a demand for justification. *En principe*, pronouncements were no longer credited by virtue of being affirmed by persons of authority" (emphasis in the original). Rational discourse does not mean a theoretically perfect mode of cognition but proceeds through a historically developed set of rules whereby the discourse is concerned to justify its assertions not by invoking authorities but rather by evoking the voluntary consent of those addressed solely on the basis of the arguments adduced. Gouldner (1976: 39–40) argues that this rationalist discourse was "historically grounded in the technology of a specific kind of mass (or public) media, printing, and its specific mode of production: privately owned, small-scale, widely-diffused, competitive and decentralised units . . . printing helped make it possible and necessary to mobilise political support among the masses." Print, with its decontextualized mode of communication, in which writer and reader were separated by location, time, and perhaps cultural assumptions, demanded more careful argumentation and greater self-groundedness, the latter a principle supported by Enlightenment assumptions about the rationality of individuals. Thus, both writing and reading as activities are highly individualized, as opposed to the essentially collective or interpersonal situation of oral communication. Print as a mode of communication helps to undermine the authority claims of traditional groups, and helps to construct the literate public as individuals ready to recombine imaginatively into other kinds of collectivities, *new* kinds of imagined communities (like classes and nations) against the traditional clerical and aristocratic authorities and their more "primordial" and hierarchical collectivities. Print therefore has extremely significant political repercussions.

Gouldner is making a radical distinction between ideology and tradition. Ideology as a form of communication depends on competition between would-be leaders for persuasive argument and methods of communicating that cajole publics into forming opinions. Tradition, however, is a method of communication in which predetermined actors issue commands that by dint of their continued social "authority" produce compulsion in the intended audience (Gouldner, 1978: 24, 200). Thus as ideal types in this argument, tradition is a model of compulsion, ideology a model of persuasion; tradition is based on certainty and closure, ideology fosters doubt and openness; tradition depends on ethos and prior social legitimacy, ideology on evidence and reason. An implicit debate with Derrida's logocentrism is lurking here, for Gouldner seems to be arguing that the Western experience of modernism now supports the privileging of writing over the spoken word, whose false immediacy as unsigned speech Derrida wants to critique. Such a debate about the contrastive power of orality over writing operates very powerfully within Islamic culture at large, and especially in its Iranian versions. The deep-rooted cultural debates about the writing of the spoken words of Mohammad into the text of the Qoran and the processes of exegesis and interpretation this particular text demands are analyzed by Fischer and Abedi (1990) and played with by Salman Rushdie in *The Satanic Verses* (1989). Fischer and Abedi summarize complex debates by saying that orthodoxy refused all proposed corrections to the Qoran to make it more grammatical or logical because "oral recitation . . . not reason . . . is authoritative" and there is "resistance to taking authority out of the dialogic face-to-face context" (105). Similarly, any attempts to dispute Khomeini would encounter his claims to traditions of Shiite jurisprudence that "assert special privilege for jurists with superior oral chains of authority and permission" (126). Perhaps Gouldner represents a tradition of political modernity out of a Christian scriptural culture that encounters an Islamic Qoranic (reading/speaking) culture. While these are only "biases" (Innis, 1951) or dominant tendencies to prefer one form of communication over another within these cultures (and both utilize many forms), they reflect powerful orientations and potentially powerful areas of intercultural conflict. However, both script and oral cultures are probably now surpassed in the internationally shared experience of image-based ethos-laden electronic culture.

Laying Claim to Authority

Beyond the summoning of religious collective identity lay the unchallenged status of the *ulema* as religio-political leaders trying to reconstruct a system of beliefs from a somewhat privatized religion to a politicized cultural identity. The great ayatollahs, *ayatollah al-ozma*, Golpayegani, Shariatmadari, and Marashi-Najafi, played an important role in helping to orchestrate the timing of demonstrations, strikes, and other special actions. From the beginning of the mass protests after the Qom demonstration in January 1978, these important *ulema* would circulate communiqués in which they proclaimed (*elam mishevad*) a national day of mourning in which they expected (*entezar darim*) the entire Moslem community to participate. Their language is neither one of persuasion nor of request but of command, with the full expectation that the religious community will follow them and fulfill religious duty.

This notion of religious duty runs through the communiqués from the grand ayatollahs and Khomeini and centers on the repetition of phrases such as *een yek vazifeyeh eslami va lazem-al ejrast*, "This is an Islamic duty and must be followed"; *een yek vazifeye elahist*, "This is a godly duty"; and *barr mellat ast*, "It is incumbent on the Iranian people." Perhaps one of the most compelling phrases was Khomeini's statement *ghiyam-e shoma baraye khoda va azadi-ye ummate Islam*, "Your uprising is for God and the freedom of the Islamic community." This was proclaimed on October 26, 1978, the Shah's birthday, which Khomeini called the beginning of Iran's desperation; he declared it a day of national mourning. Because this rhetoric constructed the movement as an expression of religious faith and a matter of duty, it brought strong social, moral, and spiritual obligations and sanctions into play that helped to ensure that people would indeed follow. Not only would there be social risks for nonparticipation, but this rhetoric threatened spiritual risks as well. Did it frighten people into action? Perhaps. It certainly underpinned the rhetorical claims with a force incomparably more powerful than anything the secular groups could use.

These obligations include the duty of believers in *amré be ma'ruf va nahye az monkar*, "enjoining the good and forbidding the evil," the political implications of which support active involvement in the struggle to overthrow a regime hostile to Islam (Enayat, 1982: 2). The social status of the ulema as learned men possessing esoteric knowledge, as the community elders, is embellished by the particular Shiite authority structure and the necessity for the *muqallidin*, the imitators, to follow the example of the jurisprudents. Possible sanctions included the transportation of guilt to the next world, where one would be forced to bear one's sins; social sanctions could include the collective labeling of a person as anti-Islamic. Thus, the construction of the popular movement as a religious activity that demanded involvement was to place a heavy burden of responsibility upon each Moslem. It meant that participation could not be seen as a matter of individual assessment and decision but as a collective duty; it was not a matter of evaluating competing claims and arguments, but of obedience to established authority. It was the apotheosis of traditional communication compelling mobilization.

This idea of religious duty incumbent on everyone is propagated in the most powerful way in Khomeini's famous communiqué for the beginning of the month of *Moharram* in November 1978. *Moharram* is the holiest month in the Shiite calendar, the time when Hossein, the son of Ali, was martyred by Yazid. Khomeini looked forward to the opportunity that this symbolic period provides, likening it to "a divine sword in the hand of the soldiers of Islam." It is

> the month in which blood triumphed over the sword, the month in which truth condemned falsehood for all eternity and branded the mark of disgrace upon the forehead of all oppressors and satanic governments; the month that has taught successive generations throughout history the path of victory over the bayonet; the month that proves the superpowers may be defeated by the word of truth; the month in which the leader of the Moslems taught us how to struggle against all the tyrants of history, showed how the clenched fists of those who seek freedom, desire independence, and proclaim the truth may triumph over tanks, machine guns, and the armies of Satan, how the world of truth may obliterate falsehood.

In this communiqué, political acts that will bring down the regime were specified and the need for continued mass mobilization explained:

> It is the duty of the entire nation that has now risen in revolt to pursue and broaden its struggle against the Shah with all its strength and to bring down his harmful, disastrous regime . . .

> The military government is usurpatory and contrary to both the law of the land and the Shari'a. It is the duty of everyone to oppose it . . .

> It is the duty of all oil company officials and workers to prevent the export of oil, this vital resource . . .

> It is the duty of those well informed about the state of the country to draw up lists of the ministers serving in this usurpatory government, or the traitors and officers who are ordering crimes and massacres throughout the country, so that the people will know what to do with them at the appropriate time . . .

> Respected preachers, dear speakers, attend even more than before to your duty of exposing the crimes of the region, so that you may hold your heads up high in the presence of God Almighty and the Lord of the Age—may God hasten his renewed manifestation—

> Dear young people at the centers of religious learning, the universities, the schools and teachers' training colleges! Respected journalists! Deprived workers and peasants! Militant and enlightened bazaar merchants and tradesmen! And all other classes of the population, from the proud nomadic tribes to the deprived dwellers in slums and tents! Advance together, with a single voice and a single purpose, to the sacred aim of Islam—the abolition of the cruel Pahlavi dynasty, the destruction of the abominable monarchical regime, and the establishment of an Islamic Republic based on the progressive dictates of Islam! Victory is yours, nation arisen in revolt! . . .

There is no excuse for any class of people in the nation to remain inactive today: silence and apathy mean suicide, or even aid to the tyrannical regime. To abandon the straightforward path of the nation and Islam would be treason to Islam and the nation, and support for the enemies of Islam and the nation . . .

I offer my congratulations to the mothers and fathers of those youths who have given their lives for the cause of Islam and freedom . . . (Algar, 1981: 242–45)

Apart from the tremendous power of the language and its effective repetitive rhythm, typical of formulaic orality, this communiqué is especially interesting because it brings together so clearly a number of central political themes. One is the by-then explicit intention to overthrow the Shah's regime, and a second is the avowed purpose of establishing an Islamic Republic. A third is the need for unity and solidarity based obviously on the centrality of Islam, which is the fourth theme. A fifth theme is the necessity for mass participation, which is to be regarded as ethical duty, and the sixth is the elevation of death in this process to martyrdom in the holy line of Hossein (Enayat, 1982). It is important to note that Khomeini frequently and specifically addressed the clergy and stressed that there was no time for pedantic debate over Qoranic interpretation but rather it was time for the members of the clergy to involve themselves in political activity to save Islam; indeed he argues that the passive, noninvolved Islam that separates religion from politics is a bastardized version promulgated by imperialism (Khomeini in Algar, 1981: 128, 139).

Not only does Khomeini employ powerful language but it is rendered accessible and comprehensible to any Iranian. Again, Khomeini's rhetoric uses Qoranic and Islamized Persian concepts in pairs of polar opposites, such that the meaning and value attached to each pole is clear. *Rah-e Khoda*, God's way, is contrasted to *gom-rah*, the lost way, away from Islam. God opposes Satan, Hossein opposes Yazid in the historic struggle of Karbala. *Mazlum*, meekness, faces *taghut*, corruption; *mostazzafin*, the disinherited, challenge the *mostakbarin*, the oppressors; *mashru'e*, a Shari'a-based religious legitimacy, triumphs over *mashrute*, the Constitution, considered to have been copied from the West and tainted by imperialism; and so on (Rajaee, 1983). The rhetoric is epideictic, highly normative, based on a traditional value system that all Iranians understand.

Khomeini's rhetoric was not the language of persuasion or gentle inducement for voluntarist participation, an inherently slow process. Nor was it the language or method of a revolutionary cadre executing the revolution with class support, a model that Iranian social structure was not "ready" for and could not support. It was the exhortatory language of a traditionalist leadership urging a still-traditional people to mass mobilization on the basis of religious duty. The struggle was portrayed as one in which every believer had a role to play, and the compulsion to participate emanates from the power of religion, the traditional power of the *ulema* in leading their community, and the charismatic power of Khomeini himself, embodied in his rhetoric. It constructed an unarmed people-in-unity as powerful against a tyrannical regime, and faith as empowering and demanding action. Undoubtedly, this call from Khomeini helped to produce the massive demonstrations of millions of people during *Tasu'a* and *Ashura*, the climactic days of *Moharram*, in 1978.

Algar (1980) supports our analysis of this crucial communications dynamic, saying "the organisational structure of the Revolution is extremely simple. It was a question of the directives being given by Ayatollah Khomeini, being distributed throughout Iran and then evoking an immediate response of obedience from the mass of the people." From the first communiqué sent from Najaf, and repeated many times thereafter, Khomeini had stressed the need for *vahdate-kalameh*, unity of word. This implied both religious solidarity around the word of the Qoran, the text to answer all contemporary problems, and political solidarity around Islamic identity, and thus the inadvisability of expressing alternative visions. Thus from early on in the movement there was strong pressure to render alternate ideologies literally unsayable. As we have mentioned before, the fact that the high *ulema* had access to esoteric knowledge provided them with valued social status, and, coupled with the institutionalization of the need for emulation of a *marja 'i-taqlid*, meant the social and political power of the *ulema* was unquestionable for most Iranians. Beyond that, the construction of political messages in religious symbolism made them particularly effective. As Hegland (in Keddie, 1983: 220) states, "because the realm of the sacred is almost by definition unquestionable and unquestioned, political 'realities' and messages couched in religious terms are all the more persuasive and powerful." The sense of the only and final word connotes, as Rose (in Keddie, 1983: 187) has noted, "a rigid ideological uniformity, characterised by belief and action aimed at reproducing the prophetic-imamic archetype of revolutionary struggle. It is further the popular force capable of initiating human self-transformation and sustaining the Shari'a milieu. In the final analysis, it is also a rubric for the suppression of dissent." Postrevolutionary struggles were thus prefigured in the rhetoric of the mobilization itself.

Charisma and Compulsion: Patriarchal Authority

Although it is true that the revolution had no evident tightly organized center but partly depended for its dynamism on the activities of many spontaneous groups, committees, and gatherings in a variety of work, educational, and religious settings, at the same time the clear direction and symbolic leadership provided by Khomeini was key to the movement's success. He represented asceticism against the conspicuous consumption and moral laxity of the Pahlavis, and manifested a political stubbornness and refusal to compromise that appealed to Iranians, so it was his own credibility and integrity, his ethos, his charisma, that helped to create a following (Fischer, 1983). This was far more important than the specific logic of his arguments. Charismatic authority is itself a model of compulsion, not voluntarism, the cathexis between leader and followers built on deep emotional ties (Weber in Gerth and Mills, 1974). Khomeini was the elderly patriarch with a long beard and piercing eyes, whose own voice was carried into countless Iranian households on cassette tapes, asking for obedience and unity. This functioned as a double displacement, the *mujtahed* as the interlocutor between God and the people, and the electronic recording speaking for Khomeini yet giving an impression of a false immediacy. Analytically, this trace of absolute presence may be shown to be illusive, based on an assumed transparency of meaning, but practically and experientially it seems to have produced very powerful effects. It is not the possession but the validation of charisma that empowers the charismatic leader, so that his actual authority depends on being accepted by a following (Norton, 1988). In its acceptance, a people reinvents itself.

Norton puts an even more complicated spin on the nature of representation, form, and religion. Arguing that Judaism is the religion of "the Father, the Law, the author, and the text" and Christianity is "the religion of the Son, the religion of representation," then Islam may be read as the realization of the third moment of divinity, "the religion of the Holy Spirit, of charisma. . . . Begun in speech, where writing is held sacred, where the only proper representation is of writing, where the Peoples of the Book are protected, Islam is the religion of the Word. In Islam God had neither face nor form, but was a Messenger" (Norton, 1988: 142). Thus the combination of the charismatic persona of Khomeini and the preexisting valued religious identity that is reauthored into a political community exert an immensely powerful force on individual Iranians to act politically. If historically within the Iranian political environment no long-enough moment of public disputation has managed to ground (write/author?) alternative bases for argumentation, and if specifically during the popular movement (up until its moment of success) no challenge to the charismatic father is laid down, this is in many ways a prepolitical, certainly preideological, struggle. From early on the centrality of Khomeini as the inspirational leader was clear. One of the demands of the Qom declaration was for the return of Khomeini from exile. Slogans rapidly elevated Khomeini to "imam," a title he did little to refute.

Again, we see the limitations of "modern" ideological politics as the model for the Iranian mobilization. Not only did the traditional forums of social/religious life provide space for the spread of political communication but also the rhetoric of Khomeini and the grand ayatollahs was a traditional form of coercive persuasion that precipitated the rapid and massive political mobilization. Political changes could have occurred in other ways, but only such religious rhetoric and such religious leadership could have produced the massive popular revolt. The argument advanced by secular politicians that Khomeini "hijacked" the revolution is somewhat fanciful; without Khomeini there would have been no popular revolution.

This argument is supported by analysis of the language, themes, and demands of the popular communiqués of the revolutionary mobilization, where it is evident that the crowd is frequently more radical than many erstwhile leaders and takes its inspiration from Khomeini. Drawing inspirations from Khomeini's pronouncements and enjoying a certain anonymity of participation, some of the revolutionary publicists maintained a continuous barrage of radical themes, which meant that any possibility of accommodation was undermined.

Two relatively simple themes predominated: the removal of the Shah and the return of Khomeini. From the aftermath of the first bloody demonstration in Qom, the popular leaflets and the prevalent slogans concentrated on the need to remove the Shah. It is interesting to note that the dominant slogan of the movement was *marg bar Shah*, literally "Death to the Shah," not "Down with the Shah," as though it was felt that he had to be erased before people could believe that the regime had truly been altered. The Shah was compared frequently to Yazid, but also to Pharaoh; he was called a fascist, a murderer, and a traitor. One early leaflet ended with the statement "Down with the anti-God and anti-people Pahlavi regime!" (Patriotic Muslim Students of Tabriz University, February 26, 1978, reprinted in *Review of Iranian Political Economy and History* II, 2: 71). Thus popular solidarity was also built around a moment of negativity, the Shah and his regime, and much less around any positive expression of the "future to come."

The lack of any "utopian" element in the slogans of the Iranian revolution is of interest. The central slogan of the French Revolution promised a new political regimen of "liberty, equality, and fraternity." The slogan of the Russian Revolution, "bread, peace, and land," promised a new political economy. The central slogans of the Iranian revolution were primarily the negative "Death to the Shah" and only subsequently *esteghlal, azadi, hokumat-e Islami*, "independence, freedom, Islamic Government." The only image of the future was the redemptive return of an Islamic community, reaching back into a mythified cultural past to reclaim a lost unity or to return to a peaceful childhood when all was secure. It is as though the pillars of despotic power cast such deep, dark shadows that the sky could not be seen until they had been toppled; by which time, the deep, dark shadow of the *mullahs* was already blocking out the light. In the Iranian revolution, it was the lost cultural past rather than any futuristic vision, nostalgia rather than hope, that inspired action. Ontogenetic certainty, the authority of the father over the sons, claimed a phylogenetic, certainly collective, memory of the early community/family that was to be reinstated. Psychological and political "regressions" support each other, as Laroui showed in his work on Arab intellectuals (1976: 99), who teetered between an abstract Marxism that cut them off from the masses or a too-ready return to an Islamic traditionalism, *salaffiya*, a form of political and cultural retardation.

Chapter 8
The "Heavy Artillery": Small Media
for a Big Revolution

. . . nothing but . . . prayers, instructions, and, to make the latter work, a single weapon: the telephone. From Neauphle, the whole of Iran was informed within hours. The calls of the Ayatollah were reproduced in hundreds and thousands of copies, taped onto tens of thousands of cassettes. Never have phone lines, roneo-machines, and photocopiers worked like this before . . . the cassettes of the Ayatollah were transformed into a heavy artillery of amazing efficiency.

Balta and Rulleau (1979: 50)

The scope of the traditional oppositional network was extended through a highly innovative use of modern communication media and telecommunications technologies to create the world's most successful example to date of alternate media mobilizing for revolution. The complex interplay and cultural resonances of traditional and modern, religious and secular, oral and printed, was what worked so well, not simply that small media were put to audacious new uses. Two main forms of "small media" were used in the Iranian movement: first, cassette tapes, which acted like an electronic pulpit (*minbar*), and second, photocopied statements, known as *elamieh*.

Cassette Tapes: The Electronic *Minbar*

The use of cassettes as opposition communication was actually nothing new in Iranian history. As early as his house arrest in Iran in 1964, Khomeini was making tape-recorded sermons from the sanctuary of his house and sending copies to important religious centers. His famous speech on 15th Khordad 1963 in Qom was recorded and became a precious commodity circulating in Tehran and elsewhere, reproduced by student activists. Tapes also appeared intermittently from his exile base, first in Turkey then, from October 1965, in Najaf, Iraq; these were carried back by Iranian pilgrims who had gone to visit the Shiite holy shrines in Karbala (Zonis, 1971: 46; Hiro, 1985: 55). Exile itself, both self-sought and regime-imposed, is a repetitive motif in Iranian political life, and was often utilized as a new locale from which to continue political activity.

There was merely a trickle of smuggled tapes in the late 1960s as pilgrims were still rather limited in numbers. Pamphlets were also brought in to Iran, including an open letter to Prime Minister Hoveyda critical of the enormous sums of money being lavished on the Shah's coronation. Lectures that Khomeini gave during this period were also published and widely circulated. Exile, literal deterritorialization, therefore did not cut Khomeini off from his followers. It is ironic to note that improvements in the relations between Iraq and Iran in the mid-1970s that aimed to settle the border disputes should have helped to strengthen this process. The Iraqis agreed to allow up to 130,000 Iranian pilgrims to visit the Shiite holy places, second only to Mecca in religious significance, so from 1976 a stream of tapes of Khomeini's speeches began to flow in to Iran from Najaf, brought back by pilgrims and visitors, and were distributed through the mosque network. The Shah became cognizant of this alternative communications network, noted briefly in his memoirs in the terse sentence "cassettes of his [Khomeini's] speeches and harangues were smuggled into our country and used by his supporters to incite the masses" (1980: 159). Hiro (1985) suggests that traffic between Iran and Iraq was drastically curtailed, returning travelers were searched at the Iraqi border, and the street price of a Khomeini cassette jumped to twenty-five dollars. This diffusion of cassettes was one of the reasons used by the Shah to persuade the Iraqis to terminate Khomeini's stay, probably one of the greatest of the Shah's ten big mistakes, as noted by Mohammad Heikal. Forced out of the comparative isolation of Najaf, and not welcome in any Arab or Moslem country, in September 1978 Khomeini found himself based in Neauphle-le-Chateau, just outside Paris. The arrangements were made by the triumvirate closest to Khomeini who came to orchestrate much of his activity: Sadegh Ghotbzadeh, Ibrahim Yazdi, and Mohammad-Hassan Bani-Sadr.

This move suddenly put Khomeini at the center of world media attention, as he was far more accessible. Many of the world's most noted journalists from major news channels journeyed to this once-quiet village to sit on the carpet and interview this new unusual revolutionary leader. The far better international telecommunications from France also facilitated expansion of the cassette-production process. In Khomeini's rented house, two tape machines were kept permanently running, recording his speeches and announcements and duplicating them for transmission or transportation to Iran. Khomeini refused to talk on the telephone directly so international lines were used for tape-to-tape recording. In Iran, followers in makeshift studios with numerous cassette recorders worked around the clock to duplicate these texts. Tehran music stores slipped in a religious tape with the purchase of musical ones. One research study (Aflatouni, 1978) revealed the decline of sales for music tapes from 1977 as religious and politically oriented materials, including international revolutionary songs, became available.

Cassettes were a most suitable format for Khomeini's lengthy sermons and diatribes against the Pahlavis. Other religious leaders such as Ayatollah Shariat-Madari, Ayatollah Kani, and Alameh Nuri also made recordings. The oral mode is culturally favored, suited the clerics' style, and allowed full play of the emotional and dramatic power of *rowzeh* mourning symbols as well as recitative repetition of the failures of the Shah's regime and the need for action. Sometimes recorded at a public preaching, these cassettes also captured the sounds of the public lamentation and prayers (*salavat*). The biggest rival to Khomeini for popular affection in the cassette stakes was Shariati. Recordings of his lectures at *Hosseinieh Ershad* in 1976 were widely distributed, sold by street vendors, and taken to rural areas where they promoted fierce debate (Hooglund, 1980). The secular opposition produced a few tapes, including recordings of the series of poetry readings organized at the Goethe Institute in Tehran in 1977, events that were significant moments in the opening up of the political environment.[1]

There was at least one instance of a hoax tape, in Tehran in the autumn of 1978. The tape purported to be the voice of the Shah, instructing the army about how to deal with the revolutionary mob and commanding the army to shoot to kill. Very hard to distinguish, this was effective like many rumors because it fitted with what people wished to believe rather than because it was factually correct. Later a famous actor, Karim Esfahani, claimed he had recorded the tape in order to shock the army and politicize the movement.

Leaflets: Xerography for Democracy

The other major form of small media utilized during the popular movement was the production of brief photocopied statements. An underground network of illegal printed material is also not a novelty in Iranian history, but it was taken to more popular and extensive lengths during the recent movement. Almost from the beginnings of a formal press in Iran, a parallel underground network has flourished, as well as a variety of exile publications (Browne, 1914; Mowlana, 1963; Behn, 1979). A response to censorship and repression, this hidden political opposition often faced harsh penalties for the publication or even possession of outlawed material. *Shab-nameh* (literally, night letters), circulated at the turn of the century, were used to arouse involvement in the growing constitutional struggle against the Qajar rulers. Another wave of underground pamphlets appeared in

1919–21 with the growth of the *Tudeh* (Communist) party, and again from 1941 and the British/Soviet occupations until 1953.

As has been underlined a number of times, when the central state was strong, a public sphere became extinct. Thus these initially limited ways of promoting public debate, through the circulation of "open letters" and poetry readings, were so significant in creating chinks in the surveillance state. These were political acts in themselves, for to begin to communicate in a situation where the processes of censorship and control were so well established was to take a brave and innovative step.

Written communiqués, leaflets, and proclamations began to surface widely after the Qom incident in January 1978. Known generically as *elamieh*, which literally means an announcement (or occasionally as *bayanie*, manifesto), these were mainly single-sheet productions. Many were handwritten, others typed, and they were duplicated single- or double-sided either by xerography or by mimeo. The office photocopy machine became the center of much activity as different groups vied for priority to use it. The photocopied materials were distributed from hand to hand, further reproduced, and passed on. They would be found in university classrooms in the morning. They were placed on car windshields. They were read aloud in mosques, teahouses, and other public places. They were pasted on walls and trees, only to be torn down by SAVAK and the military. Duly renewed and removed, a thick layer of glue and tattered remnants together with erased and repainted graffiti transformed the hitherto bleak exteriors of high-walled streets and alleys into a dynamic concrete canvas that witnessed the growth of political activity. Indeed, the production of *elamieh* was the self-inscription of people into the political process.

Many *elamieh* were open anonymous statements of condemnation of the regime without an attribution, like the traditional *Shab-nameh*. Others were signed by a variety of political, religious, and professional groups, many of which were named into being precisely for the purpose of putting out such a statement; after the publication, they perhaps found further mobilizing activities to enact or perhaps remained dormant until the need was felt to publish another statement. Although the popular movement did see the renaissance of many old formal political parties and organizations, it also witnessed an astonishing ebb and flow of grouplets of often no more than a handful of people who wished to name themselves and circulate the fact of their political involvement for others to see. This element of uncoordinated spontaneous activity using small media is part of what makes the Iranian process so special. The next chapter provides a narrative of the year of revolutionary mobilization and describes the duet played out between the state media and these alternative forms of communication.

Here, some analysis of the functions of these communiqués is presented. Perhaps the first widely circulated communiqué was sent by Khomeini from Najaf, in which he extolled the "brave fighters of Islam" who had been killed in the bloody demonstration in Qom in January 1978. In asking the Iranian people to commemorate their deaths, the ritual forty-day cycle took on a political flavor and initiated a political crowd that assembled and dispersed almost without beckoning, according to the known rhythms of Islamic mourning.

In the autumn of 1978 distribution of underground materials was facilitated by the period of intense darkness created by the nationwide electricity cuts that began at 8:30 P.M. each night. The military curfew began at 9 P.M., so a thirty-minute "witching hour" remained for covert political action. The main nightly newscast on television was also blacked out. The dissemination of materials was a "free press" in all senses: anyone could participate, it was indiscriminate as to content (although it was almost totally oppositional), and everything was distributed free of charge. Beyond the two dominant forms of cassettes and photocopied publications, a plethora of other kinds of communication grew, including many kinds of posters (often representing Khomeini in classic Renaissance Christian poses; see figs. 5.1–5.3), stenciled images spray-painted onto walls, and elaborate calligraphy, new and traditional art forms being called upon to serve the movement (Fischer and Abedi, 1990; Hanaway, 1985). The ever-evolving slogans and graffiti messages testified to a great talent for political satire and trenchant comment that had lain dormant for a long time.

The Function of Revolutionary Communiqués

The revolutionary process in Iran produced a mélange of leaflets, flyers, communiqués, manifestos, and other brief documents, materials that are sometimes referred to as the "ephemera" of revolution, but which are here considered central to the political process. It is impossible to know exactly how many leaflets were produced during the revolutionary period. The analysis that follows is based on an extensive personal collection, as well as on an archive established at Iran Communications and Development Institute in 1978. Both these collections contain hundreds of documents, which include not only Tehran-based items but also circulars originating in Qom, Tabriz, and Isfahan. Many were collected personally at demonstrations in Tehran and Isfahan. Others were collected through the university network and through Ali's participation in the strike-coordinating committee, which brought together representatives from a wide cross section of institutions in the autumn of 1978. Others were passed on by friends and contacts in political groups, other work areas, and from other cities. Neither collection is "complete" but the materials represent a spectrum of religious and secular opinion, a variety of groups and geographic spread. There are also several published collections of such materials (*Qiyam*, 1978 [1356], three volumes in one; *Nedaye-Hagh*, 1979 [1357]; *Asnad*, 1979 [1358]).

The essential function of many *elamieh* was a combination of exhortation to action, i.e., mobilization, and prescription for further action. This pattern was set by Khomeini's first communiqué from Najaf after the Qom demonstration in January 1978. In it he commended the brave martyrs of Qom for their actions. He lambasted the regime, criticizing the development projects and the "White Revolution" as promoting Westernization, and declaring the change of calendar, the attacks on the clergy, and political freedom for women to be profoundly anti-Islamic. Already at that relatively early point in the popular movement, he called the demonstrations a "referendum for the Shah's abdication" and gave instructions for the commemoration of the deaths of the Qom martyrs. He also asked each stratum of the nation to maintain solidarity, Vahdat-e-kalame, through Islam and criticized those who demanded constitutional rights because that implied acceptance of the corrupt Pahlavi regime. The central rhetorical and political motifs of the movement were thereby established. Death was elevated to martyrdom, something glorious rather than terrifying, thus empowering an unarmed people and belittling any regime threats. Much has been made of the enduring power of martyrdom in Shiite thought (Enayat, 1982), but much less has been made of the symbolic power of death within contemporary secular movements. As Glucksman (1979) argued, "Dying power changes the world . . . is what constitutes the strength of social movements," building rather than destroying solidarity in many social movements. Khomeini rejected any compromise or intermediate settlements with the regime from very early on. Unlike the initial secular intellectuals who addressed the regime directly and tried to persuade it to open up and grant specific requests (in the manner of most social movements), Khomeini turned his back to the regime, which is typified as contaminated, ritually unclean (najess), as well as tyrannical. The entire focus of Khomeini's propaganda is addressed to the people of Iran who are pak, clean/innocent, for the maintenance of solidarity to achieve the overthrow of the regime. The functional argument for solidarity in Islam is also a prefiguring of the total dominance of this perspective over all others that was the outcome of the movement.

Future communiqués would elaborate on these themes and also provide precise, practical instructions about politico-religious activity, acquiring a tactical role. The seven- and forty-day mourning cycles would have occurred anyway, but their orchestration into political events was conducted by communiqués issued by leading religious figures. Communiqués by Khomeini and other ayatollahs ordered the first general strike day on May 15, 1978, and similar communiqués preceded subsequent strikes. The various opposition groupings and competing leaders may have come to accept Khomeini's leadership and coalesced around him only in the autumn of 1978, but the evidence from the popular leaflets, slogans, and pattern of mobilization suggests that the popular movement centered on him from January 1978.

Ayatollahs Taleghani, Ghomi, Golpayegani, Shariat-Madari, and Saddoughi all issued elamieh during the popular mobilization (Qiyam 1:83–88; Asnad, 70:98–99). Lesser religious figures, including Tehrani, Khamene'i, Rabbani, and many others, also made proclamations. Secular groups such as the National Front and later the *Fedai'i* publicized similar communiqués to conduct demonstrations of their own as well as supporting the broader demonstrations and helping to organize the strikes. Other political groups produced communiqués in support of a proposed activity and invited supporters to join in.

Identification and agitation were important functions of *elamieh*. A crucial element in any political movement is defining the "enemy," setting limits to legitimate targets of political action, and in the process reinforcing the collective "we" of revolutionary actors. Political labeling was an important device to reinforce the parameters of insiders (movement participants) and outsiders (groups/individuals supporting the regime) and neatly symbolized the political and economic nature of the regime. A number of leaflets were written and circulated that accused both individuals and groups of complicity with the regime in various forms. Some of these were simply lists of names, including a list of supposed SAVAK members and a list of Iranians purported to have CIA connections. Much of this information was of dubious veracity, but its effect was immense. Some named individuals did not dare go to work, creating chaos in an already-disturbed work environment. Rumors and gossip abounded, and collective pressure increased for individuals to align themselves positively and openly with the movement. A list that circulated during the premiership of Sharif-Emami purported to reveal that most of the members of the cabinet at that time were freemasons brought to power through a British intelligence plot. After the revolution, two lodges were found in Tehran whose membership lists did substantiate some of the claims, although not the British complicity (see also Ra'in, 1968). These lists played on the popular myths about foreign conspiracies and used the accusation of a foreign connection to ruin many reputations. That many of the secular opposition figures of the popular movement would themselves be later accused by the Islamic Republic of being not only Westernized but actually "American spies" and agents would be one of the biggest ironies of the revolution.

Some communiqués made allegations about financial finagling and corruption as well as accusations of political duplicity. In December 1978 a group of people who signed themselves Employees of the Central Bank produced a list of 180 Iranians who had allegedly transferred a total of 2.7 billion dollars out of the country in the preceding few months. Like the other lists, there was probably an element of factual accuracy here compounded with a lot of fabrication, but the communiqué was widely believed, suggesting immense corruption within the government and reinforcing awareness about the tremendous gap in wealth that existed in Iran, and it aroused considerable anger. A similar statement emanated from employees of the Pahlavi Foundation, a charitable foundation that sent money abroad to support university students; the list of contributors to the foundation included names of young children, indicating that many people were sending money abroad under false pretenses. Another statement described the wealth and assets of the royal family; circulated later in a pamphlet satirically named "Octopus," it revealed the extent to which national wealth was being siphoned off into the Pahlavis' private hands and the dramatic extent of the family's economic involvements. A public inquiry was demanded, and the Shah himself promised investigations, but nothing happened. Thus these leaflets, concocted with political agitation in mind and based on a judicious mix of fact, gossip, and fantasy, had a profound catalytic effect. They appeared to reveal the extent of antipopular and antinational political connections, as well as the amount of both petty and gross corruption, and helped to increase the level of popular agitation.

The function of agitation cannot be easily distinguished from another purpose of these leaflets, the provision of analysis and counterinformation against the government standpoint presented in the media. Leaflets were distributed from the first demonstrations in Qom and Tabriz and after, providing sharply differing accounts than those of the government about the dynamic of events and about the levels of violence. Often media reports of events are quoted in the leaflets and explicitly refuted. For example, one leaflet written by students of Tabriz quotes an *Etela'at* article from February 20, 1978, that reported that the army had "reestablished order" in the city by noon, and then cheerfully rebuts this account by claiming the demonstration went on into the evening and was followed the next day by outbreaks in four other places in the city ("Report," *Review of Iranian Political Economy and History*, June 1978: 60–71). With military control of the media in the autumn of 1978, this function of rebutting government arguments, figures, and claims was one of the most important roles of the clandestine communications network.

Leaflets also reported episodes of government callousness, such as blood donors being turned away from hospitals to which wounded had been taken. There were stories of bodies being piled into army trucks and being sent to unknown destinations, so that the bodies were not available for burial and no accurate casualty count could be made. Many communiqués were issued after the tragic Cinema Rex fire killed more than four hundred people in Abadan; the fire was generally perceived at that time to be a SAVAK plot to discredit the movement, and the leaflets attacked the government for its premeditated murder of innocents. Similarly, after the Jaleh Square incident leaflets utterly contradicted government announcements and death tallies.

In this internal confusion about the true "facts" pertaining to events, the BBC became elevated to an objective third party perceived by many to have reliable information. Yet obviously the BBC coverage was only as good as its available sources and resources would allow. The opposition became adept at feeding information to the BBC correspondent so that in general coverage probably lent in the direction of the perspective of the opposition movement. In the absence of a solid baseline of certain fact, the popular movement won the propaganda war, gaining internal credibility as well as external recognition. A different kind of information was provided by employees of the Bureau of Statistics. They presented figures on the level of inflation in housing costs, food, and other economic variables over the few years of the Pahlavi regime, giving some "objective" measure of the economic squeeze that so many people were experiencing.

Another important role of many of these leaflets was the expression of solidarity, often by apparently spontaneous groups that began to coalesce across the country, frequently after the immediate experience of a popular demonstration. Leaflets appeared after every bloody demonstration. Some were left unsigned, but many were the products of a multiplicity of small groupings that suddenly came together after such an event. There were student groups like "Patriotic Muslim Students of Tabriz," and groups of clerics such as "The Society of Militant Clerics" (*Review of Iranian Political Economy and History*, June 1978; *Asnad*, 1978: 129). There were bazaari groups, from the general "Merchants of the Tehran Bazaar" to the more specific "Isfahani Merchants and Artisans Resident in Tehran," who immediately expressed their solidarity with the Qom demonstrators, struck on January 10 and 11, 1978, and called a general closure of the bazaar across the country for January 19, 1978. Other groups were called "Revolutionary Workers of Islam," "Vengeance," "Dawn of Islam," "Seekers of God," and "Heirs of the Blood of Hossein" (*Asnad*, 1978: 131–33; *Qiyam*, 1978: 133). Many of these groups were composed of a few individuals, had no previous political history, and diffused as the revolution ended—but their very ephemerality is essential and specific to the dynamic of this mobilization. There were no extant "political" organizations to carry the revolution. This coalescing of numerous groups comprising different sectors of the population across the country was a central part of the revolutionary mobilization, the means through which many people made their commitment explicit, and the first chance for many to be actually involved in political activity beyond marching in a demonstration, even if this participation was "only" the production and distribution of a leaflet. Undoubtedly, these leaflets and the appearance of groups had a contagion effect, signifying the expansion of the opposition, which then encouraged others to follow.

The manifestos of occupational, interest, minority, and other groups represented another kind of communiqué that revealed the depth of penetration of the popular movement. By autumn 1978 and with the widespread strikes, the number of communiqués increased as each group put out its declaration. Both white-collar and blue-collar workers were involved. An incomplete list of participants includes employees of the Plan and Budget Organization, Iran Air, the water industry, the electricity service, the Tabriz Tractor Factory, and teachers across the country. These communiqués proclaimed the economic demands of each group for higher wages as well as political demands. Teachers demanded the right of association, the termination of mandatory attendance at pro-Shah events, the release of political prisoners, and the lifting of martial law. Tehran Water Board employees sent out regular bulletins that cataloged opposition activities and regime responses. A section of the First Army in Tabriz (*Artesh-e Yekom*) also proclaimed its revolutionary tendency in a leaflet, which, by revealing another significant breach in the apparatus of repression, had an inspirational effect. One significant statement was signed by the strike-coordinator representatives of twenty-three of the most important government ministries, banks, and other institutions such as the Plan and Budget Organization, the universities, the Finance Ministry, the Atomic Energy Commission, the telephone company, and Central Bank. It stated their aim to coordinate militant activity in governmental and national institutions throughout the country under the leadership of Khomeini. They supported stands against imperialism and despotism throughout the world, and pledged to fight any compromises with the regime. As an expression of the rejection of the regime by bureaucratic and technocratic elements, the white-collar middle class who had appeared to be well accommodated to the system, this was a stunning leaflet, revealing the total institutional collapse of the regime.

The oil workers, on strike from the end of October 1978, produced a series of statements detailing the purpose of their strike and their determination to prevent the exportation of any oil, restricting use to domestic consumption. They included in their political demands the abolition of martial law, the opening of the universities, the freeing of political prisoners, the elimination of SAVAK, the continuing battle against corruption, and the removal of American advisors (9 Azar 1357, *Syndikaye Moshtarak-e Karkonan Sanat-e Naft*, United Syndicate of Workers/ Employees of Oil Industry). The spontaneity of the oil workers' movement should also be noted. On being asked who gave instructions to strike, oil workers replied, "No one in particular. Everyone agrees. There is really no organization. It's too bad. But by firing on us, the army has forced us to organize ourselves. We listen to Khomeini and read the tracts of the Mojahedin" ("Fear Reigns in Abadan," *MERIP Report*, 1979: 75–76; see also Bayat, 1986).

Even minority religious communities such as the Zoroastrians and the Jews produced communiqués of solidarity with the popular movement. One communiqué, for example, was produced by the "Organization of Jewish Intellectuals." The importance of the involvement and militancy of these professional and highly skilled groups can hardly be overstated. This was predominantly a social sector that was well- and Western-educated, part of the Shah's technocratic base that had been compliant until this point. That they too were mobilizing revealed the widespread repugnance felt for the Shah's regime, and qualifies the totally religious nature of the movement. Khomeini was recognized as a powerful and militant leader, with little or no discussion about what the political system "after the Shah" would be like.

A few leaflets were oriented to the need for and development of armed struggle. After the violent events in Tabriz in February 1978, some leaflets provided justifications for each of the targets selected for attack: *Rastakhiz* was renamed *rosvakhiz*, the scandalous party; Saderat Bank belonged to the Pahlavis and was a "big landowner and comprador"; cinemas were "centers of corruption"; shops were "sellers of junk houseware" ("From Qom to Tabriz—Solidarity with the Bloody Demonstrations in Qom," Patriotic Muslim Students of Tabriz University, *Review of Iranian Political Economy and History*, June 1978: 47). Another leaflet ends by supporting "the necessity of arming the patriotic forces, as Imam Khomeini has said: The 'righteous person should be armed' . . . Victory to the armed struggle of the Moslems in Iran and all over the world!" ("Report of the Patriotic Muslim Students of Tabriz on the Tabriz Uprising," *Review of Iranian Political Economy and History*, June 1978: 71). Another group that called itself "The Group of the *Towhidi* Line" claimed responsibility for planting a bomb that had killed several people in a North Tehran restaurant, Khansalar, frequented by foreigners. It pledged to avenge every last drop of blood shed by "this bloodthirsty regime and imperialism" ("The Group of the *Towhidi* Line," Military Communiqué No. 1: 22, 13 August 1978). As their members were released from prison and the guerrilla groups of *Fedai'i* and *Mojahedin* began to regroup in the winter of 1978, there was more public discussion about the possibility of armed struggle, but generally this was not a prevalent theme of the popular leaflets.

The occasional unclassifiable communiqué also appeared. For example, in September 1978, as Prime Minister Sharif-Emami was wistfully commenting that someone was bound to blame the government for the Tabas earthquake, a five-page document with diagrams circulated. It claimed that there had been no earthquake but rather the event was the result of the testing of a U.S. underground nuclear device in the Dasht-e-Lut desert. Signed by the *Hezbollahs*, it played on the readiness of Iranians to accept conspiracy theories, the more preposterous the better, and it remains as one of the more confusing of the revolution's creations. A similar type of story grew after the unsuccessful U.S. mission to rescue the hostages in the summer of 1980. Instead of accepting the crash of the U.S. helicopters as accidental, rumors spread that the Soviets had been shooting down the helicopters with lasers.

Other communiqués created to cause confusion and mistrust were those purportedly distributed by SAVAK. Only a few leaflets were alleged to be the work of SAVAK, recognized as such because very early on in the movement the organization deliberately tried to sow dissension and make accusations about popular figures quite against the general tone of solidarity of the genuine movement. Khomeini warned against SAVAK's attempts to cause confusion and undermine the movement, as in its accusing the movement of starting the Cinema Rex fire (leaflet of 3 Shavval 1398). Only after the establishment of the Islamic Republic was it learned that a religious group had started the fire in order to discredit SAVAK.

This considerable volume of photocopied and mimeographed literature not only was crucial to mobilization and politicization but also reflected the extent of popular involvement and presented channels for participatory political communication. It effectively challenged the big media of the regime, becoming more credible and effective as the movement progressed.

The Growth of an Alternate Press

Most of the leaflets were one-off circulars, often produced in response to a particular event. A more continuous, formally organized underground press emerged with vigor in the autumn of 1978. When the military government was appointed on November 6, 1978, the mass media of radio-television and the national press went on strike. Almost instantly a regular underground newsservice, with two main publications, was put into operation. One was produced by the Journalists' Syndicate, which was well aware of the national need for information at such a critical period but not willing to cooperate with the military and its demands regarding censorship. Its Strike Bulletin, *Bulletin-e Ehtesab*, carried "people's news and information": it described the different strikes in progress around the country; opened bank accounts and called for contributions to support strike activity and to cover its own publishing costs; and printed letters of solidarity. One bulletin was produced every week for the duration of the military government. Occasional statements were also released that demanded a return to civilian government, argued against censorship, and condemned the Pahlavi regime.

The second underground publication was a weekly news bulletin called *Hambastegi* (Solidarity), which was organized by the National Organization of Universities, *Sazman-e-Melli Daneshgaian*, and published in conjunction with the Writers' Syndicate and the Committee for the Defense of Political Prisoners. Ali wrote for this bulletin, and helped distribute it around Tehran. As well as this regular publication, the university organization also produced communiqués that demanded academic freedoms and scientific and cultural freedom, protested censorship, and called for a revolutionary transformation of social institutions in Iranian society.

From August 1978 many of the more formal political groupings were also publishing tracts and journals. The National Front had its *Khabarnameh* (Newsletter); *Tudeh* began to republish its newspaper, *Mardom* (The People); even copies of *Kar* (Labor) of the *Fedai'i* guerrilla organization began to appear. Haj Seyyed Javadi published his own *Jonbesh* (Movement), and Moghadam Maragheh put out *Nehzat-e-Radikal* (Radical Movement). This flurry of spontaneous organizations and public communication was the political heart of the revolution. While serious strikes were hurting the economy, this publicity network not only was in itself an impressive manifestation of political involvement but also helped to bring to the streets some of the most massive demonstrations of contemporary history. Here was a forum for secular intellectuals long denied any autonomous political and cultural practice; here was room for young clerical activists, students, workers, and many others to learn the rudimentary steps of political organization and writing; here were possibilities for public participation, debate, and involvement the likes of which had not been experienced in Iran since the early 1950s. The public was forcefully expressing its opinions.

Rumor: Collective Construction of Reality

Another manner in which the public made its ideas and opinions felt was in the extensive and powerful rumor network that operated as an informal communications channel. The context for rumor production accords well with Shibutani's (1966: 62) classic description that "an unsatisfied demand for news—the discrepancy between information needed to come to terms with a changing environment and what is provided by formal channels—constitutes the crucial condition of rumor construction." Despite the widespread suspicion of the news and information reporting of the formal media channels in Iran, they had provided a baseline from which to make judgments and draw conclusions. When these formal channels were silenced during the lengthy strike of November 1978-January 1979 the alternate channels of the opposition as well as foreign channels were widely used instead, and the rumor circuit was yet another way in which people were trying to make sense of the events occurring around them (see also Pliskin, 1980).

The basic condition for rumor generation was provided by the political struggle itself. Rumor was generated through the political forecasting that abounded, future possible scenarios being rapidly translated into likely sets of events. Shibutani (1966: 50) points to a similar process: "Often people are able to 'sense' momentous events in the making . . . many rumors turn out to be fairly accurate forecasts of coming events." Among all the competing rumors about, for example, the likely return of Khomeini to Iran, one might have hit on the correct date and thus the network would in a sense be validated. The stories that were generated about the Cinema Rex fire in Abadan were attempts by a population suspicious of government ploys and propaganda to try to invent meaningful political scenarios for itself.

Some rumors were deliberately developed as weapons in an ideological war against the regime and its propaganda, working on the reverse dynamic of what we have just described: if something was widely publicized, that might hinder its actually coming to pass. When it was learned that a plan had been mooted to set fire to Evin jail (a notorious center for political prisoners) to burn the remaining political prisoners, including some top ex-officials who then would be unable to expose the regime and blame others, the event was deliberately undermined by spreading this idea publicly, forewarning the crowd. It remains unclear whether the rumor was effective, and indeed whether such a plan ever seriously existed. Similarly, the notion of a possible military coup attempt during the Bakhtiar period, heightened by the Huyser mission, was intentionally kept alive by some people in the hope that if it were public knowledge such an event would be less likely to be acted upon. Forewarning the public was also forearming it. Some rumors developed because people could not come to terms with things they did not want to believe, such as the hard fact that the army that had fraternized with the people one day would turn to shoot the crowd the next. Hence the spread of rumors about the importation of Israeli troops to do the Shah's dirty work in the Jaleh Square incident.

At times rumors were an extension of gossip dealing with the health and welfare of individuals. Rumors abounded in the summer of 1978 about the Shah's ill health, yet these were always parried by his own comments that he had never felt better and that subversive circles were spreading these ideas as part of their grand strategy to undermine Iran. Rumors also spread in December that General Azhari was dead, adding to the popular idea that the country was unstable and leaderless. Azhari had had a heart attack but survived. Other rumors were also radicalizing, such as that about the cause of the Tabas earthquake being an underground nuclear test, which helped maintain anger at colonial interference. A rumor that all the crown jewels had been removed from the vaults of the Central Bank alerted people to the possibility of the royal family's departing and taking a chunk of the public wealth with them. Despite refutations by the bank's manager, there were sneaking suspicions that the gems in the vaults were fakes.

Rumors often ran counter to logic and other available evidence, flourishing in a situation where multiple meanings were competing for credibility. One rumor in particular vividly illustrates the process of collective self-delusion. In the autumn of 1978 a story spread that Khomeini's face was visible on the surface of the moon. People craned from windows and rooftops, exulted in seeing his visage on high. In Hamadan a sheep was sacrificed to celebrate this amazing phenomenon. Clergy in Hamadan then released a communiqué saying that such rumors were the work of the enemies of Islam who were trying to misrepresent the movement as reactionary and superstitious. Even Khomeini issued a statement from Paris asking people not to be fooled by such deliberate attempts to confuse them. Once the myth was broken, people became very angry and demonstrated against what was felt to be the government's fomentation of such a rumor.

As rumors developed to cope with crisis and out-of-the-ordinary situations, they were often contradictory, mutually incompatible, and sometimes plain wrong. Yet they were important means of negotiating the ambiguity and tension of the period. They were effective because they were perceived as correct, and often provided more popularly acceptable definitions of current events than those available from other sources. It was often hard to separate news from rumor, fact from fiction, and the confusion was increased by the use of rumors by the BBC and by the Iranian press. Rumor often slipped into humor, and the growth of political jokes and satire reflected another means of dealing with the ambiguity and stress of events.

The International Connection

After the cacophony of voices of the revolution, international information sources were used by the opposition to fill out the gaps and distortions in internal news reporting. By the mid-1970s an estimated nineteen international stations broadcast in Persian, and widespread listening to shortwave broadcasts from Moscow, Monte Carlo, Cologne, Tel Aviv, and London increased in direct relation to the growing awareness of the lacunae in the coverage of government-controlled media. International channels were seen as the repositories of "objectivity" and factually correct information, and their credibility and status rose as that of the internal mass media fell. Such a phenomenon is not particular to Iran. As Gauhar (1979) has written, "a weak and suppressed information system invites foreign cultural infiltration. By suppressing the national press the governments do not suppress news. They only make it easier for foreign news agencies to report news to their people with much greater impact."

The BBC in particular became an invisible actor within the Iranian political drama, so much so that Prime Minister Sharif-emami in October 1978 enjoined the Iranian press to provide better coverage of domestic events so that people would not turn to foreign channels; he referred to the BBC by name. The regime in the person of Ameli-Tehrani, Minister of Information under Sharif-Emami, addressed directly "those Iranians who are working for the BBC," saying that the channel's comments had "caused sabotage, destruction, and certain cases of arson" (*Kayhan International*, October 30, 1978). At the end of November a formal complaint about BBC coverage was lodged with the British ambassador, showing that the Iranian regime did not understand that the BBC is an autonomous institution but instead held the British government responsible for its output. The regime also tried to brand the BBC as the voice of colonialism. In the autumn of 1978, amid a highly volatile situation and rapidly moving events, the BBC took to reporting items under the heading of "It has been rumored in Tehran," partly reflecting the connections made with the opposition by the BBC's Tehran correspondent, and partly reflecting the sympathies of the Iranian staff working for the Persian service in London. Yet the BBC correspondent was allowed to continue working in Tehran; only a *Guardian* reporter and a UPI correspondent were forced to leave Iran during the revolution because of regime displeasure with their coverage.

With the national mass-media strike from November 1978-January 1979, both the internal channels of information through small media and the international channels became vital sources of daily news and analysis. The BBC compiled nightly reports of the day's events across Iran and thus provided Iranians with a complete picture of their national struggle in a way that only extensive long-distance phone conversations could have replicated internally.

Shortwave radio was probably the most crucial international channel in the

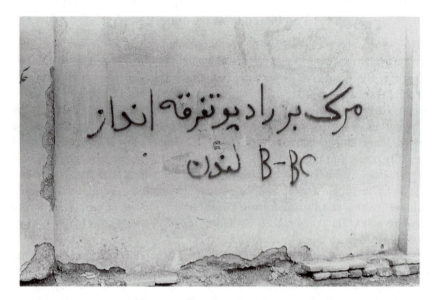

Figure 8.1. Graffiti on a Tehran wall reads, "Down with the BBC radio, whose message creates disunity."

revolutionary mobilization, but it was not the only one. Khomeini was at first highly suspicious of the international press. In the first interview he granted a foreign correspondent, Lucien George of *Le Monde* in Najaf in May 1978, he made his mistrust clear: "The international press is concerned chiefly with pomp, pretension, show, and official ceremony: things like Persepolis, the Shah's coronation, and so on. At the most, it will show some interest in the price of oil, but never in the misfortunes of the Iranian people or the repression they are suffering. The Shah is said to spend 100 million dollars a year on propaganda abroad . . . I have been told that your newspaper is independent and concerned with the real problems of Iran: torture, massacre, and injustice. I hope that this interview will contribute to making known the goals of my people" (interview in *Le Monde*, May 6, 1978; reprinted as "An Exile's Dream for Iran," in Nobari, 1978). Khomeini's assessment of the role of the media vis-à-vis Iran did not differ greatly from that of many Western analysts such as Dorman and Farhang (1987) or even Said (1981). Khomeini's move to Paris in early October 1978 landed him at the center of world media networks, and a decision seems to have been made to make more active use of the foreign media. Within the first two months of his Parisian exile, Khomeini had given interviews to at least France-Press and Associated Press; to French, German, Austrian, Luxembourgian, Swedish, and Greek broadcasting stations; to Mike Wallace of CBS; and to *Al-Mostaghbal* and the *Guardian* newspapers. The collected messages, speeches, and interviews of just these initial two months amount to 458 pages of Persian text (*Nedaye-Hagh*, 1979 [1357]). Not only were Khomeini's analyses and plans given international publicity in this way, but the background pieces played an important role of image-making. The glimpses of his asceticism, the reports that he ate a simple Persian stew for lunch, sitting on Persian carpet, and offered tea to visitors, also accommodated on the floor, provided vivid contrast with the pomp and ceremony of the Peacock Throne. Khomeini was a most unusual media "star."

As events became more violent and more critical during the autumn of 1978, Iran began to take over the covers of news magazines, depicted through photographs of Khomeini, violent events at Tehran University, and the burning of the Shah's photograph. This material circulated inside Iran, and even for those unable to understand the English-language reports it was clear that events of international importance were in the making. This publicity produced a sense of pride that finally the Iranian people, and not the regime, were making history. By February 1979, when Khomeini had returned to Iran, Tehran hotels were transformed into world news centers, although a lack of fluency in Persian kept many reporters propping up the bar rather than probing for a story (one *Los Angeles Times* correspondent, however, was killed while covering a violent demonstration). At least one leaflet circulated that expressly welcomed the attention of the foreign press corps "for bringing the plight of our people to the world's attention. You brave people, who run into hazardous situations yourselves, are carrying a greater share of responsibility now that our own press people are not free to do their part" (*MERIP Report*, 1979: 75–76).

The disjuncture between the internal and external perceptions of the role of the foreign press is quite interesting. Inside Iran, these channels were used to supplement and validate other sources of information, and gave Iranians a sense that the whole world was watching their making of history. Abroad, dramatic news photos and tropes such as "Islamic fundamentalism" played against the myth of the Shah as the progressive modernizer to reinforce an Orientalist hostility toward Moslem fanaticism that would poison international relations for some time. To argue that international channels were utilized inside Iran is in no way to endorse their content or to reject the telling criticisms of Said (1981) and others.

IV
The Revolutionary Process

Chapter 9
A Communication-based Narrative
of the Revolution

We provide in this chapter a narrative eyewitness account of the revolutionary mobilization that focuses on the particular junctures at which communications of various kinds played a critical role. We highlight small media as a public space of confrontation between opposition movement and the regime, small media as integral elements to the developing and maintaining of an alternative history and set of heroes to mobilize and foster solidarity, and small media as forms of political participation in and of themselves. As participants in many of these events, we also hope to share some of the atmosphere, the excitement and the danger, of being part of such a massive political upheaval.

Although political activities in the universities and among the secular intellectuals had already started, a bizarre occurrence brought on a very different cycle of demonstrations, moving the revolution onto the streets. On January 7, 1978, *Etela'at* newspaper suddenly carried an article that berated the antiregime clergy and lashed out at the conspiracy of "black and red reactionaries" trying to undermine the Shah-People Revolution. Dariush Homayoun, the Minister of Information at the time, said much later that the piece was ordered directly by the Shah. Further allegations were made against Khomeini in the article: he was not truly Iranian, he had British connections, he led a dissolute life, and he wrote Sufic poetry. The purpose of this article was unclear, but its effect was crystal clear. The seminary and bazaar in Qom closed, and 4,000 theology students and others demonstrated, calling for a public apology and shouting, "We don't want the Yazid government." The theology students formed an Educational Society and developed a manifesto of twelve demands that included the implementation of the Constitution, the dissolution of *Rastakhiz*, and the return of Khomeini. An ensuing clash with police left people dead and injured; numbers varied greatly between the opposition's claimed seventy deaths and the regime's reported two. Such conflict over exact numbers was to continue throughout the movement. The next day a communiqué from Khomeini began orchestrating the opposition response, and the period of predominantly secular middle-class revolt was over. The so-called initial liberalization was shattered and the revolt moved out to the streets.

From Mourning to Mobilization: Communiqués from Exile

Khomeini's communiqué from Najaf, Iraq, was probably the first tactical leaflet of the revolution. In it he thanked the militant clergy and brave students of Qom for their heroic support against *taghut* (decadence). He criticized the regime, asked the entire nation to maintain *Vahdat-e-kalame* (unity of the word, by which he meant ideological solidarity around Islam), and warned that supporting the Constitution meant acceptance of the corrupt Pahlavi dynasty. Thus from the start of the popular mobilization Khomeini voiced a very radical position that was increasingly reverberated through the popular movement. From this moment on communiqués from Khomeini, as well as from Ayatollahs Shariat-Madari, Golpayegani, and Marashi-Najafi, guided and encouraged opposition activities, their messages being read aloud in mosques by local clerics. The ritual seven-day and forty-day Islamic mourning cycles began to determine the rhythm of events and provided powerful moments for public wrath and political demonstrations whose early form was the outcome of actions by local activists, religious leaders, and small groups.

On February 18, bazaars and universities shut as memorial marches were held in Tehran and many provincial cities. Events in Tabriz were particularly volatile. A demonstration of ten thousand to fifteen thousand people was broken up by police and a demonstrator was shot. For two days the city was in the hands of the people, mainly Islamic and leftist youth, who ransacked and burned selected targets such as Bank Saderat, liquor stores and cinemas, *Rastakhiz* party headquarters, and other public offices. The army was required to quell the city, with considerable loss of life.

Small media had already been used to prepare the people, trying to bolster solidarity and goading the population to action. Cassette tapes of Ayatollah Shariat-Madari (who was from Tabriz) speaking at the Azam mosque in Qom after the first bloody demonstration there, with loud audience lamentation audible in the background, had been widely circulated in Tabriz before this event, stirring emotion and helping to prepare people for action (interview with "earwitness" Moghadam Maragheh from Azerbaijan, March 1985; see also *Review of Iranian Political Economy and History*, June 1978: 2). The regime and its security forces, refusing to acknowledge the growing mass revolt, tried to explain the event by claiming that Soviet Azerbaijani forces had crept over the border. The chief of police of East Azerbaijan, the head of the Tabriz SAVAK, and the governor general of Tabriz were all removed.

Both the Iranian press and NIRT covered this event, with pictures of the damage and the cleanup. They facilitated a "demonstration" effect, carrying the news throughout the country and providing other groups with a cue and model of activity. The Tabriz events helped to shatter the myth of SAVAK omniscience and total regime power, and empowered the further development of the political crowd. Leaflets distributed after this event explained rationales for the attacks on these particular targets and also presented a narrative of events that differed from that given by the mass media (*Review of Iranian Political Economy and History*, June 1978). From this point the network of small media played an important role of counterinformation, rebutting and correcting the regime version of events, body counts, and so on.

Another reaction to the Qom event, and a tactic that would develop into a major weapon of the opposition, was the one-day closing of the bazaar in Tehran, Mashhad, and other cities in solidarity, and the inevitable production of leaflets signed by a variety of groups supporting the demonstrators and their demands. Each event was used by various groups for expressions of solidarity and pressure for further action; after Qom, the Committee for the Defense of Human Rights, student groups, and religious leaders all issued statements, and the concerted actions showed how the movement cut across traditional and modern divisions, across religious and secular lines. Groups, many small and spontaneously created, formed and cohered around the production of such statements. This was an important way in which the growing participation could be rendered public, part of a "spiral of mobilization" where once-different groups began to express their support and solidarity. Other economic sectors and interest groups also rushed to declare themselves. Economic strikes were organized, by the Tehran postmen and tobacco factory workers among others, for better salaries and welfare benefits, to which the regime quickly acceded, hoping to take the steam out of the growing movement. Political prisoners also organized a hunger strike against torture, which was widely publicized abroad by the Committee for Defense of Political Prisoners.

The first general strike on May 15, 1978, was called by Khomeini in another *elamieh* from exile after a violent spate of demonstrations. The government tried to quash the "rumor" of a strike with the state media's urging people to go to work as usual, but the same press noted the next day that the bazaars were closed everywhere and that huge demonstrations had been held on various university campuses.

Regime Reaction and Counterreaction

While maintaining its rhetoric of liberalization, the regime's initial reaction was toughness. In April 1978 *Rastakhiz* created the Resistance Corps to trace "saboteurs and agitators" and to locate "caches of subversive literature" (*Kayhan International*, April 16, 1978). It also broke up student meetings and mosque gatherings. SAVAK organized its own group, the Underground Committee of Revenge, which was mainly concerned with the secular opposition and arranged bombings of homes and offices. The regime warned that it would not tolerate disorder and rioting and used tear gas and troops to disperse the crowds.

The regime also stepped up the ideological offensive, and any remaining illusions that may have been harbored about the neutrality of NIRT were shattered. The ideological label of "Islamic Marxists" became the standard description used in domestic news broadcasts. NIRT news bulletins called the demonstrations "the work of a left hand protruding from the sleeve of black reaction" that was manipulating the Iranian masses for its own interests (NIRT Radio, April 19, 1978). Media time was given to Mahmoud Jafarian, a key regime ideologue as deputy general of NIRT, the director of PARS news agency, and deputy to the secretary general of *Rastakhiz*, who warned of the dangers of "red imperialism." The Shah himself, in an interview with the British newspaper *Sunday Times* that was broadcast on Iranian radio, spoke of the "old unholy alliance of black reactionaries and red revolutionaries" who had a common interest in preventing the progress of the country (NIRT Radio, April 16, 1978). Khomeini continually rebutted any such alliance as an impossible contradiction.

From May 1978 another political about-face seemed to occur, with signs of changes among the political elite. Cracks began to appear within the *Rastakhiz* party. The Shah expressed regret at its poor performance. A third and more critical "wing" of the party developed, but the heads of the other two wings resigned in June, to be followed by more resignations in July. Some Majles deputies defected to resurrect defunct old political groups, and there were suggestions that promised elections would be open to non-*Rastakhiz* candidates. This contrasted vividly with the initial threats of retribution against all those who did not join *Rastakhiz*.

There were other more visible alterations in the regime's position. On the day after the second national strike, June 6, General Nassiri, the head of SAVAK since 1965, was "transferred" to an ambassadorial position in Pakistan, and General Nasser Moghadam, considered a more moderate figure, was appointed instead.[1] New procedures for military tribunals were proposed, and the Shah announced a code of conduct for the royal family that included curbs on excessive profits from business deals (*Kayhan International*, July 3, 1978). A plan for greater university autonomy was also mooted (*Kayhan International*, June 28, 1978).

By the summer of 1978, then, considerable changes in the upper echelons of the political structure had been undertaken, with talk of more to come. In his Constitution Day message on August 5, the Shah announced plans for Western-style parliamentary democracy with elections that would be "100 percent free" (*Kayhan International*, August 6, 1978, front page). But, as everywhere, democracy had its limits, which in Iran meant "one may not turn the monarchy, the throne, and the destiny of Iran into playthings of a handful of people." Khomeini, however, repeatedly spoke of the street demonstrations and strikes as a "popular referendum"—an unusual use of constitutionalist language—against the Shah, where the popular cry was *Marg bar Shah*, "Death to the Shah."

Visually the otherwise blank exteriors of public buildings, high walls of private houses, telephone booths, and buses had all been converted into dynamic canvases of the changing face of the popular movement. They were covered with slogans and elaborate calligraphic graffiti. Spray-painted stencil images appeared everywhere: of Khomeini's face, of an armed guerrilla, or even of local images, like Armenian symbols that appeared in the Armenian section of Julfa, Isfahan. Colored posters also began to appear, often with political cartoons, and were plastered on public buildings, which also displayed the ragged tatters of the leaflets that had been plastered up and then torn down by the security forces. Images of old and new heroes spread. Huge blown-up photographs of Khomeini, Mossadeq, Fatemi, Golesorkhi, and Takhti were carried in demonstrations. Mossadeq was the national democratic prime minister who nationalized oil in 1952 and pressed the Shah for constitutional reforms, and who had suffered internal exile by the Shah after the 1953 coup d'état. Fatemi had been Mossadeq's foreign minister and was executed by the Pahlavi regime. Golesorkhi was a revolutionary poet, condemned by military tribunal and blinded before being executed. Posters and volumes of his poetry became widely available after the revolution, and an old military film of his "trial," never before seen publicly, was shown frequently on Islamic television. Takhti, a popular Olympic medal-winning wrestler, was also killed by the regime. These figures had become political icons, powerful examples of "anamnestic solidarity" and the reconstruction of an alternative, oppositional history with its own dates and heroes, in whose path the contemporary movement marched and whose symbolic power further galvanized the movement.

In August new and old political groups were publishing newsletters and circulars, campaigning and focusing on issues such as SAVAK brutality, regime corruption, and the need for explicit guarantees of support for the Constitution. Clerical leaders such as Shariat-Madari also condemned the ruthless slaughter of Moslems and pledged that the movement would persist until liberty and social equality had been secured. The tone of these would-be leaders remained comparatively moderate and their demands might have been satisfiable within the parameters of a constitutional monarchy, but continued regime vacillations and aboutfaces, coupled with the militancy of Khomeini's communiqués, and hence of the crowd, made that an increasingly impossible option from the summer on. A cas-

Figure 9.1. A series of stencils on the walls of Julfa, Isfahan, which has a large Armenian community. The stencils include drawings of Dashnak party heroes of the Armenian cause in Turkey.

sette of Khomeini that circulated in Tehran in August urged pressure on the government and insisted on the overthrow of the monarchy in response to the bloodshed of the past months. He also began to urge the military not to cooperate and particularly not to shoot civilians, their Moslem brothers [*sic*].

In Isfahan in early August, Ayatollah Taheri, released from jail, spoke in the bazaar and at the Friday sermon, and was arrested again. This precipitated violent demonstrations in which the luxury Shah Abbas hotel, cinemas, banks, and Westernized boutiques were attacked and slogans for Islamic rule were popular. A dusk-to-dawn curfew was then imposed in Isfahan and three other cities, Najafabad, Homayounshahr, and Shahreza. Tanks appeared on the streets of Isfahan and all assemblies of more than three people were forbidden. The regime renewed its ideological war, claiming that leftists were working behind the facade of Islamic rhetoric, that religious reactionaries wanted to put back the great development initiatives of the past decade. The regime pointed to crowd violence to emphasize the difficulties of implementing democracy in a backward society, directly undermining its own claims about being close to the gates of the Great Civilization (*Kayhan International*, August 14, 18, 19, and 29, 1978; also NIRT broadcasts at this time). In an interview the Shah spoke ominously of subversive elements working for a foreign power who wished to divide Iran up to create little

Figure 9.2. Posters on the walls of the U.S. embassy in Tehran. The one on the right calls for the unity of the people of the world against U.S. imperialism; the one on the left, with its fat U.S. officer astride the globe, reads, "Down with U.S. imperialism, the bloodiest imperialism in the world."

Iranestans, and who only offered the Great Terror against the Great Civilization (*Kayhan International*, August 14, 1978). Fear of a communist conspiracy was being manipulated in an attempt to conciliate moderate elements.

August 19 was also 28th Mordad, the twenty-fifth anniversary of the coup that had brought the Shah back to power. *Rastakhiz* demonstrations were held, the Shah celebrated, and the usual block advertisements from industries and banks dominated newspaper space with good wishes for the Shah and the glorious Shah-People Revolution. The same day an explosion and fire in the fully occupied Cinema Rex killed more than four hundred people in Abadan. The disaster was made worse by the fact that many of the doors were locked: it was obviously arson. Previous attacks on cinemas had been by angry crowds and directed at empty buildings, cinemas being considered examples of Western cultural penetration but also a lucrative business owned by the Shah's patrons. There had also been rumors that SAVAK kindled some of the blazes as symbolic counterpropaganda, aiming to present the movement as reactionary and anti-Western.

No single incident revealed more clearly the extent of the nation's mistrust of the government and its media network than the Cinema Rex fire. The rapidity with which the government attempted to make political capital out of the event suggested to many that it had been planned. Homayoun, the government spokesman and the Minister of Information, implicated the opposition, and "foreign elements" were mentioned (*Kayhan International*, August 21 and 22, 1978). A circular from Khomeini immediately appeared in which he suggested that "the available evidence points to a conspiracy by the brutal regime of the Shah to cast blame on the opposition groups and condemn the humanitarian principle of Islam" (Nobari, 1978: 186–87). While rumors abounded, the general mood was to hold the regime responsible and violent demonstrations broke out across the country over the next few days. After the revolution, an Islamic group confessed to starting the fire as a way of further discrediting the regime, which it did.

The liberalization program was shattered. The media were further discredited as passive instruments of a corrupt regime. NIRT installations now had to be protected by barbed wire and armed guards, and images of the NIRT lion surrounded by barbed wire circulated. The combined security forces of police and troops failed to preserve the peace. On August 27, the resignation of Prime Minister Amouzegar and the appointment of Sharif-emami to that position were announced.

Sharif-emami and Press Freedom

Sharif-emami's strategy was to maintain as large a distance from *Rastakhiz* as possible, and he embarked on a course clearly designed to appease the clergy. In his first speech to the Majles he pledged his government to observe Islamic tenets and show respect for religious leaders. He changed the Shahanshahi calendar back to the Islamic calendar. He banned gambling and pornography. He abolished the Ministry of Women's Affairs and created a Ministry of Religious Affairs. He apologized to Ayatollah Shariatmadari for invasions into his house in Qom and spoke of releasing religious figures such as Ayatollah Taleghani from prison.

During the month of Ramadan, hundreds were killed in demonstrations around the country. But quite exceptionally, on Eid-e-Fetr, the celebration of the end of Ramadan (Monday, September 4), a huge march in Tehran passed peacefully. A colossal gathering said prayers in the streets, presented cakes and flowers to soldiers and police, and articulated again the growing themes of the popular movement: Independence, Freedom, Islamic Government, *Istiqlal, Azadi, Hokumat-e Islami*, and the return of Khomeini. This was the beginning of both mass and massive demonstrations, which included women and children and cut across age and class differences. For many these demonstrations were quite exuberant moments of participation in the political crowd. Messages circulated about another demonstration on September 8. Television coverage, however, was preoccupied with the traditional Salaam ceremonies at Niavaran Palace, at which the Shah warned about national disintegration.

Massive demonstrations during the next few days left Tehran resounding to the slogan of "Death to the Shah" and reeking with the stench of burning tires. This

Figure 9.3. Posters in Tehran, supporting the revolution and International Labor Day.

brought a prohibition on all demonstrations and the long-anticipated imposition on Thursday, September 7, of martial law on Tehran and eleven other cities. On Friday morning the media broadcast over and over the communiqués of the martial-law administrators, who were headed by General Oveissi. A crowd began to gather in Jaleh Square in south Tehran. By 8:00 A.M. the army was firing tear-gas grenades to make the crowd disperse, and Alameh Nuri requested that the crowd sit. Yet some stood and shouted slogans, and suddenly the troops fired into the crowd with machine guns, killing veiled women, children, and men. The government said fifty-seven people were killed; the opposition claimed a massacre of thousands, citing mortuary numbers as evidence. Gruesome photographs circulated of bodies at the mortuary marked with identification numbers in the thousands, visual verification of opposition claims.

That evening numerous opposition figures, including Mehdi Bazargan, Karim Sanjabi, Dariush Forouhar, Rahmat Moghaddam Maragheh, and Ayatollahs Ruhani and Nuri were arrested. Bazargan called this "the point of no return," and even the moderate opposition leaders felt that compromise with the monarchy was impossible. A joint declaration by Ayatollahs Shariatmadari, Golpayegani, and Marashi Najafi on September 12 denounced the tyrannical regime and said that people "desire the uprooting of the autocratic and colonial regime . . . the establishment of an Islamic order and the implementation of the commandments of the glorious Qoran" (September 12, 1978; document in private collection). Telephone calls of support for the Shah and public statements from Jimmy Carter and Zbigniew Brzezinski fueled the anger against "imperialist aggression." Most important, ordinary people, workers, professionals, shopkeepers, and so on, had vivid evidence of the regime's attitude toward the people, and they began to take part in the rapidly developing events. A rumor spread that the Shah had brought in three hundred crack Israeli commandos to perform the massacre, as Iranians were unwilling to believe that their own army's soldiers, with whom they had fraternized only days before, were actually responsible.

Khomeini's cassettes and leaflets encouraged the "brave Iranian people" in their struggle against the brutal regime. The radical division between the nation, *mellat*, and the state, *dowlat*, was clear, and each possessed its own communications system to counter the other. For example, after the Tabas earthquake on September 23, 1978, a communiqué from Khomeini ordered Iranians to help their troubled countrymen and women directly or through the mosques but not to contribute to the government relief scheme. Prime Minister Sharif-emami, aware of the public mood, commented that he would not be surprised if someone blamed the government for the tragedy. As we have already mentioned, a five-page leaflet did circulate that argued that the earthquake was caused by U.S. underground testing of nuclear weapons in the Iranian desert.

Sharif-emami recognized the extreme crisis of credibility that the regime was suffering, and the increasing importance of the rumor circuit in defining reality. He noted that "if we say it is daytime when it is daytime, people will deduce it is nighttime." Partly as an attempt to improve this image, his Minister of Information, Ameli-Tehrani, put forward a press bill on September 23, proposing a five-member Press Commission to be chaired by the deputy information minister, with a built-in official majority and wide discretionary powers. There was considerable opposition, some arguing that the Constitution alone would be a sufficient guarantee of press freedom. The *Tehran Journal* believed that professional journalists had to be involved and described the proposals as "another nail in the coffin of a free press . . . a document for an establishment press" (*Tehran Journal*, September 24 and October 1, 1978). *Kayhan* similarly argued that "the press bill was tailored to ensuring the continued raj of the ministry in matters of the press" (*Kayhan*, September 25, 1978). The text of the press bill was published on October 1. The mere existence of public discussion of this matter was an indication of how the atmosphere had dramatically changed.

On October 7 the Shah inaugurated the new session of Parliament and addressed both houses. He made a plea for "unity and oneness to preserve the independence, freedom, and sovereignty of Iran" (*Kayhan International*, October 8, 1978). In perhaps the most extensive public self-criticism he was to make, he admitted "mistakes, excesses, and misappropriations" had fueled the present crisis but promised that further liberalization measures would be undertaken. The next day, as though to test his word, the press presented an ultimatum for freedom in a seventeen-point document that demanded withdrawal of the proposed law, revoking of current press laws, and an end to censorship and the banning of writers. Journalists expressed their intention to strike if the demands were not met. The daily press also began to carry news articles and extracts from foreign papers of interviews with Khomeini about his move to Paris. This was the first time (apart from a series of photographs that had been printed in August) that Khomeini's name had appeared in the Iranian press since the 1960s. The foreign press was still coming in to the country, and the vivid color photographs of Khomeini and the popular movement on the covers of *Time* and *Newsweek* created excited discussion at the newspaper kiosks, being taken as evidence that important things were indeed happening in Iran and that the world was paying attention. The press also began to carry articles from lawyers that asked for the freedom of political prisoners, and there was extensive discussion of events in the universities and schools.

Recognizing the burgeoning social importance of the press, suddenly on October 11 military censors arrived at the offices of *Kayhan* and *Etela'at* and notified journalists that all domestic and foreign news coverage had to be cleared in advance by a military censor. The liberalization seemed once more to have been abruptly reversed. Those journalists immediately went on strike, as did those of the two other dailies, *Rastakhiz* and *Ayandegan*. Discussions were held with Prime Minister Sharif-emami and Minister of Information Ameli-Tehrani, and on October 14, quite unexpectedly, a communiqué guaranteeing press freedom was issued. The first editions of these newspapers after the strike on October 15–16 were euphoric. "I write, therefore I am," punned *Kayhan*. *Kayhan International*'s headline read simply "Freedom at Last." *Etela'at* stressed the need for responsible journalism, and *Tehran Journal* said there was now a chance for the press to build a reputation for objective journalism that it had never enjoyed. Numerous articles by secular intellectuals, such as Eslam Kazemi, Nasser Pakdaman, Fereidun Adamiyat, and Simin Daneshvar, were carried; some warned against the continuing danger of self-censorship out of habit and urged the press to take up serious journalism. Political graphics abounded, many playing with the image of a pen being released from a cage. *Kayhan* scooped a front-page picture of Khomeini with an interview by its own reporter. Even the street vendors draped colored lights over their booths and displayed signs that read "Censorship no, truth yes."

Media professionals found the ground rules to be curiously fluid. Sharif-emami himself was moved to suggest that it was because the internal media carried so little domestic news that people were forced to turn to foreign channels, and he mentioned the BBC by name. A political cartoon in *Kayhan* had already parodied the situation: it pictured an NIRT news announcer, saying, "And now, for the domestic news, will you please turn to the BBC!"

For a few weeks in the autumn of 1978, from October 15 to November 6, a unique period in Iranian media history was enjoyed as media content was perhaps for the first time guided by professional standards and social commitments rather than by heavy-handed control from above or outside. This was a time of the most explicit news coverage ever seen on Iranian television, particularly of coverage of violent demonstrations at Tehran University in early November when a number of students were shot. The new media openness played into the hands of the opposition movement, for it showed too much too late to help the regime. As already mentioned, numerous grizzly photographs of shootings and of cadavers lying in the morgue were circulating among the population, grim visual records of regime violence "against an unarmed people," as the slogan went. But to suddenly show this domestic violence on television throughout the country was horrifying, intensifying the slogans against regime brutality and bringing more people into the movement. In the press there were unprecedented analytic pieces on the workings of SAVAK, the appalling conditions in prisons, and problems in the legal system. Ehsan Naraghi, known as a court ideologue, even explained some of the confusions within the ruling group. There was a series of discussions about censorship and cultural policy; one piece was entitled "Iranian Cinema Is the Garbage Can of the West" (*Kayhan*, October 17, 18, 24, and 25, 1978). Newspapers carried more photographs of demonstrations, of soldiers in city streets, of people praying in Tehran University. Political cartoons proliferated. Suddenly the media were playing an agenda-setting role, bringing to life a host of political and social issues that had been buried from public debate. The press enjoyed an excellent circulation, and items would be read aloud in offices and teahouses and were the subject of intense discussion. From being the instruments of regime policy, the media were invited by the same regime to be more open and critical; yet instead of saving the system, this helped speed its collapse. In typically contradictory fashion, the huge block advertisements in the press wishing the Shah a happy birthday on 4th Aban (October 26) still appeared.

In October Khomeini made his fateful move from Najaf to Paris, having been refused entry by other Middle Eastern states such as Kuwait. He began to orchestrate the revolutionary mobilization by telephone from Neauphle-le-Chateau. Relatively inaccessible in Iraq, he was now the focus of world media attention, and even a cursory glance at the international press from this time on shows a dramatic rise in the amount of coverage given to Iranian affairs and the number of front covers given to depictions of Iranian events.

By mid-October the movement began to involve the professional middle class in a more widespread and systematic way. Universities had become free spaces for meetings and the centers for distribution of literature, and students and schoolchildren were actively involved in disseminating and discussing materials. The nation was engulfed in strikes encompassing millions of blue- and white-collar workers, including employees of the telecommunications company, the Tehran Water Board, the Tavanir Company, the State Tobacco Company, the Abadan Water and Electricity Services, the Karun Agro-Industrial Complex, and Iran Air, as well as taxi drivers, postal workers, hospital workers, bank employees, university professors, ministerial workers, and, most important, National Iranian Oil Company (NIOC) employees.

By October 29, the Abadan refinery was at a standstill, oil production had been cut by 75 percent, and the national economy was paralyzed. The government was forced to cancel various military and nuclear purchases in order to meet wage demands. In November, employees of twenty-three government ministries also went on strike and put out leaflets of solidarity with the popular movement. Bureaucratization had been imposed without the development of a bureaucratic mentality and without the sense of commitment to the organization that the notion entails. Always tempered by corruption and *parti-bazi*, the Iranian penchant for finding a "connection" in order to enact business, the large bureaucracies were often facades for inefficiency and corruption, another example of the superficial pseudomodernization.

These strikes are of particular interest for a number of reasons. Many started with economic demands, but when these were satisfied by a government in no mood to add to its difficulties, the demands became political and manifestos were drawn up demanding the release of political prisoners, a return to the Constitution, and so forth. For many people this was their first taste of self-organization and of political involvement, and the production of statements was an important experience in this process. Ironically, even while on strike government employees continued to receive salaries. Opposition to the regime now encompassed both wage earners and salaried middle classes, the technocratic elite who had appeared to be co-opted into the system.

Evidence now reveals how spontaneous and decentralized much of this activity really was. For example, a representative of the Tehran electricity workers came to the offices of the Committee for the Defense of Human Rights (which played a coordinating role between various sectors of the movement) saying that the workers had the capacity to create electricity cuts and wanting to know from Bazargan when the most effective time to do this would be. At the same time, the representative made quite clear that this did not imply political support for Bazargan, for the workers followed only "the Imam's line," i.e., Khomeini (story told by Moghaddam Maragheh, the committee member present that day; personal interview, March 1985). Groups began to cohere and to organize separately and only later sought how to support the activities of others, provoking a number of "coordinating committees" in various sectors. Under the leadership of Ayatollah Beheshti, a secret Revolutionary Council was forming to plan and organize activities. Sometimes the core of a group would be two or three dedicated individuals, and others were far larger, but the spontaneous and evolving nature of this phenomenon cannot be overemphasized. This was a general learning process for most people, who had no experience of such activity, an embryonic participatory democracy.

For the Shah's birthday at the end of October, one thousand political prisoners were released. The press spoke out about prison conditions and torture, and some of the tense and dramatic debates in Parliament were broadcast by NIRT.

Yet in early November 1978, Sanjabi, the National Front leader, returned after a secret meeting with Khomeini in Paris to announce that no compromise with the Shah was possible anymore. The movement had reached a point of no return. During November the Shah's statue was toppled from its position at the gates of Tehran University, which had become a central meeting place and arena of debate, and more than thirty student demonstrators were shot dead. Participants in this demonstration, we witnessed some soldiers join the crowd. After such events, the streets of Tehran would resound with the screams of ambulance sirens and the honking of ordinary cars that were trying to carry supplies of bandages, sheeting, and medical supplies to the hospitals where the wounded had been taken.

The Tehran bazaar shut the next day, which later became known as "Red Sunday." Students and young men took to the streets to vandalize selected targets: foreign businesses like airline offices, luxury hotels, and international banks, and anti-Islamic operations such as liquor stores, cinemas, and restaurants. As was the general pattern for such attacks, the targets were politically symbolic, damage was done to property not persons, and no looting took place—bottles of liquor were broken, not stolen. In the releases of political prisoners, some members of the *Fedai'i* and *Mojahedin* guerrilla groupings had been released. The *Mojahedin* became active as security for demonstrations, and were involved with others in storming the British embassy and gutting one of its wings, an ominous event for the foreign community, which was gradually beginning to pull out. Some violent guerrilla actions against foreign targets, such as Bell helicopter employees and German technicians, had also increased, and the atmosphere was becoming progressively more anti-American.

The day after "Red Sunday," the Shah acknowledged, live on television, that his civilian coalition had failed. He confessed to past mistakes but promised that "unlawfulness, cruelty, and corruption will not be repeated." He ordered an investigation into the wealth of the royal family and a review of the Pahlavi Foundation, as if to appease the opposition once more, but at the same time he declared himself compelled to appoint a military government under General Azhari. The entire country was put on a 9:00 P.M. to 5:00 A.M. curfew. NIRT news showed the Shah with his new military cabinet, suggesting that the full range of coercive powers were being mobilized to stop the movement. Yet even then the Shah's own vacillation and seesaw policy of mixing increasing repression with steps toward liberalization did not end.

Military Government and the Demise of the Big Media

Rapid signs of the Shah's intention to "clean up" his own regime came with the rounding up of many top political figures who were placed in detention without

Figure 9.4. A section of city wall in Tehran, with posters for the *Fedai'i* and political prisoners along with remnants of other posters, writing, and bloody handprints.

trial. These included Nassiri (the ex-head of SAVAK), Hoveyda (a loyal prime minister for thirteen years), Homayoun (a *Rastakhiz* leader and court ideologue), and other figures who had been key officials and served the Shah well over the past few years.

Nothing was more instant than the military government's recognition of the powerful role being played by the media in publicizing and analyzing the unfolding of political events, and it acted to change this. Almost its first act was to dispatch military censors to the offices of the national press. Five editors were arrested, thirty journalists were charged with inciting public unrest, and the press was ordered not to publish. Censors were also sent to NIRT. Gradually the roles reversed as the military government decided to get newspapers back on the streets; journalists and printers refused to help and reiterated their old demands for press freedom. NIRT workers supported the journalists and circulated their own communiqués that urged Iranians to turn off their radio and television receivers and not to listen to the voice of the military. Leaflets were printed showing yet another change of NIRT logo: the two lions rampant were now clad in war helmets and were brandishing bayonets.

By holding the media responsible for promoting political activity through their provocative reporting, the military caused an unexpectedly radical reaction: their silence. The daily press maintained a total strike for two months beginning on

Figure 9.5. An altered logo for NIRT during the period of the military government, November 1978 to January 1979. The slogan reads, "Fellow Iranians, this is the voice of the military, not our voice!"

November 6. The professional staff of NIRT struck, leaving only a skeleton group that ran the organization together with the military for over three months. To fill the gap of news and information, a variety of alternate sources were quickly organized, an underground alternative. Daily broadsheets, including one produced by the striking journalists, were published by a number of groups and pasted up in public places. The media professionals acknowledged the great responsibility they had taken on themselves by engaging in this struggle and depriving the public of its usual channels of information at such a critical time, but they argued that the struggle against censorship was an integral part of the struggle against domination currently being fought in Iran. One strike bulletin published in red ink, proclaiming that it was recording these great historical events in the blood of martyrs ("Fifty-eight Days of Press Strike," *Hambastegi* 8, Tuesday, 12 Dey, 1357). People tuned in with regularity to Persian-language and other broadcasts of foreign channels on shortwave radio, and bought up the foreign press. The rumor network also heated up in the classic manner to fill the absence of more precise and verifiable information, with everyone becoming a potential source of information and an analyst of events. As Alloway noted, "the absence of newspapers caused a wave of rumours in the city, helped by the sparsity of official announcements" (*The London Times*, November 8, 1978). After a period in which the "big media" had gained some credibility and extended their coverage to deal with opposition attitudes and activities at some level, coexisting with the alternate small-media network, they were suddenly silenced. Tehran and other cities were under a military occupation.

Strikes continued and by early December the oil-workers' strike was causing unparalleled public inconvenience, as domestic supplies of petrol and kerosene dried up. Mile-long queues of parked cars outside gasoline stations created congestion the likes of which even Tehran had not seen before. Adapting to the difficult circumstances, people would deposit their plastic canisters on a rope in the morning, and return in the evening to buy a few liters of kerosene necessary for heating, cooking, and lighting. From November 28 a massive strike of electricity employees began to cut off the power supply across the nation nightly from 8:30 to 10:00 P.M. as an objection to the military government and specifically blacking out its evening television newscast at 8:30 P.M. The government made excuses about technical difficulties, but it was well known that the cuts were political acts by the opposition, especially when the lights were kept on for the nights of December 25 and December 31, out of respect for the Christian communities. The blackouts also provided a half hour of intense darkness before the curfew began at 9 P.M.; these thirty minutes were actively used for distributing leaflets and underground papers and for writing graffiti.

A new nightly lifestyle evolved that entailed the filling and preparation of oil lamps and kerosene heaters, setting up the battery shortwave radio for foreign newscasts, and making the telephone accessible for reports from friends about events in other areas. We would gather around a *korsi*, a traditional heating device, comprising a low wooden structure, heated from below by a bucket of hot charcoal or an electric element, and covered with quilts, toward which everyone placed their feet like spokes of a wheel. It provided a cozy, even romantic, way to survive those difficult and often very frightening nights. With the start of the mourning month of *Moharram* in early December, another nightly ritual was initiated. At the start of curfew time, shrouded by darkness, people emerged onto balconies and rooftops and shouted *allah-hu akbar*, God is great, intermixed with *Marg bar Shah*, death to the Shah. When the military government remarked that these were just cassette-tape recordings of people shouting, this comment was then incorporated into the nightly repartee as the invisible crowd taunted, "So you think we are only tapes?" It was a bitter winter, and the still, cold air allowed this repetitive, rhythmic chanting to waft over the city; sometimes over the telephone one could hear similar sounds from other parts of the city, and sometimes one could hear machine-gun fire. In many places, young men dressed in *kaffan*, the white shroud of the dead, poured out to the streets and proclaimed their readiness for martyrdom in front of the military. The military was in an ambiguous position, on the streets yet with no clear orders about when and how to use its weapons. Yet every night machine-gun and other fire could be heard and numerous youths were killed.

Moharram, the Shiite month of mourning, had been anticipated as a climactic period. Khomeini sent an important communiqué from Paris describing *Moharram* as the month when "truth triumphs over corruption" and urged the movement to continue pressing for the Shah to go. The mourning month culminates in the two days of *Ta'asua* and *Ashura*, which commemorate the killing of Hossein at Karbala by the forces of Yazid in the eighth century. A massive march was organized for *Ta'asua* with groups starting from a number of locations in Tehran to converge at the Shahyad Monument, popularly named Azadi or Freedom Square, to listen to speeches.[2] Coordinated by Ayatollah Taleghani's office, through telephone contact with the Liberation Movement, the Committee for Defense of Political Prisoners, and so on, with *Mojahedin* as security, this was the biggest demonstration ever held in Tehran, gathering some millions, and was repeated in many provincial cities. Slogans were kept low-key. At various demonstrations there were scuffles as Islamic men demanded that women cover their hair, which was often furiously refused by university and other women while others agreed to do so as it was a religious day and solidarity was essential to success. Some women gathered in large female sections that were then surrounded and protected by a chain of men holding hands. The mood was buoyant, almost jubilant, despite the ever-present fear of regime reprisal.

When this demonstration passed quietly, the mood of the equally large crowd the next day was more overtly political, with a variety of factional banners being displayed and slogans that included the commonplace "Death to the Shah" but also "We will kill Iran's dictator and destroy Yankee power in Iran" and "Hossein is our savior, Khomeini our leader." A seventeen-point program was read aloud for popular approval, recognizing Khomeini as the leader of the movement, appreciating the valuable leadership of the clergy, and demanding the overthrow of the Shah's regime for one based on Islamic justice. On both of these days there

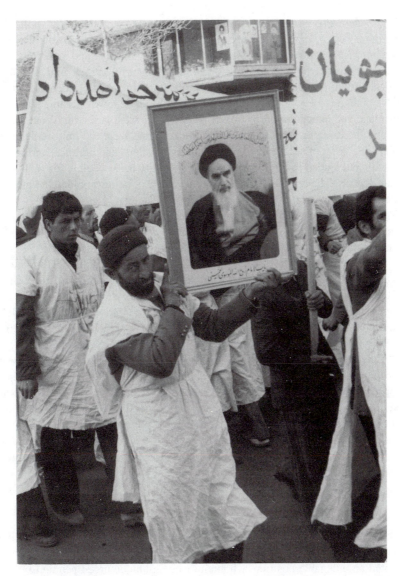

Figure 9.6. Demonstrators wearing the *kaffan,* shroud of the dead, in Tehran, spring 1979. The slogan reads, "Our movement is Islamic and our leader is Khomeini."

were extensive rumors of regime plots to break up the demonstrations by land mines, by bombing the procession, and by bringing in troops. Actually, opposition leaders had met with some generals to agree on peaceful marches, much to the displeasure of the hard-line military.

There were also growing rumors of a Vietnam-type "scorched earth" policy or of a military coup, as the regime seemed unable to negotiate or press its way out of the impasse it had helped to create: an increasingly massive and united opposition confronting a fragmented and demoralized security system and a broken political structure. Indeed, in December various provincial cities such as Qazvin and Najafabad were singled out for vicious attack. These towns became places of pilgrimage and excursion, attracting crowds who gawked at the burnt-out buildings and the random shoes and broken crockery that were the only remains of family life. News of such events spread through leaflets, photographs, and word-of-mouth and tended to reinforce opposition hostility to the regime for such anti-human actions. The regime again accused the BBC of being a colonialist mouthpiece when it broadcast news of these violent attacks.

The popular movement appeared unstoppable as it rallied behind Khomeini, rejecting compromise with the Shah and not cowed but galvanized at the great burden of martyrs it was accumulating. The strikes and daily discomforts continued, but were tolerated. Before Christmas Khomeini issued another communiqué in which he called for the help of all Christian nations, including the "great United States," to help the popular struggle against the Shah.

In December General Azhari had a heart attack. Various opposition elder statesmen such as Sanjabi, Sadighi, and Amini were approached to form interim civilian governments to facilitate the Shah's departure, but all refused. There was talk of the Shah's abdicating in favor of his son, with Queen Farah as vice-regent, and rumors abounded. No one seemed to be in charge and the situation was highly unstable. On December 29, 1978, the Shah handed power to Shahpour Bakhtiar, agreed to the formation of a regency council, and agreed to leave the country for a vacation. Bakhtiar was immediately expelled from the National Front, from which he had broken rank anyway; the political group rejected this last-ditch attempt to rescue the Shah. Khomeini urged from exile that the struggle should continue until final victory.

Bakhtiar and the Adversary Media

Bakhtiar pledged to abolish SAVAK, to institute freedom of speech and political organization, to lift the curfew rapidly, and to defuse the situation. But he had accepted an untenable position. Khomeini's communiqué urged people to "continue your battle, do not hesitate a single instant or the blood that has been spilled until now for Islam and liberty will be lost and you will receive such a blow that your breath will be cut off and your cries stifled" (communiqué dated January 8, 1979; reprinted in *Kayhan* the following day). Khomeini provided specific instructions about how to proceed. New ministers should be prevented from entering their ministries. No government bills, including those for taxes, water, electricity, or telephone, were to be paid. All groups were to denounce the illegality of the new government. The nightly sloganizing and troop-baiting continued, with a new rhyming taunt, *Bakhtiar, nokare bi ekhtiar*, "Bakhtiar—servant without any power." The struggle of the people against the state had not ended. Khomeini urged the oil workers to produce only enough oil for domestic consumption and Ayatollah Shariat-Madari sent Bazargan to Khuzestan to assure the oil workers that no oil would be exported.

On the media front, the end of the military government meant the pretext for the press strike had gone, and on January 6, 1979, after sixty-two days, newspapers reappeared and declared once more that there would no longer be any censorship from government. Khomeini sent a special communiqué to newspaper workers. Another period of investigative reporting dawned and full-page spreads appeared about the former ministers and officials currently imprisoned. The new military chief of staff, Gharebaghi, was not pleased by the open press and claimed it was undermining the spirits of the armed forces. The reference was partly to reports that General Oveissi, military governor of Tehran, had fled the country, amid the prevalent reporting about rumors of a coup.[3] The strength of the rumor network is clear when the mass-media reference it and use it as an information resource. Bakhtiar denied the possibility of a coup, arguing that the Iranian class base was quite dissimilar from that of Chile. Foreign reporters were actively chasing stories while domestic reporting lagged behind, still formed and cowed by a different press tradition, and thus major news items and stories in the Iranian press were culled and translated from foreign coverage. The domestic press was also upset at Bakhtiar's penchant of giving interviews to the foreign but not the domestic press; *Kayhan* devoted an editorial to his disdain for the domestic press. The Iranian press began to print a rumor column and reprinted texts of some of the major communiqués of this period. Gradually the press slipped into an adversary role against the government, a position unprecedented in recent Iranian history, and big and small media worked together. When the Shah left the country on January 17, 1979, there was dancing, and free candy was poured onto the streets. Gloves perched on the end of windshield wipers waved deliriously, and *Etela'at* ran its biggest-ever headline, *Shah raft*, "The Shah's Gone." But Khomeini had declared himself ready to establish an Islamic Republic and even to head it (already backtracking on earlier comments that he would return to Qom and stay out of politics), and huge demonstrations were held on *Arbai'in*, the fortieth day of *Moharram*, January 19, 1979.

The press began to carry reports of demonstrations and lectures being broken up by violence. The once-unified crowd had split into three: those who supported Bakhtiar and his constitutional pledges and organized demonstrations amid widespread criticism and hostility; the secular left, which was developing an independent voice, already warning of religious domination and promoting a democratic or people's republic; and the religious majority, which rallied around the slogan of "Islamic Republic." The press became prey to these various factions. On January 21, for example, a group of Islamic students occupied the premises of *Kayhan* newspaper and demanded that the paper print a twenty-page article to counteract the excessive space it had given to "leftists." The next day the paper's editorial pointed out the dangers of "press freedom being used to impose the opinion of the majority" and said that many nonreligious participants in the revolution were confused about the lack of definition of what constituted an "Islamic Republic" and warned of the call for "one voice, one step" from the Islamic majority as leading to a new religious dictatorship (*Kayhan*, January 22, 1978). In a new dynamic, the press found itself buffeted in many different directions at once and unable to satisfy any of them. Yet circulation was healthy: *Kayhan* enjoyed double the circulation of the days of stricter censorship.

Bakhtiar's powers were limited by the continued existence of martial-law authorities. The open demonstrations seemed to end on January 26 when troops violently broke up a gathering at Tehran University and the press faced difficulties when some journalists were arrested for reporting on the events. NIRT was beginning to adopt a more open policy and covered the demonstration and shootings, similar scenes not having been shown on television since before the military government in October. Discussion of Khomeini's return seemed to presage further media liberalization.

Since the day the Shah left the public clamor had built for Khomeini's return. After various false starts, including *mullahs* on a hunger strike at Tehran University, and a barricade of the airport, the all clear was finally given for his return on February 1. The head of NIRT announced elaborate plans to cover this historic event live and said that even still-striking workers would cooperate for this program, setting up mobile units at the airport and along the route and writing background materials in the event the broadcast was less than satisfactory. A crowd of some millions packed Tehran streets to greet Khomeini, while millions more around the country watched the televised pictures of the welcoming party at the airport, the landing of the Air France jumbo jet, and Khomeini as he descended the steps of the plane and was helped into a waiting car. Then the screen went blank. After some minutes a voice-over explained that "because of loss of sound and other technical difficulties" the telecast could not continue. Suddenly a picture of the Shah was shown and the national anthem was played. In some places people threw their television sets out of windows in rage. Tehranis demonstrated that the proposed televising of Khomeini's arrival had been a plot to keep them off the streets. Bakhtiar blamed "leftists" for the disruption, and NIRT employees explained that army officers had entered the studios and stopped the broadcast.

From the day of Khomeini's return a situation of dual power existed: Bakhtiar still refused to resign, while a majority of people recognized Khomeini as their leader. Khomeini's first visit was to Behesht-Zahra, the cemetery in south Tehran, where he thanked all the different groups who had brought the movement so far and exhorted continued solidarity until the Shah and his "foreign hands" were cut out of Iran. A clamor of different voices, expressed through a variety of channels, rose to a crescendo. A new wave of photocopied communiqués were plastered everywhere, calling for Bakhtiar's resignation, the trial of army officers, the dissolution of Parliament, and also including proclamations of solidarity to Khomeini by certain military groups. Khomeini actually presented his own prime minister, Mehdi Bazargan of the Liberation Movement, as head of a provisional cabinet. Khomeini set up headquarters at the Refah school in Tehran and was visited by waves of people every day, including large contingents of army personnel. When such photos were printed in the press, Bakhtiar rejected them as forgeries, a sign of his growing desperation. Khomeini's reaction to the media was expressed at his first press conference on February 3 when he said: "All I have to say is that the printed media as well as radio and television must be at the service of the people. Governments have no right to the supervision of the activities of the media. In this respect, the ex-Shah and his governments used to violate all internationally accepted norms" (*Kayhan International*, February 8, 1979). Perhaps the ultimate in alternate communication was the pirate television station that operated from the Refah school with equipment and help provided by some striking NIRT workers. Some members of the audience suddenly found a picture on their screens, and passed the message along. Later leaflets appeared, explaining that houses within a five-mile radius could receive the signal, which was considered to be "the hottest show in town" (*Kayhan International*, February 8, 1979).

The final action that toppled the Bakhtiar government and resulted in the establishment of the Islamic Republic was also precipitated by a media event. NIRT, still occupied by the military but pursuing a more lenient policy, had advertised that an edited film of Khomeini's arrival was to be shown the evening of Friday, February 9. There was considerable eagerness to watch this film that had earlier been denied a showing. At Doshan Tappeh air base in Tehran, air force personnel gathered to watch and began to shout pro-Khomeini slogans. The air force had enjoyed a reputation as the most oppositional military force. When security guards could not quell this demonstration, tanks were brought in, and then the Immortal Guards, the Shah's personal, highly trained, and committed unit, were called in. The armed clash lasted through the night and by morning outfits of revolutionary soldiers, including *Mojahedin* and *Fedai'i* guerrillas, had arrived on the scene. The next two days saw unprecedented street fighting in Tehran, centered on barracks and strategic sites and shifting focus as one after another of the supposed fortresses of the Shah's regime fell.

A final attempt to keep control by imposing a 4:30 P.M. curfew on the city on February 11 was widely disregarded—even women and children were spilling onto the streets, eager to find out what was happening. Localities put up sandbag barriers, women helped to make Molotov cocktails, and preparations were made for a new level of resistance against the military. City residents witnessed chaotic street scenes of young men in a military vehicle racing down Tehran highways in one direction while a similar group careened in the opposite direction, or of young *cherik* (guerrillas) in army jackets and kerchiefs, and with automatic weapons, directing traffic, shouting commands, and generally taking charge of city organization. But the army command was taken over by revolutionary forces and the remaining Armed Forces High Council declared its neutrality in political matters and pulled its troops back into the garrisons from where they had barely fought.

Almost the last bastion of the military to fall was NIRT. On the evening of February 11, however, the old faces and voices of the long-striking staff of radio-television reappeared on the screen, stretching out their clenched fists in solidarity with the popular struggle. Film was shown that had been taken earlier of the army tanks being driven away from the central production facilities of NIRT to the cheering waves of a large crowd. Revolutionary music and graphics of red tulips embodying the blood of martyrs made up the background to the first program, an endless reading of congratulatory telegrams and messages from all the popular grouplets. Mehdi Bazargan was internationally recognized as prime minister of a temporary government of the Islamic revolution, with Ayatollah Khomeini as its symbolic head.

The revolution was over, and only just beginning.

Chapter 10
The Islamic Republic and the Process of Islamicization

Communication and Cultural Politics under the Islamic Republic of Iran

The Islamic Republic was declared on February 11, 1979, under the charismatic leadership of Ayatollah Khomeini, who rapidly proclaimed himself *vali-e faghih*, the supreme jurist. It has since weathered many crises, including a massive bomb blast in Tehran in 1981 that killed many members of the Majles; the takeover of the U.S. embassy and the "hostage crisis," the exchange of weapons for hostages under Irangate, and the still-frosty relations between Iran and the United States; a number of military coup attempts; declining oil prices; and, most devastating, eight years of intensive warfare with Iraq at a toll of 135,000 dead and 500,000 injured and a cost of billions of dollars, still maintained as an uneasy ceasefire under U.N. supervision. The Islamic Republic has even survived the death of Khomeini, in June 1989. Despite the hopes and warnings of monarchists, secular and religious leftists, and liberal democratic oppositions, the regime has not crumbled, and no exile faction has made significant inroads in popular affection.

Any revolutionary government faces a myriad of problems and the challenge of translating its rhetorical goals into practice, especially amid confusion and conflict. The theocratic state launched a project far more hegemonic in scope than Pahlavi modernization, attempting to "Islamicize" Iranian culture and promote religion as the core of social and political life, a project with a far greater remit than most secular ideologies, claiming authority over most areas of public and also what in the West would be considered "private" life. Essentially we will argue that, regime rhetoric and Western media analysis to the contrary, the new official culture and communications environment of the Islamic Republic is still emergent, not fixed, and that it is far more porous than first appearances suggest. We will examine the cultural and media policies of the Islamic Republic during the past fourteen years, focusing especially on the rerise of state media, and the demise of small media through internal censorship and the frustrations of exile, and we will present some repetitive motifs of Iranian political and cultural life.

From Revolutionary Transition to Islamic State

On February 11, 1979, revolutionary forces were finally successful, and Khomeini invited Mehdi Bazargan to form a temporary government. This government had nominal control over what remained of the state bureaucracies and institutions such as the army, police, and civil service. Yet a competing center of power grew up alongside the formal center: the Revolutionary Council, headed by Khomeini, which controlled the Revolutionary Guards and took upon itself various policing and security duties. Despite Khomeini's earlier pronouncements that he intended to return to the religious city of Qom out of the political front line, this never happened, and Bazargan wryly commented that the situation of dual power and the competing revolutionary organizations made Tehran like a city run by a thousand sheriffs, an interesting metaphor to appropriate from American popular culture. The wide differences in political perspectives that had been masked or held in abeyance by the solidarity of the mobilization began to surface, and there were great struggles for power as the secular groups tried to gain access to government, and also among the clerics as more radical and more liberal positions emerged.

The postrevolutionary atmosphere was highly charged with revenge and purge, notably in the army, state bureaucracies, and education. The few high-ranking members of the Pahlavi state who remained or were found were executed quickly, against arguments for bringing them to trial. Old managers were purged, those who had "cooperated" with the old regime were removed, and those unsullied by past affiliations and of a religious disposition were instated. An atmosphere of revolutionary purity developed, in which allegiance to Islamic ideology was of far greater worth than any professional qualifications; this still remains true in 1994, despite talk of the need to expand Iran's technocratic base. Pressing problems were numerous: economic dislocation and considerable loss of oil revenues; a rise of ethnic and tribal demands that had not been articulated since the 1950s; the demands and concerns of women, active participants in the mobilization but without their rights "at the dawn of freedom," as the slogan ran; fear of counter-revolution from monarchist forces, and even fear of external intervention. In this context, as the new Islamic state tried to consolidate and return to business as usual, perhaps one of the biggest ironies of the Iranian movement is the rapidity with which the complex network of small media was stifled once again and the

Figure 10.1. The first *Fedai'i* commemoration, Tehran University, during the "spring of free-dom," 1979.

big media were incorporated as a central weapon of the new hegemonic Islamic state. It is possible to give here only the briefest indication of the immensely complicated political struggles that developed after the declaration of the Islamic Republic; we will concentrate on the emergent cultural and media policies and their implications for Iranian political and social life. First we will look at the brief "Tehran spring" of open debate; second, the reestablishment of big media, specifically the Islamicization of radio-television; third, a brief comment about the contradictory position of the exile press and international communication; and fourth, the new modes of cultural resistance that sprung up even inside the hegemonic Islamic Republic.

"Tehran Spring" and Islamic Frost

January to May 1979 saw the freest and culturally and politically most dynamic period of recent Iranian history. More than 250 publications flourished, including those by a wide spectrum of leftist and other secular political factions, women's groups, regional tribal and ethnic groups, Jewish intellectuals, and many other groupings (Hamzeloo, 1979). Magazines and journals banned under the Shah reappeared, and new ones were started. Book publishing enjoyed a heyday, with reissues of previously banned writers, great quantities of translation including large numbers of Marxist and leftist texts, religious pamphlets, and so forth. Cas-

Figure 10.2. Revolutionary decoration of Farabi University, Tehran, March 1979. Pictures draped at the top of the building represent, from the left, Assadabadi, Ali Shariati, Ayatollah Taleghani, and Golesorki.

sette tapes of all kinds of music, but especially of revolutionary international songs and classical Persian music, were mass-produced. The main street along Tehran University, once called *Shahreza* but now renamed *Enghelab* (Revolution), became an open bazaar of cultural goods and a major meeting place. Drama groups produced first performances of prohibited plays, and cinemas were packed for viewing previously banned films such as *Z* and *State of Siege*. University campuses played host to photography exhibitions documenting the revolutionary movement, to endless meetings, and to huge rallies held in homage of past heroes, such as the *Fedai'i* guerrillas who fell at Siahkal. For a brief moment, it did feel like the very dawn of freedom—but one of the earliest oppositional slogans ran, "at the dawn of freedom, the place of freedom lies empty" (subsequently recast as "the place of women lies empty"). From the beginning of the Islamic Republic the mass movement that had been held together in the common purpose of removing the Shah splintered into a range of competing parties and groupings, new and old, and formally clerical, religious, and secular. It became clear that a real "public sphere" of political debate would not be allowed to last for long. Already there were debates about the naming of the new structure, with "Islamic Democratic Republic" or "Islamic People's Republic" rejected as unnecessary qualifiers to an Islam that guaranteed all necessary rights. There were debates about social and economic policy (we did not make this revolution for "cheaper melons and cheaper houses," said Khomeini) and debates about the nature of the constitution: a clerical one that supported *velayat-e-faghih* and the power of the clergy, or a modern one that considered everyone equal under the law (the former proposition, supported by Khomeini, winning). All arguments were met with a similarly unassailable Islamic rhetoric as had mobilized the popular movement in the first place. Liberals such as Bazargan and other former human-rights activists were considered insufficiently radical, and "liberal" became a term of disparagement; Western-educated politicians were tarred with the general brush of being tie-wearers, *fokul-cravati*, and West-struck, *gharbzadeh*. Secular groups were further labeled devilish (*taghut*) or atheist (*cafer*), and inevitably *zed-e-enghelab* (counterrevolutionary). Islam and anti-imperialism were always on hand to reinforce solidarity and alienate those who dared to criticize.

The new Minister of Information, Propaganda, and Charity, Mehdi Momken, made warnings about publishing material that "infringed on the people's rights" or about illegal publications that had no right to operate. Islamic unions inside the newspapers pressured for more articles about Islam or about the *moztazzafin*, the poor who had made the revolution. On the streets self-proclaimed groups of Islamic youths, commonly known as *Hezbollahi* (from their slogan *Hezb faqat Hezbollah, rahbar faqat Rouhollah*, the only party that of God, the only leader Rouhollah), took it upon themselves to guard the Islamic Republic, arrest suspected *taghutis*, cause disruption at the secular radical/liberal rallies, and destroy publications of which they did not approve. By May 1979 the tension between "freedom of speech" and adherence to a single Islamic line led *Ayandegan* newspaper into trouble. It had published an interview (*Ayandegan*, May 8, 1979) with Khomeini conducted by Eric Rouleau of *Le Monde*, which angered Khomeini, and the paper was accused of being "communist, Zionist, idolatrous, the organ of the former regime, imperialist, and dissembling" (*Ayandegan*, May 12, 1979). *Ayandegan*, which had maintained as critical and independent a role as was possible under the Pahlavis, reacted to the threats against an independent press by publishing a symbolic four-page paper with three blank pages, writing on its single page that "it is the duty of a journalist to put the people in the picture and keep them informed of what is going on, not to sweeten everything or present it as divine guidance, so that no one knows exactly what and how bad the probable ills of the people are," and declaring that, until the government clearly spoke in defense of free speech, "it is no longer possible to continue at present" (*Ayandegan*, May 12, 1979). The state news agency PARS put out a statement, echoing state radio, that added to the list of epithets used against those who supported an independent, freely organized press: they were the "agents of foreign powers" and "lackeys of Zionism and imperialism" who had abused the freedom inside Iran for their own antirevolutionary purposes and attacked other newspapers in the same manner.

By early summer the name of the Ministry of Information was changed to the Ministry of National Guidance, nominally indicating the role that the press was to be expected to play in Iranian society. *Etela'at* newspaper had been taken over by a senior clergyman, Hojatol Islam Doaie, and had begun to reflect the views of the Revolutionary Council; *Kayhan* was sold to a syndicate of bazaaris; and Bani-Sadr's new paper *Enghelab-e Islami* (Islamic Revolution) appeared. To protest the growing press censorship and general erosion of freedoms, a huge demonstration was organized by the National Democratic Front of Matin-Daftari, and more than one hundred thousand people turned up; so too did a large and well-organized group of *Hezbollah* and *chomagh-be-dast* (club throwers) to beat up the demonstrators. The inevitable press law passed in August 1979 gave Islamic judicial backing to press control, and justified the banning of forty-one newspapers, including *Ayandegan*. Only small-circulation newspapers and weeklies, including the satirical *Ahangar* and *Haji Baba*, remained as independent voices. Thus already by the end of the summer of 1979, an Islamic frost had stilled the independent and critical voices of many revolutionary participants, the revolution expelling or, worse, devouring its own children. Eventually all political groupings other than the dominant Islamic Republican party would be banned (including the *Tudeh* and *Mojahedin* who supported the regime for some time; the *Fedai'i;* the secular democratic and human-rights groupings; and even the lay Islamic groups such as Bazargan's own *Nehzat-e Azadi*). Indeed, with the demise of Bani-Sadr, the first elected president of the Islamic Republic, from June 1987 a fully clerical state had been created. While unemployed lumpen elements were deployed to upset left/liberal activities, the bulk of the population was being demobilized, essentially kept busy in the daily struggle to find foodstuffs, fuel, and other necessities.

From NIRT to VVIR: Big Media Reinforce the New Big State

NIRT had been "liberated" on February 11, 1979, when the occupying military forces were ordered back to barracks after a ninety-nine day occupation. That evening well-known staff returned to the screen, the two lions of the NIRT logo were shown holding flowers, and a favorite newscaster clenched his fist in solidarity with the "radical" people of Iran and showed his delight with the spring of freedom. For the next few days, television broadcast from 7:00 P.M. to 11:00 P.M. a selection of newly composed revolutionary Islamic songs to a background of edited film and photographs of the revolutionary mobilization, a sort of instant historical replay of the revolution, along with new political graphics and poetry readings from previously banned writers such as Golesorkhi and Mirzadeh Eshghi. Endless salutations to the revolution were read from, it seemed, every organization, office, and school in the country, somewhat like a revolutionary postcard claiming "We were there, too." The first political content was provided by Bazargan, prime minister of the temporary government. An impish old man with glasses who fidgeted continuously, making for uncomfortable viewing, he spoke of the vast array of problems facing Iran, evocatively describing how the previous tenants had wrecked the house, and asked for public patience and cooperation in the rebuilding effort. Also broadcast were speeches from Khomeini in his temporary headquarters in south Tehran, where thousands upon thousands poured in to pay homage and to be treated to a sermon on the evils of imperialism. Any statement by Khomeini was instantly newsworthy, and he came to dominate so completely the news broadcasts—which lasted as long as his often very long speeches—that it was once asked somewhat quizzically if anyone would dare to interrupt him even to announce the start of World War Three.

The title of the organization was changed to Voice and Vision of the Islamic Republic (VVIR) and it was soon clear that radio and television were to become major weapons on the ideological front, to wage war not only on the West and imperialism but also on internal dissidents, and to (re-)enforce Islamicization. Sadegh Ghotbzadeh, one of the triumvirate who had joined Khomeini in Paris and had been rewarded with important positions after the revolution, became the first head of VVIR.[1] Rather brash and fractious, he soon ran into difficulties with the old guard in RTV who knew far more about the processes and practices of production and transmission than he did. In his first televised speech, Ghotbzadeh criticized the frivolous, uncommitted tone of past RTV content and promised that henceforth VVIR would be the voice of the "barefoot people" of Iran who had made the revolution, and not the voice of government (*Kayhan*, February 17 and

Figure 10.3. Bare-headed women protest encroachments on their freedom at a demonstration at Tehran University, March 1979. Slogans read: "The freedom of women shows the freedom of the society" and "Sitting at home is our shame; freedom is our claim."

March 1, 1979). He developed this populist strain further by inviting the barefoot to become involved with media production, an idea that further alienated the professionals but never became a reality. One of his earliest tasks, paralleling similar operations in other government bureaucracies, was *pak-sazi*, "cleansing." Known and reputed SAVAK agents, as well as old directors and heads of departments, were all dismissed from the organization. This was a formality, for most top NIRT people had fled well before the end of the revolution. Touraj Farazmand helped some monarchists establish a radio broadcasting station in Iraq, and is now in Paris; Iraj Gorgin is in Los Angeles; and Reza Ghotbi, the former director general, is in Washington, D.C. Parviz Nik-khah, the head of public affairs and news analysis, and Mahmud Jafarian, first deputy director of political affairs of NIRT and head of PARS news agency, were both executed during the first month of the revolution, in February 1979.

The farther down the organizational hierarchy, the more such accusations were based on hearsay and were increasingly arbitrary. *Pak-sazi* called into question the responsibility of all who had worked in Pahlavi Iran for the injustices that had occurred; those who had lived in Paris or Texas, waiting until the Shah had gone, were purportedly purer and free of contamination, a bizarre twist on the logic of "cultural imperialism." Two core ideas—a notion of "pure Islam," *Islam Rastin*,

Figure 10.4. Mobilization of religious women, with weapons, as part of "an army of twenty million," late spring 1979.

and the slogan "Neither East nor West"—became the criteria for televisual content and the weapon of the emergent state, but for a brief period there was an interesting interchange of views between the still-independent press and the state-controlled VVIR about censorship of the latter. This censorship allowed for interviews to be cut short if unsuitable opinions were expressed, for leftist commemorations and demonstrations to be ignored, or for minimal coverage to be given to the first-ever celebration of International Women's Day, which coincided with Khomeini's affirmation that female government employees must be veiled at work and ended in assaults on the participants by *Hezbollah* thugs. Within one month of the revolution, the issue of the veil had become a symbolic battleground in a wider struggle about the position and rights of women in Islamic Iran, and women staged numerous sit-ins and demonstrations at VVIR to protest the lack of coverage and discussion of these issues (*Kayhan*, March 13, 14, and 15, 1979).

Figure 10.5. Women played significant political roles both during and after the revolution. Here, a women's section of a demonstration, late spring 1979.

Obviously, the clerical political project did not include the slow development and maintenance of a civil society and an autonomous sphere of debate. Instead of opening up, the clergy clamped down—on the left, on women's groups, and on VVIR. In July 1979, Ghotbzadeh was replaced by a clergyman, who was himself later replaced by a council of three clerics. Television was becoming more and more a broadcasting pulpit. The style of programming was quickly Islamicized. Initially there were no published programs, so one simply had to watch to find out what was on. The screen was dominated by turbaned talking heads who, in the best clerical style, could sermonize for hours. It became common practice to start a speech with a *bis-millah*, "in the name of god," and by July even the newscast began in this way, a useful truth claim in the face of mounting opposition to the selection and presentation of news stories, and to regime policies in general. Few women were shown on television, many having resigned from their positions rather than wear Islamic headgear, and there were moments of crisis when a seemingly innocuous film with a positive social message suddenly revealed too much female body, at which point the broadcasting plug would be thrown, and screens across the nation plunged into darkness while the film was wound on.

Programming for a Theocratic State

Much programming was directly religious in content. There were interpretations of the Qoran, sermons by leading *mullahs,* extensive coverage of Friday prayers at Tehran University and other places around the country, and formal lessons proving the existence of God using blackboard and chalk (one famous *mullah,* Hosseini, could write with both hands simultaneously). The tone was moralizing and didactic, while the style—often based on a single camera with unchanging focus—was tedious and direct. Essentially the pacing and modes of oral communication were transposed into broadcasting, which fits well with Ong's (1982) model of secondary orality's reverberating many of the same qualities as pristine orality. The social ethos of the clergy and Khomeini himself were carried by VVIR into Iranian homes with the least artifice, almost bracketing or minimizing the mediation of television itself. The extended broadcast time, pacing, and lack of editing and cutting mimicked closely the experience of being present at one of these events, binding the millions of home viewers to the live participants. Electronic media thus supported and extended the preexisting social legitimacy of the clergy, having failed to create such legitimacy for the Pahlavis.

In yet another parallel to the rhythms of traditional life, when Ghotbzadeh pronounced that television was bad because it broke up family life, programs were limited to midevening, from roughly 6:00 P.M. to 11:00 P.M. Even a popular film that had been advertised was not shown; the announcer explained that it was too late and people should go to sleep. With typical Iranian sarcasm, VVIR was soon nicknamed "mullahvision."

Figure 10.6. A satiric logo for the new mullahvision; the legend reads "Iranian Akhundi Radio and Television."

The Islamicizing of domestic content was matched by a negative stance toward most Western cultural materials. In an interview with Oriana Fallaci, Khomeini described music as a powerful drug that created erotic feelings, and on his instructions all Western and Iranian pop music, jazz, and even the Western classical tradition were banned from broadcasting. Military marches and revolutionary songs were allowed, dominating the airwaves during the Iran-Iraq war, and traditional lamentation was also acceptable.

Inventing a theocratic state has not been easy, and the state institutions are still subject to change. A new Ministry of Islamic Guidance, *Vezarat-e Ershad Islami*, had been created to orchestrate the policy of Islamicization. In December 1986, the Majles decided to enlarge the scope of this ministry, changing its name to the Ministry of Culture and Islamic Guidance (*Kayhan*, December 16, 1986). The ministry was to have control over the Islamic Republic of Iran News Agency (IRNA); all charities, endowments, and *Haj* (pilgrimage to Mecca) organizations; the Islamic Tourism Organization; all printing and publication organizations, both public and private; the Farabi Foundation and all film production, regulation, and licensing associations; and the Center for Documentation of the Islamic Revolution. VVIR remained independent of this ministry. A council of three men, the Guardian Council, was appointed by Khomeini to represent the judiciary, legislature, and *Velayat-e-Faghih* (the leader of the Islamic revolution) in order to supervise and cooperate with the director general of VVIR on all matters. The two organizations were supposed to work together in a mutually reinforcing elaboration of Islamic culture (Sreberny-Mohammadi and Mohammadi, 1991). Thus, simply from the organizational standpoint, the Islamic state has taken a far more centralized and directive role over culture than the Pahlavi monarchs ever did. One element of continuity from the Pahlavi period is that just as the Shah trusted sensitive political issues to a few individuals who acted as his "antennae," so many of the new "Islamic antennae" are relatives of or clerics close to Khomeini. For example, in the spring of 1989 the head of the Judiciary Council was a direct representative of Khomeini, his son-in-law was the political deputy-general of VVIR, and the brother of President Hashemi Rafsanjani was director general of VVIR. In many ways VVIR had become a family business, and personal allegiance seems a more trustworthy adhesive even than ideological purity (from interview with member of Guardian Council, Tehran, January 1988). It was often noted that one thousand families controlled Pahlavi Iran, but some suggest that a mere handful of families now controls the Islamic Republic.

Since the end of the war with Iraq in September 1988, direct propaganda and religious broadcasting have given way to a peacetime scheduling that reflects an embryonic kind of Islamic television. There are serials such as *Tanzavaran* (The satirists), which pokes fun at Iranians in exile, and *Bad banha* (Sails), a historical dramatization of the constitutional revolution and the role of Modarres, a key political figure. Didactic programs like *Akhlagh-e dar Khanevadeh* (Ethics in the family) teach basic social skills. On the lighter side, an Iranian version of *Candid Camera* called *Durbin-e Makhfi* (Hidden camera) is very popular although questions have been raised in the Majles about its incipient criticism. The Guardian Council has also censored programs it considered "un-Islamic," and a new generation of television producers is being trained and socialized into the acceptable modes of Islamic representation. Broadcasters face a new double bind in which nothing that can be construed as anti-Islamic should be broadcast, while at the same time they are enjoined to be critical, honest, and not give in to flattery. Even Khomeini once warned the Guardian Council that "you have to employ all your

Figure 10.7. The U.S. embassy during the hostage crisis, January 1980.

efforts that radio and television remain neutral in terms of independent opinion or political group. Otherwise the broadcasting institution becomes a means to justify ends, and consequently honest people will lose their trust in broadcasting and the results become unpredictable. If you do not let the news, facts, and analysis reach the masses, they would turn to foreign radio from East and West" (*Soroush* 318, November 1985, quoting a speech by Khomeini in January 1981).

Early in the postrevolutionary period, there was a general proscription of American cultural products and Hollywood film as part of the cultural campaign against the "great Satan." Only foreign films with a suitable political orientation were allowed. Yet some television imports do appear, including even American programming such as *Little House on the Prairie*, which was considered wholesome and family-oriented, and a 1984 British serial *One by One*, which centers on a veterinarian in a rural practice. In the spring of 1989 by far the most popular program on television was the historically based Japanese serial *Oshin*, a fascinating cross-cultural identification. Western programming no longer dominates in amount or as only source, with a much greater variety of programming and film from Eastern Europe, the Soviet Union, and the Third World now available. The large amounts of foreign materials partly offset the disruption and difficulties of domestic cultural production. A new Islamic cinema is evolving, however, and from 1983 the state started to sponsor filmmaking at the rate of about fifty films per year, although even among these films many do not pass the Islamic censor or are so badly cut as to dilute the original intention completely (Naficy, 1987; *Index*

Figure 10.8. Revolutionary demonstrations in Tehran in spring 1979, with a focus on U.S. policy.

on Censorship, 1992). A recognition of the importance of producing popular culture with an Islamic imprint has not escaped the regime, which realizes that these materials are not only to be used in internal socialization and indoctrination but also to be exported. Rafsanjani, when still Speaker of the House, went so far as to declare at the Fifth Islamic Film Festival in Tehran that "in order to export the Islamic Revolution, we have to make effective films and not let Hollywood be the dominant influence. We have to change the attitudes of people. Instead of giving grants for building mosques, we should give grants for building cinemas and making films!"

The Impotence of Exile and Small Media

There have been several waves of Iranian exile. The earliest groups were monarchists, leaving as the movement mobilized or escaping afterward. Secular middle-class liberals and radicals, participants in the revolution but who once again found no place for their voice or vision, or even their modernist mode of rational discourse, in the Islamic Republic, left from late 1979 to 1981. Later, younger, often more radical, lower-middle classes left; they had weaker contacts and less experience abroad, and more naive hope in the promise of the Islamic Republic, supporting it for a considerable time only to be more deeply disappointed as its clericalist, antipopulist mien became evident (see Abrahamian, 1989). Finally, many fled to avoid conscription for the war with Iraq. This outflow of Iranians has been estimated to be over two million; the largest numbers went to Western Europe and the United States, but significant new Iranian communities have grown up in China, Japan, Australia, and Costa Rica.

By 1985, an estimated forty opposition radio channels beamed into Iran. Opposition leaders produce and distribute cassette tapes. Exile publishing is a growth industry, located predominantly in Western Europe, the United States and Canada, and Australia, with over one hundred regular titles available in 1989 (Mohammadi, 1989). The sheer volume of material is far greater than the materials that circulated under the Shah, and if any single example were needed to refute the notion that "small media" by themselves cannot create political change, this would be a clear candidate. Indeed, the bulk of the material circulates among exiles, although occasional items do get into Iran and very occasionally the Islamic media mention the contents of an exile channel. Essentially the exile communications network is disconnected from politics in Iran, not only ideologically but now also territorially. The tragedy of the educated middle class in Iran, finding no real political role under the Shah, precipitating the mass movement, and now finding itself shut out of the Islamic Republic, has to be one of the most devastating sagas of Third World intellectuals that we have witnessed. The limitations of exile as a strategy for political change must also be confronted, for it is most likely that this class has shut itself out of Iranian political life for some time to come, ultimately making things politically easier for the new Islamic regime (Sreberny-Mohammadi and Mohammadi, 1987, 1991; Fathi, 1991: 205–27). A particular conjuncture of forces—small media, unity in negativity, populist ideology based on religious popular culture, a charismatic leader, economic crisis, regime disarray—brought the Islamic Republic to power, and no simple mimicking of its ideological weaponry is going to dislodge it, especially not from outside. Although the exile community is the source of many new and interesting hybrid forms of cultural expression in film, television, and the plastic arts, as well as fascinating intellectual analysis, of greater interest is the cultural resistance inside Iran, where somewhat surprisingly a considerable amount of non-Islamic cultural material circulates.

The Growth of an Unofficial Culture: Passive Resistance

Foucault (1988) argues that power is not a possession but a set of relations, or discourses, that inevitably set in motion various kinds of resistances. In many repressive systems, where formal political activity is extremely curtailed, such resistances may have important political implications and reveal the difficulties of maintaining ideological and cultural hegemony in the contemporary world. As well as the internal dynamics of resistance within the would-be hegemonic structures, which we have outlined, there are many signs of a broader cultural resistance to the fanaticism and puritanism of the official Islamic culture, even by people who would consider themselves good Muslims.

New bookstores have appeared all over Tehran and in Isfahan, and although the distribution of paper for printing is deliberately controlled and restricted by the government, publishing activity is extensive. Some argue that the lack of variety and the dreariness of television fare has pushed people back to books. A considerable amount of original work in Persian is being published, including historical research, economic and social critiques of Western capitalism, religious writings, and fiction and poetry. Despite the ban on Marxist political parties, a great deal of Marx and Marxist writing, including Althusser and Gramsci, is readily available in Persian. Much translation work is in process; among the most popular translated authors of recent years were Erich Fromm, Herbert Marcuse, and Alvin Toffler. Ironically, Salman Rushdie is also a popular writer; both *Midnight's Children* and *Shame* have been translated, and the latter won a prize in 1988 for the best translation.

Tired of the incessant war coverage and sermonizing, television audiences have turned to videocassette recorders, preferring to rent videos rather than watch the available programming. A videocassette recorder costs approximately one hundred thousand toman, about one thousand dollars at black-market currency rates, and the machines are now widespread among urban families. In big cities, especially Tehran, the numerous video stores of 1983 have been reduced to a handful, yet the most current foreign films and soft porn are available on the extensive "cultural black market," brought in via Dubai and the Arab Emirates. In the winter of 1991–92, underground video home-delivery service operated in Tehran and many provincial capitals, while the regime continued to justify the ban on open video rental as necessary to support the domestic film industry.

There is a large market for audiocassettes within Iran, both of Persian classical and of foreign music. Weekly news cassettes that provide information, analysis, and music and are sold by street vendors have also been devised.

Iranians' love of elegance remains undaunted. The chic boutiques in Tehran are still there, selling both imported and homemade clothing, including excellent shoes, fine leatherwear, and handmade knits. Iranians who visit from the United States return talking about the excellent shopping in Tehran! On Tehran pavements all sorts of black-market goods are available.

Alcohol and opium, and increasingly heroin, can be found in Iran, although both consumption and trafficking are highly illegal and dangerous. Many families produce their own liquor, *Araq*. Despite Khomeini's own "war on drugs" (including execution of many accused of drug dealing, an offense used to cover political repression), drug habits are not easily altered, particularly when the trauma of war, economic dislocation, and social instability present the kind of extreme conditions in which drug use grows. Iranians love to recite verses from the poet Khayyam that talk of the brevity of happiness because life has no meaning, and the massive collective tragedy of the war has encouraged deeply ingrained attitudes of fatalism and passivity. But even beyond such a logic of drug consumption, it appears that people who barely drank under the previous regime now produce their own alcohol, in a cultural cussedness against the regime, its puritanical official culture, and its over-long reach into private life.

Thus a dynamic "popular culture" flourishes distinct from, and mainly in opposition to, the "official culture of Islam." The "popular culture" is not all un-Islamic but reveals a synthesis of cultural forms, a refusal to accept the stark fundamentalism of the "official version," and a lust for life and good times that the "official version" certainly does not celebrate. Private family parties continue with gusto, providing good food, music, and drink, as well as a chance to dress up, while the public visage has to conform to *Hejab* (veiling) and Islamic demeanor. Dissimulation has a long history in Iran, and the cultural split between the private and public worlds of the Islamic Republic is where this is currently being played out. In the early postrevolutionary period, people were arrested for possessing liquor, unmarried men and women were detained if found together (leading to widespread use of *sigheh*, or temporary marriage papers), groups of *pasdaran* would invade elaborate family parties and carry off the food "for the poor," and private space was interrupted at will by the state. Latterly, this has quieted, and the regime has pulled back from such intrusive strategies.

Similar pushes and pulls have taken place in other areas of social and cultural expression as regime repression is met with resistance, as the boundaries of the possible are tested by segments of the population, and as the regime itself decides what it will and will not tolerate. This dynamic of cultural politics has gone in waves. In the early period of postrevolutionary zealousness, women wearing makeup were publicly apprehended and forced to clean their faces, and some were even imprisoned for their so-called anti-Islamic conduct. Slowly, lighter-colored headscarves began to break the monotony of black, a lock of hair could be shown without fear of reprisal, and urban boutiques still offer an interesting array of non-Islamic apparel.

A period of comparative relaxation in 1983–84 led to a plethora of video rental outlets in Tehran and elsewhere, but in 1987 the regime reacted violently against the re-creation of what it described as *facade* (decadent) culture. Islamic motorcycle gangs trashed the video shops and Khomeini made proclamations against the sale of Michael Jackson T-shirts. When the regime felt its power slipping or when social discontent became too verbal, such anti-Western slogans still worked to galvanize lower-class elements to culturally police the more middle-class enclaves of northern Tehran. Yet from the summer of 1988, a new period of accommodation and relaxation appeared evident again.

Chapter 11
A New Cultural Atmosphere

Suddenly in the summer of 1988 a new cultural atmosphere developed in Iran. Some analysts attribute the changes to the sudden acceptance by Khomeini in September 1988 of U.N. Resolution 598 and the cease-fire in the war with Iraq, after eight devastating years of conflict. The war had created a grim collective determination, a central national purpose, and a ready policy for the media. With the end to the fighting—which carried no immediate gains for Iran—there was an evident easing of cultural pressure, perhaps in recognition of the immense pressures and toll that the war with its urban missile attacks and economic dislocation had had. There were signs that the tight Islamicization of the past nine years was giving way to a marginally more relaxed cultural atmosphere, and criticism and debate about social reconstruction began to be heard.

In September, Khomeini gave his official blessing to musical instruments and reallowed the playing of chess, which had been banned after the revolution (Simpson, 1987). During Friday prayers in Tehran over the summer, Rafsanjani referred to Khomeini as a progressive leader of pure Islam, *Islam-e-nab*, who had broken with certain dogmatic Islamic notions in allowing chess and music once again, and proclaimed that these were great steps for progressive Islam against the more traditionalist clerics (*Resalaat*, 3 Dey, 1367 [January 1989]: 10).

Another big story developed when a young woman broadcast on a call-in radio program admitted that she identified more with and took more readily as a role model a character in the very popular Japanese soap opera *Oshin* rather than the daughter of Mohammad (*New York Times*, February 10, 1989). Khomeini was offended by the broadcast, and ordered the head of radio imprisoned and the directors of VVIR's Islamic ideology group sentenced to fifty lashes. Only on the intercession of the Chief Justice, Ayatollah Mousavi-Ardebili, who argued that public opinion did not support Khomeini's overreaction, did Khomeini pardon the participants.

Such occurrences are vivid instances of cultural struggle, of a new Islamic television being worked out through the testing of limits and the evolving of standards and criteria. This dynamic has existed since the formation of the Islamic Republic, but what is important about these recent incidents is that they occurred in public, with material already aired and then criticized and retracted. Controversies about programming had previously been dealt with in the confines of the media organizations, whereas now the cracks in Islamic hegemony are probed in public. The official culture has vacillated on many issues, despite the continued reaffirmation of the basic values of Islam. Among the many reasons we might identify is the difficulty of producing enough cultural products at home, as many media professionals are in exile and the training of a new cadre of Islamic media professionals takes time. A second issue is the expense of importing the necessary hardware and materials for domestic media production at a time of general national fiscal crisis. VVIR spends about twelve million dollars each year on equipment and consumption of chemicals for development of film, and on hardware parts, mainly from Kodak Corporation. Because of the U.S. economic embargo, Iran has faced serious shortages of materials and has been forced to buy on the international black market (Seminar on Production and Broadcasting in Islamic Republic, Aban 1363 [November 1985]). A third issue is one that we addressed under the Pahlavi regime, the very deep "internationalization" of urban Iranian culture that took place under the Shah, creating a large urban population with sophisticated cosmopolitan tastes and interests. This material is cheaply available on the international market, Iran is still not signatory to international copyright conventions, and demand is high, so it is not surprising on all counts that considerable international cultural fare is accessible in Tehran, ideological protest to the contrary.

Who would have thought that one of the most diverse examples of Third World postmodern cultural bricolage could be found inside the Islamic Republic of Iran? In early 1994, the state itself supports the publication of four magazines concerned with cultural matters: *Soroush* is put out by VVIR, and *Rasaneh* (Medium), *Nameh-Farhang* (Cultural news), and *Film* are all published by the Ministry of Culture and Islamic Guidance. Current evidence of the "internationalism" of the cultural offerings in Tehran can be gathered by examining the listings in the "What's New?" column in *Soroush*, which provides information about current cultural activities in Tehran. Much of the material in *Soroush* is translated from international film and arts magazines, often without credit. Only on the last few pages does *Soroush* review new Persian books and films, and describe the internal and external radio and television programming. Recent issues carried an interview with a young Iranian filmmaker, and photographs of the four best teachers of the year, three of whom were young women in Islamic covering.

The representation of women has continued to be one of the most problematic issues. As Naficy (1987) has suggested for film, the most significant strategies are the avoidance of stories involving women and the acceptance of a rigid code that requires that Moslem women be shown as chaste, God-fearing, and maternal, but neither commodified nor sexualized. Even the Majles has on occasion debated the suitability of television images, as in 1988 when the neck of a young woman protruded from under her headscarf in a then-popular serial *Pai'z Sahra* (The plains in autumn). Khomeini resolved the issue by a *fatwa* (religious pronouncement) that approved the program as Islamic. One ayatollah continued to object, whereupon Khomeini's answer was that every beholder (male, of course) should control his passions. Another debate about coverage of female athletes in the Olympic Games, which had been spartan in 1984, was by 1988 decided in favor of increased coverage (Petrossian, 1988). Occasional articles about the marginalization of women in Islamic Iran do appear now within the press and magazines, and it remains one of the key issues for the Islamic Republic. Women themselves "stage" their own stylistic war with the regime. By 1994, purple, mustard, and blue have become popular colors for the *rou-poush,* a stylish long coat that is worn by women in public, a symbolic move against the black of the early revolutionary period.

Beyond the eclectic internationalism of film and television offerings is a new atmosphere of public criticism and concern about culture, again most interestingly expressed in the pages of *Soroush* and other privately published cultural journals such as *Adineh.* There is evidence of considerable internal criticism and confusion. Although the solutions for many social issues may be found in verses of the Qoran, recipes for Islamic media policy are not readily found there. Beyond the broadest of value orientations, Islamic media are being invented as they go along, and differences of opinion once fought out within the media organizations are beginning to be articulated publicly.

For example, the propagandistic nature of Iranian news coverage was criticized by the chief of news broadcasting himself in an interview that was printed in *Soroush* in which he described the dilemmas facing news broadcasters (interview with political deputy director general, January 25, 1989). He argued that news was the most important program broadcast because it conveyed the beliefs and morals of the Islamic Republic and the way it saw the world; hence the considerable time allocation to news coverage on radio and television, so that twenty-four hours of radio carries three hours of news, and seven hours of television has two hours of news. He argued that Western news coverage was subtle propaganda that was persuasive and helped to undermine other cultural identities, stating that "in my view the Western method of news broadcasting is the best because they cover their propaganda in a complex, artistic form, in a very clever way, and are indirectly persuasive to the audience. So the BBC broadcasts news in a way that shows and feels how wonderful and objective the BBC is while in reality it follows the general British policy and influence. It attracts our trust." Islamic news tried to "awaken those nations that are under dictatorial and imperialistic regimes" and "to develop Islamic values." Very self-critically, he admitted that "we use direct methods of propaganda in our news broadcasts that have a negative impact; if we use Western methods, we might have a better impact. Most people in charge of our communication system are not familiar with this medium and don't know the methods that other countries, especially in the West, use."

Here is articulated the notion that when ideological hegemony reveals itself too crassly, it will inevitably create resistance. Western media methods are seen to work better because their value orientations are more subtle, less readily perceived, and therefore more readily accepted as "objective truth" rather than being seen as propaganda. Such an argument sounds rather like Foucault himself, and certainly echoes arguments recently put forward in regard to the U.S. media by Herman and Chomsky (1988). The director general of VVIR, in a recent interview, described the organization as possessing "the expressive language and the sensitive eyes and ears of people of Iran," and stated that its mission was to reflect the needs of the people and thus engage in criticism of the government (interview with director general of VVIR, "Criticism Is the Mission of the Mass Media System," *Soroush* 451, Aban 14, 1367 [November 1988]). He defined criticism thus: "What I understand by criticism is to evaluate and to review honestly the problems and the performance of the current affairs in the country; in criticism a person should be like a mirror, to reflect the strong and weak points of the current affairs. One should be responsible not only to criticize the ugly side but also to show the positive side . . . that is, one should be constructive and aim to improve the social and political affairs of society." He complained that many government officials could not tolerate criticism, evidenced by official discontents about talk-show programs that allowed the public to air grievances, often directed at governmental inefficiencies. He couched the task of the media in general terms: "Our position should be to carry out our duty, which is to be resilient, to carry out the principles of our Constitution, and to execute what the *Majles Shoraye Islami*, the Islamic Parliament, defines as our policy. We have to follow Islamic values, the revolution, and most importantly, to be inspired by the prophetic guidance of the Imam, God bless him, in order to protect the interests of the revolution and the people, and seek mercy from God." Again there is a retreat into generalizations, with no concrete guidelines proffered as to day-to-day policy regarding content. Yet, for the first time, the ambivalent role of the media is publicly aired and explored openly.

The new atmosphere of criticism is revealed in an unsigned piece in *Soroush* dealing with the lack of entertainment to occupy leisure time, entitled "The Culture of Corruption and Addiction: Our Social Diseases" (*Soroush* 431, 21 Khordad 1367 [June 1989]: 3–5). The argument is made that Islamic administrators should create cultural activities for leisure time, or otherwise drug addiction and the "Pahlavi culture," Western corrupt consumer culture, will return because people have nothing to do and nowhere to go during their leisure time. Tendencies that are a threat to the very foundation of the revolution are exemplified in "clothing, bad *hejab*, the loose relations between men and women, and the social addiction to opium and heroin." The author writes, "In Tehran today heroin is cheaper than cigarettes and easier to find than a packet of Winstons!" This is an astonishing admission for a major government magazine to publish. Within the regime, then, there are voices questioning the purpose and efficacy of cultural policy, while there are abundant signs of broad cultural resistance to the imposition of a univocal Islamic voice. Clearly, it is one thing to describe the ebb and flow of cultural policy, the moments of repression and the moments of loosening, and the contradictions apparent within the broadcasting and cultural policies and practices of the Islamic Republic; it is quite another thing to make good sense of what the deep contradictions we have described within the cultural policy and practice under the Islamic Republic reveal about the enduring and deep-rooted effects of Pahlavi Westernization inside Iran. Even with the loss of a sizable segment of the educated middle class, interest in Western cultural products and desire for knowledge about Western cultural trends are very strong.

The Islamic Republic had tried to stem such interests and to re-create a sense of indigenous cultural worth and pride in authentic collective identity that was being undermined by the rapid Westernization process. It has failed, perhaps for two main reasons. First, it has simply been unwilling to acknowledge the depth of popular interest in such products; second, and more fundamentally, in its own rigid enforcement of a univocal Islamic line, new eradication of political alternatives, and harsh censorship, it has undermined the conditions for an efflorescence of Iranian-Islamic culture within Iran. That space has been discovered by exiles across the globe and extensive experimentation and hybridization of Iranian with all kinds of Western forms in writing, plastic arts, and film is under way.

For those who search, however, pockets of "postmodern" cosmopolitan culture can be found in Iran. Many are trying tentatively to reclaim a creative space inside the Islamic Republic. New art galleries have opened, cassettes of Western classical and global music as well as Iranian music are plentiful, a considerable amount of fiction is being published, and, behind closed doors, new *dowreh* of poetry and politics develop.

It remains to be seen how far the Islamic Republic, so inimical to democratic participation from the beginning, will allow this still rather marginal element of cultural relaxation to go. Although a considerable number of political prisoners were released on the fourteenth anniversary of the Islamic Republic in February

1993, many members of the *Mojahedin*, and *Tudeh* organizations were executed. The Rushdie affair, now five years old, shows little sign of resolution in the spring of 1994. But the election of Rafsanjani as president in April 1992 was another sign that the pragmatists may indeed be in the ascendancy, and thus the space for cultural diversity may develop further. Such rapid changes of direction reveal the intense political negotiation ongoing among the upper echelons of power-holders inside the Islamic Republic. It is little surprise, therefore, that cultural and broadcasting policies also show contradictions and abrupt changes of heart.

Cultural Invasion

In 1994 these issues continue to rage inside Iran. There are still heated debates in the pages of the main newspapers and cultural journals, and contradictions are evident between the cultural habits of certain subcultures (particularly but not only youth) and the convoluted practices of the regime.

On the one hand, regime rhetoric still professes concern about cultural invasion. But now the press sarcastically asks why, some fourteen years after the revolution, television programs consist of English, American, Japanese, or Russian films and cartoons, summing up the issue in military terms: "If today the war is the cultural war, why do we consume the cultural products of the enemy? . . . Tehran has become a city without gates, unable to protect itself from the onslaught" (*Kayhan Havaii*, May 26, 1993).

The onslaught takes many, sometimes sanctioned, forms. At the Sixth International Book Exhibition in May 1993, over sixty thousand foreign book titles at a worth of $3.5 million dollars were purchased, albeit mainly in engineering, medicine, and other academic fields (*Kayhan Havaii*, May 26, 1993). But one of the most popular areas of the exhibition was a corner where monitors connected to satellite dishes were downloading the BBC World Service Television, CNN, and Asia TV; many visitors spent hours in these booths just watching foreign television broadcasts. The joke of the conference was that the gardener tending the grounds of the exhibition also watered the satellite dishes, saying that he hoped they would spread like his flowers did. In an interview carried in the cultural magazine *Soroush* under the title "Isn't Tomorrow Too Late?" Ali argues on the basis of such evidence that there is no option for the Islamic Republic except to provide alternative channels and improve the quality of television programming of VVIR (*Soroush* 652, June 1993).

In some radical yet incompletely thought-through actions, the Ministry of Guidance and Islamic Culture assigned a team in July 1993 to develop video clubs, to buy film and video rights selectively from international television production companies, and to develop cable television in order to prevent the expansion of black-market video piracy and the spread of illegal satellite dishes (*Soroush* 656, July 1993). The latter crimes have developed so extensively that in Isfahan alone four hundred people have been arrested for satellite piracy and for reproducing international films for underground video rental, and their dishes have been confiscated. Another regime strategy is cultural deterrence, so VVIR has begun during the summer of 1993 to prepare an extensive series of programs called *Shab-i khun* (*Invasion by night*) that examines cultural issues, particularly different modes of cultural influence, and includes a focus on cinema, television, and music, to be broadcast on VVIR in the autumn.

Yet even so the *Jomhuriye Eslami* paper (22–2-1372) criticized the "cultural soup" that the cultural planners were concocting and said it was a joke if they tried to fight cultural invasion yet installed satellite dishes carrying CNN to every government office. Reports from Iran, including radio and print stories filed by Stephen Sackur, the BBC Middle East correspondent (*New Statesman and Society*, July 2, 1993), focused on the Nintendo games, rap and heavy-metal music aficionados, and the fashionable male peacocks of Tehran youth in their Levis, checked shirts, and trainers. For women, fashion is, of course, a private, domestic phenomenon as public decorum still demands Islamic covering and public social life consists mainly of walking in the park or—in Isfahan—strolling by the banks of the Zayanderud River. Yet the shops are filled with the latest European modes, exotic, colorful materials for home dressmaking are plentiful, and cosmetics and perfumery are widely available.

Thus Iran under the Islamic Republic remains torn between two apparently conflicting cultural pulls, toward the indigenous and the religious or toward global popular culture stemming mainly from the West. If anything, the interest in and demand for the latter is stronger than ever, not eliminated but perversely encouraged by regime sanctions, a true return of the repressed.

The desire for and tendency toward hegemony are visible in broadcasting as in other spheres of the polity. But the ideological definitions are still evolving, and the fundamentalist version of Islam does not provide a coherent definition or a clear set of criteria for the functioning of a modern bureaucratized media system, however encompassing and interventionist it wishes to be. Cultural resistance may show many different motivations and desires. Iranians have endured an abundance of daily difficulties, including food and commodity shortages, rampant inflation, and extensive electricity cuts, even since the active war effort has quieted. The "circuses" of contemporary mediated culture may thus provide a very brief respite from all the other tribulations that exist.

For many, in the absence of democratic rights in the Islamic Republic, a reaffirmation of cultural resistance that includes international cultural consumption is as much a protest against the Islamic extremism of Khomeini as the return to the veil was a protest against the extreme Westernization under the Shah. The popularity of heavy metal and punk rock, Nintendo, and the door-to-door video rental system serves as various indications of this. In both regimes, the political system has tried to control the cultural arena, albeit in different ways for very different purposes. Iranian resistance to both reveals a cussedness and refusal to be coerced by the state, a spirit that unfortunately has usually been forced to operate in the negative mode.

It may well be that politically repressive regimes buy themselves a longer lease on life by relenting in the cultural sphere, loosening controls on music, film, publishing, and so forth. Perhaps only time will tell whether this does work as a deliberate "bread and circuses" phenomenon in Iran, or whether these cultural phenomena begin quietly to probe political areas and become new forms of public mobilization. If the cultural sphere opens up somewhat, return by some exiles may also become a possibility, with further repercussions for cultural and political life inside the Islamic Republic.

The problem with the big state/big media model is that it overstates the univocality and range of power of authoritarian states; the problem with the "cultural resistance" model, however, is that it overstates the real effect and political impact of, for example, drinking vodka inside the Islamic Republic. As Foucault (1988: 96) says, there are occasionally "great radical ruptures, massive binary divisions" (the Iranian revolution itself) "but more often one is dealing with mobile and transitory points of resistance, producing cleavages in a society that shift about, fracturing unities and effecting regroupings, furrowing across individuals themselves, cutting them up and remolding them . . . the swarm of points of resistance traverses social stratifications and individual unities." In Iran the crucial issue becomes the relationship, if any, between the individualized cultural resistance we have described and the development of new forms of solidarity and new social stratifications; whether cultural resistance is the beginning of new "relations of force" as Gramsci (1973) describes them. We would argue that a more diverse and less controlled cultural space has a value in itself. Some space is better than no space, cultural diversity better than state-imposed hegemonic culture, and its solid establishment would be a progressive step forward in the politics of the Islamic Republic. It offers the possibility for the articulation of other identities, other ideas, which might eventually be translated into more specifically political discourses, demands, and organizational structures. Some public space is the precondition for political activity. Not the world-historical moment, or the prior internationalization of Iranian culture, or the internal divisions among the clergy, helps the hegemonic project of Islam. And though the clergy are highly politicized, they are not actually experienced politicians and are not particularly well versed in running a modern polity. The expectation of coherence and competence may in itself be wrong, and the pushes and pulls of cultural policy may be exactly what we should expect in a new political system trying to establish its boundaries and limits of tolerance. The Islamic Republic is making its own history but not in circumstances of its own choosing. So too are the Iranian people. After fourteen years, there is still great uncertainty in many areas, especially the political and economic, but major cultural questions have not been resolved either.

Conclusion:
The Importance of the Iran Experience

The analysis of the Iranian revolutionary process shows how effective traditional channels of communication and small media could be in undermining a strong regime with universal mass-media reach, in mobilizing a massive popular movement in opposition to the Shah, and in providing long-awaited opportunities for political organization and political communication.

The argument has shown the lacuna of communications focus in not paying sufficient attention to traditional/indigenous channels of communication that may express cultural continuity and identity. It has also suggested the immense political potential of new "small media" in developing public spaces in contexts where none seems possible, and the authority of international broadcasting channels where domestic mass-media coverage is publicly discredited. At the same time, communications issues have been inserted directly into the economic, political, and cultural spheres, and the communications dynamic has been analyzed within a detailed historical perspective about both mass media and opposition forces. We have tried to guard against elevating communications to an isolated sphere of study; indeed, many of the comments about mass-media "power" outlined at the beginning have taken on a generic quality precisely because analysis of mass-media institutions in non-Western societies has so often been nonhistorical and nonanalytic, importing the frameworks, assumptions, and methods of Western research with little attention to the very different international, historical, and social structural contexts.

In Iran, precisely because the mass media were identified with the Pahlavi regime and lacked autonomy, as the regime lacked legitimacy so did the mass media (unlike a communications model that would suggest that mass media endow a regime with legitimacy). The mass media played a role in the processes of uneven development, in political repression, and in cultural dissolution, which were the underlying themes of political opposition. The regime severed whatever tenuous ties it had with the traditional social forces at a time when it was itself economically weakening and in political flux. In not allowing the modern classes any autonomous organizations or political practice, and being unwilling even at the end to provide for these, the regime eroded the possibilities of accommodating a more moderate political transition. It *produced* the dualistic culture in which traditional monarchical despotism using the modern mass media was pitted against traditional religious authority and religiously based popular culture.

What had essentially been repressed in Iran was any modern, secular, ideological, competitive political communication. The lack of political development produced the two opposing yet traditional images of Iranian society, monarchy or Islam. While a movement of solidarity against the Shah was achieved, the differences of outlook within the movement were evident from the beginning, as the comparison between the initial secular progressive "speaking out" and the politicized Islamic rhetorics show. Secular modern intellectuals were among those most alienated from the Shah's regime who initiated political dialogue in the hope for change. Yet the secular groups lacked mass appeal, and the analysis of the small media reveals a populist radicalism that developed rapidly. Ultimately this group sided with the religious mobilization, only to become the central target of the new repression by the Islamic state.

Issues for Communications

In general it appears that the dominant focus on mass media has meant neglect in studying other communications channels, particularly traditional/indigenous forms of communication. A much greater focus on the entire communications environment of a society seems to be required, with analysis of the linkages between different forms of communications practices; the connections between communications practices and broader political and economic institutions, both modern and traditional; and the relationship between internal and international channels of communication.

Although some early analysts of the potential of mass communications in the development process, such as Pye and Schramm, underlined the importance of maintaining links with traditional and interpersonal channels, that advice has often been ignored by Third World countries that are rushing to establish modern mass media as symbols of development and ideological servants of strong states. Gaps are created between educated elites who dabble in global cosmopolitan culture and rural and poor urban masses for whom mass-media content may be incomprehensible, incredible, and inadequate.

This problem may be exacerbated by two other issues. One is the limited development of literacy and a countervailing "public sphere" of social debate and criticism, and the second is the dynamics of economic and cultural dependency. One reason for Iran's extensive polarization was the skipping of what appears to be a crucial stage of media, but also of political, development: the expansion of mass literacy. The blocking of independent centers of opinion and competing ideologies further contributed to the polarization. Lack of internal democracy and political feedback, and inadequate arenas for the articulation of grievances and discontents, may render traditional forms of cultural participation the sites of political/cultural struggle. As modernization undermines traditional identifications, so countermodernizing tendencies may also develop and "primordial" identities be revitalized. The weakness of a synthesizing middle strata allows the dramatic polarization evidenced in Iran, but the politics of Islamic identity are emerging throughout the Middle East and elsewhere.

We have also raised the question of the relationship between particular media and forms of discourse. The European experience tied literacy to the growth of ideology and rational discourse, independent judgment, and the demise of truth claims based solely on tradition. Media development in the Third World, like broadcast media everywhere, reinforces the earlier social patterns of oral cultures, including a stress on verticality, status, and cognitive domination. It is precisely in the stage that is leapt over, the lack of development of literacy, of a "public sphere," of open and challenging political debate, that the dilemma and tragedy of Third World intellectuals and the limited nature of political discourse is located.

The politics of identity is also the counterside of perceived excessive Westernization/Americanization in which the mass media are often central players. Cultural contact should not be confused with effect, which is the central mistake of much of the writing on "cultural imperialism," because countervailing tendencies may develop. These may include the formulation of national communications policies and the self-conscious revitalization of indigenous culture and traditions. This is evident in developed countries such as Canada, which is concerned about its dependency on the United States, as well as in the communications/informations policies of developing nations like Tanzania, Mozambique, and Peru (Hamelink, 1983; Mattelart and Siegelaub, 1983). Indeed, it is indicative of global cultural and economic power that concern about the "erosion of cultural identity" has grown since the issue was articulated by Europeans, embodied in recent French film industry concern about GATT, from when it was debated with vigor by the Third World in the 1970s. The relevance of traditional religious culture as an expression of identity is clear, but what the Iranian experience suggests is how that may become a new "jargon of authenticity" used to justify the imposition of a rigid single vision on a society. There may well be competing claims among a variety of traditional elements, linguistic, ethnic, or religious, and again a democratically conceived policy would need to give room for each of them to flourish.

Insistence on the importance of authentic cultural development in the face of Western cultural penetration, which is currently argued for by critical communications scholars, is not in itself a solution but the site of another struggle whose dimensions need careful study.

Clearly too, populism should not be confused with democracy. The other systems of authoritarian populism in history include fascist states, which organized themselves on a different politics of identity, that of race. Identity politics is not simply a problem of undeveloped polities, and race and gender issues are of central importance in Western political communication. The growth of fascism was the context in which earlier arguments about the power of mass media were developed. The evidence from Iran points to a different conception: mobilization on the basis of traditional affiliations and locations in the social structure, or the importance of primordial identities in counteracting unacceptable influence from the mass media. The mass-society/mass-media model assumes the loss of prior identifications, while the new evidence suggests those may be the most crucial. This of course raises the question of where "newer" identifications come from. This study has mentioned the blocked identification with nationalism that was part of the Pahlavi legacy, and the limited development and effectiveness of contemporary ideologies of class. Because the regime with its mass media appeared unable to satisfy the need for a coherent and meaningful collective identity, particularly in a period of dramatic social change, there was a return to the central traditional one, religious identity. Yet that has also changed in the process, from being a taken-for-granted element to becoming a self-conscious and highly politicized identity, one competing against others. In that sense, religious identity has now become relativized, framed in a contemporary manner, one "ideology" among others. It would be important to study the shifts in religious rhetoric from a mobilizing and oppositional one to the justificatory and propagandistic voice of a contemporary state.

This ties up with another fascinating communications problem: how traditional culture can be synthesized with contemporary broadcast media and how broadcasting can be employed in ways that better fit the moods and styles of the national heritage. The analysis of small media and of international communication channels that we have presented suggests that state attempts to control the ideological sphere are going to become more and more difficult in the future as national boundaries become increasingly porous and the nature of the new communications forms becomes almost impossible to control.

In the West the debate about the social impact of the "new technologies" like interactive cable, direct satellite broadcasting, and electronic publishing is heated. Unabashed optimists believe that the easy access, low cost, and distributed intelligence of modern means of communication are a prime reason for hope, and that these are nothing more than "technologies of freedom" (Pool, 1983). Others argue that the dominant tendencies in the West are such that communication is increasingly privatized (as privately owned systems encroach upon public-service systems, as leisure time is increasingly privatized, and as audiences are increasingly fragmented into specialized taste cultures, witnessing the demise of the "general public") and consider democracy to be on the defensive in the West.

In Iran the combination of traditional channels of communication, rooted in urban social life, coupled with small media based on contemporary media technologies, promoted an indigenous identity and opportunities for participation, unlike the despotic state and its mass media. The greatest irony, of course, is that the theocratic state then imposed that religious identity against the expression of all others, and severely limited political and communications participation.

Lasswell and Kaplan (1965) have suggested the terms "demosocracy," describing a system wherein popular trust and affection are vested in leaders, and "ethocracy," representing a system in which people recognize the moral competence of their leaders. While Khomeini and the clergy may be seen as natural or organic leaders, enjoying popularly based power, they are also literally the demagogues who determine the vertical flow and nature of communications. Their basic values are closer to the core values of the mass of Iranians than were those of the Shah, but the period of mass mobilization and participation has given way to limitations on democratic participation and communications diversity that are more extreme than ever.

Still lurking are deeply unsettling questions about Third World development. Despite the bad press that "reason" has received recently in the West, and acknowledging the limited development of the project of the Enlightenment within Western modernity, we are left with the sense that only by working through the "project" of modernity can the Third World create truly democratic, participatory, and egalitarian societies. It certainly appears that the route of "authenticity" and "identity" alone cannot provide the emancipatory possibilities once imagined. Orwell argued that all revolutions are failures, but they are not all the same failure. The Islamic revolution has, in many respects, been a tremendous failure, only clearly achieving its central goal of removing the Shah from power, and not implementing a regime of democracy and tolerance that many of its participants had dreamed about. But that is the cunning of history, and the beginning of another story.

Meanwhile, our daughters consider themselves members of a number of global cultural clubs, as yet perhaps not fully aware of the complexity of their inheritance. The new hybrids, they feel at home in many locations in the global cultural ecumene. But for us, the wandering Jew, the Iranian exile, we two grow old and sometimes do wear the bottoms of our trousers rolled, and echo along with so many participants of the revolution, "No, that is not it at all; that is not what we meant, at all."

Notes

5. Oppositions: Secular and Religious

1. See the glossary at the end of this book for definitions of all Persian and Arabic terms used. These are also discussed further in the text that follows. There is some discrepancy in the reporting of these figures among various sources; these figures come from Abrahamian (1982), except for the information on theology students, which is taken from Akhavi (1980).

2. The *sahm-e Imam*, portion of the Imam, was half of the religious tax, *Khoms*, that would help support the clerics and religious students. Akhavi (1980: 124–29) provides a fascinating discussion from the 1960s among progressive clergy over the danger of a conservative public controlling the economic viability of the religious institutions.

3. The history of clergy/state relations is still the subject of much controversy, both in relation to doctrinal issues of the rejection of the legitimacy of all temporal rulers, and in regard to the actual history of those relations in Iran. Some analysts such as Lambton (1956) and Algar (1972) assert that opposition to monarchical despotism has been a fundamental characteristic of Shiite Islam. Others, including Floor (1983) and Arjomand (1984), argue that the clergy was inserted into the power structure as part of the traditional power elite, and is profoundly socially and politically conservative.

4. The attitude of the Islamic Republic toward Shariati has been mixed. Much of what he considered to be *akhundism*, clerical reaction and dogmatism, seems ironically to be most manifest under Khomeini's regime. Mehdi Bazargan became the first prime minister of the Islamic Republic, and in 1994 still maintains a lonely critical presence in Iran.

6. Cultural Criticism, Secular and Religious

1. Those jailed included Adamiyat, Saedi, Beh-Azin, Sultanpour, Tonokaboni. The two writers mentioned but not named by Abrahamian (1989: 443) were Tonokaboni and Reza Baraheni. Saedi's "confession" was published in *Kayhan*.

7. Language, Authority, and Ideology

1. Already here are the seeds of an intense ideological struggle between the left and secular nationalists such as the National Front after the revolution. On one hand, the National Front would be accused of being supernationalistic and not supporting the international anticapitalist proletarian struggle. On the other hand, certain groups on the left would protest the imposition of a strong Persian (Farsi) language and culture over ethnic minorities such as Turks (Azeri speakers) and Kurds (speakers of Kurdish).

8. The "Heavy Artillery": Small Media for a Big Revolution

1. A commemorative volume from the poetry readings was also published, *Dah Shab* (Ten nights), edited by Nasser Mo'azzen of the Writers' Association (Tehran: Amir Kabir, 1357).

9. A Communication-based Narrative of the Revolution

1. Nassiri turned out to be one of the staunchest defenders of the Pahlavi regime. On trial before the Islamic Republic, he rejected all accusations and was executed in March 1979.

2. Hence the title of Manny Shirazi's latest novel *Siege of Azadi Square* (London: The Women's Press, 1991).

3. Later analysis of the U.S. General Huyser's mission to Iran and talks about military options revealed that the rumors were not without some foundation.

10. The Islamic Republic and the Process of Islamicization

1. Abol-Hasan Bani-Sadr was elected the first president of the Islamic Republic, only to flee for his life in 1981 after disagreements with Khomeini about the conduct of the war; he now lives in Paris.

Glossary of Persian and Arabic Terms

akhund	A cleric.
ayatollah	"Sign of God"; the highest-ranking scholars of Islamic law, the leading *mojtahed*.
ayatollah al-uzma	"Greatest sign of God"; the supreme *mojtahed*.
bazaar	A covered row of shops.
bazaari	A merchant or one who has a shop in the bazaar.
chadur	A tent; a veil for women.
dasteh	Procession of men during Moharram.
elamieh	An announcement; a leaflet or communiqué.
Etela'at	A daily newspaper in Tehran.
Faghih	One who knows *sharia* or the Islamic laws and tradition.
fatwa	The view of the Imam or Moslem religious leader on Islamic matters.
Fedai'i	Left urban guerrilla group.
fokul-kravati	A "tie-wearer," a Westernized person.
gharbzadeh	"Westoxicated"; one who admires the Western way of life.
hay'at-e mazhabi	Religious group gathering.

197

Hezbollah; hezbollahi	The Party of God; member of the party, a religious hooligan.
hojjat-al-Islam	"Proof of Islam"; a cleric qualified for religious preaching.
hosseinieh	Community centers.
howzeh-e elmieh	Seminaries, centers of religious learning.
ijtehad	The right to make interpretations of the law.
Imam	For Twelve Shiites, the legitimate leaders of the Islamic community.
kafer	Infidel, pagan.
Kayhan	A daily newspaper in Tehran.
khatib	Religious man, one who delivers a *khotbeh* (sermon).
khoms	"One-fifth"; a religious tax.
luti	A believer who combines physical strength with moral steadfastness.
madraseh	School.
Majles	National Assembly or parliament.
maktab	Religious elementary school.
marja-e taqlid	(plural, *maraji-e taqlid*) Source of guidance, supreme authority on the law.
mazlum	Meek.
minbar	Pulpit; steep stairs on top of which the preacher sits.
Moharram	Mourning month for Shiism.
Mojahedin	Islamic urban guerrilla group.
mojtahed	One who exercises *ijtehad*, interpretive reason.
mostakbar'in	The oppressors.
mostaz'afin	The oppressed.
mullah	A cleric, one of the *ulema*.
najes	Ritually unclean.
pish-namaz	A prayer leader.
Qom	A religious city in the central province of Iran.
Qoran	Holy Book of Islam.

Ramadan	Ninth month of the Islamic calendar, requiring abstention from food, drink, and sexual activity during daylight hours.
Rastakhiz	Resurgence, the name of the single political party developed in 1975.
rowzeh; rowzeh khan	Homiletic sermon; a reader of homilies, a preacher.
sahm-e Imam	Half of the *khoms* (religious tax), used to support clerics and religious students.
SAVAK	Acronym for *Sazman-e Etela'at va Amniyat-e Keshvar*, National Information and Security Organization.
Sepah-e Din	Religious Corps.
shab-nameh	Secret letters; clandestine printed materials.
sofreh	Literally, tablecloth; a ritual feast.
ta'ziyeh	Passion plays about the martyrdom of Hossein.
taghut; taghuti	Idol; believing in idols, decadent.
takyeh	An open area used for homiletic preaching.
tallabeh	Religious student.
toman	Monetary unit (in 1977, seven toman equaled one dollar).
towhid	Oneness of God, unified worldview.
ulema	(singular, *'a'lem*) Religious leaders; men learned in the Islamic tradition, especially its laws.
Velayat-e faghih	Guardianship of Islamic laws and traditions.
wa'ez	A preacher or orator.
waqf	Religiously endowed land.
zakat	An annual property tax paid by Moslems for charity or government expenses.
ziyarat	Pilgrimage to holy place.
zolm	Cruelty, despotism.

Bibliography

Abrahamian, Ervand. *Iran between Two Revolutions*. Princeton, N.J.: Princeton University Press, 1982.

——. *Radical Islam: The Iranian Mojahedin*. London: I. B. Tauris, 1989.

Ahmad, Aijaz. *In Theory*. New York: Routledge, Chapman and Hall, 1993.

Akhavi, Shahrough. *Religion and Politics in Contemporary Iran*. Albany: State University of New York Press, 1980.

Al-Ahmad, Jalal. *Plagued by the West*, trans. Paul Sprachman. New York: Caravan Books, 1982. Originally published as *Gharbzadegi*, 1964.

Algar, Hamid. *Religion and State in Iran, 1785–1906*. Berkeley: University of California Press, 1969.

——. "The Oppositional Role of the Ulama in Twentieth-Century Iran." In Nikkie R. Keddie, ed., *Scholars, Saints and Sufis*. Berkeley: University of California Press, 1972.

——. "The Year of the Revolution." In Kalim Siddiqui, ed., *The Roots of the Islamic Revolution*. London: The Open Press, 1983. 99–130.

——, ed. *Islam and Revolution: Writings and Declarations of Imam Khomeini*. Berkeley: Mizan Press, 1981.

Alter, Jonathan. "Prime-time Revolution." *Newsweek* (January 8, 1990): 25.

Althusser, Louis. *For Marx*. London: Penguin, 1969.

Anderson, Benedict. *Imagined Communities*. London: Verso, 1983.

Appadurai, Arjun. "Disjuncture and Difference in the Global Cultural Economy." *Public Culture* 2, no. 2 (Spring 1990): 1–24.

Apter, David. *The Politics of Modernization*. Chicago: University of Chicago Press, 1965.

Aristotle. *On Rhetoric*, trans. G. Kennedy. Oxford: Oxford University Press, 1991.

Arjomand, Said Amir. "Traditionalism in Twentieth-Century Iran." In Said Amir Arjomand, *From Nationalism to Revolutionary Islam*. Albany: State University of New York Press, 1984. 195–232.

——. *The Turban and the Crown*. Oxford: Oxford University Press, 1988.

Ash, Timothy Garton. *We the People: The Revolution of 89*. London: Granta, 1990.

Ashraf, Ahmad. "Bazaar and Mosque in Iran's Revolution." *MERIP Reports* 113 (March-April 1983).

Asifnia, Aryana. "The Rise and Fall of Iran's Underground Press." *Tehran Journal* (November 2, 1979).

Assadi, Ali, and Marcello Vidale. *A Survey of Social Attitudes in Iran.* Tehran: Iran Communications and Development Institute, 1977.

Balta, Paul, and Claudine Rulleau. *L'Iran Insurge.* Paris: Sinbad, 1979.

Banani, Amin. "The Role of the Mass Media." In Ehsan Yarshater, ed., *Iran Faces the Seventies.* New York: Praeger, 1971.

Bassets, Luis. "Clandestine Communications: Notes on the Press and Propaganda of the Anti-Franco Resistance, 1939–1975." In Armand Mattelart and Seth Siegelaub, eds., *Communication and Class Struggle. Vol. 2: Liberation, Socialism.* New York: International General, 1983.

Bateson, M. C., J. W. Clinton, J. B. M. Kassarjian, H. Safavi, and M. Soraya. "Safa-yi Batin: A Study of the Interrelations of a Set of Iranian Ideal Character Types." In L. C. Brown and N. Itzkowitz, eds., *Psychological Dimensions of Near Eastern Studies.* Pennington, N.J.: Darwin Press, 1977.

Bayat, Assef. *Workers and Revolution in Iran.* London: Zed Press, 1986.

Beeman, William. *Culture, Performance and Communication in Iran.* Tokyo: ILCAA, 1982.

——. *Religion and Politics in Iran.* New Haven: Yale University Press, 1983.

Behn, Wolfgang. *The Iranian Opposition in Exile: An Annotated Bibliography of Publications, 1341/1962 to 1357/1979.* Weisbaden: Otto Harrasowitz, 1979.

Benjamin, Walter. *Illuminations.* London: Jonathan Cape, 1970.

Bernard, Cheryl, and Zalmay Khalilzad. *"The Government of God": Iran's Islamic Republic.* New York: Columbia University Press, 1984.

Bharier, Julian. *Economic Development in Iran, 1900–1970.* Oxford: Oxford University Press, 1971.

Bill, James. *The Politics of Iran: Groups, Classes and Modernization.* Columbus, Ohio: Merrill, 1972.

Borthwick, Bruce. "The Islamic Sermon as a Channel of Political Communication." Unpublished Ph.D. dissertation, University of Michigan, 1965.

Bourdieu, Pierre. *The Algerians.* Boston: Beacon Press, 1962.

——. *Outline of a Theory of Practice.* Cambridge: Cambridge University Press, 1977.

Boyd, Douglas. "The Janus Effect? Imported Television Entertainment Programming in Developing Countries." *Critical Studies in Mass Communication* 1, no. 4 (1984).

——, Joseph Straubhaar, and John Lent, eds. *Videocassette Recorders in the Third World.* New York: Longman, 1989.

Boyd-Barrett, Oliver. "Media Imperialism: Towards an International Framework for the Analysis of Media Systems." In James Curran, Michael Gurevitch, and Janet Woolacott, eds., *Mass Communication and Society.* London: Edward Arnold, 1977.

Brecht, Bertolt. "Radio as a Means of Communication: A Talk on the Function of Radio (1930)," trans. Stuart Hood. *Screen* 20, nos. 3/4 (Winter 1979–80).

Brinton, Crane. *Anatomy of Revolution.* New York: Vintage, 1965.

Browne, Edward G. *The Persian Press and Persian Journalism.* London: John Hogg, 1913.

——. *The Press and Poetry of Modern Persia.* Cambridge: Cambridge University Press, 1914; republished, Los Angeles: Kalimat Press, 1983.

Bumpus, Bernard. *International Broadcasting.* Paris: International Commission for the Study of Communications, 1978.

Byram, Martin. "People's Participation Demands Change." *Media Development* 27 (1981).

Cabezas, Omar. "The Voice of the People Is the Voice of the *Pintas.* In Armand Mattelart, ed., *Communicating in Popular Nicaragua.* New York and Bagnolet: International General, 1986.

Castoriadis, Cornelius. *The Imaginary Institution of Society.* Cambridge: Polity Press, 1987.

Cole, Juan R. "Imami Jurisprudence and the Role of the Ulama." In Nikkie Keddie, ed., *Religion and Politics in Iran.* New Haven: Yale University Press, 1983.

Coraggio, Jose Luis. "Social Movements and Revolution." In Armand Mattelart, ed., *Communicating in Popular Nicaragua.* New York and Bagnolet: International General, 1986.

Cottam, Richard. *Nationalism in Iran*. Pittsburgh: University of Pittsburgh Press, 1979.

——. "The Iranian Revolution." Unpublished paper, 1984.

Crome, Len. *Unbroken: Resistance and Survival in the Concentration Camps*. New York: Schocken, 1989.

Curran, James. "Communications, Power and Social Order." In Michael Gurevitch et al., eds., *Culture, Society and the Media*. London: Methuen, 1982.

Curzon, George. *Persia and the Persian Question*. London: Sidgwick & Jackson, 1892.

Darnton, Robert. *The Business of Enlightenment: A Publishing History of the Encyclopedie, 1775–1800*. Cambridge: Belknap Press, 1979.

——, and Daniel Roche, eds. *Revolution in Print: The Press in France, 1775–1800*. Berkeley: University of California Press, 1989.

Davidson, Phillip. *Propaganda and the American Revolution*. Chapel Hill: University of North Carolina Press, 1941.

Davison, W. Phillips. *International Political Communication*. New York: Praeger, 1965.

Deutsch, Karl. *Nationalism and Social Communication*. New York: Free Press, 1963.

Dissanayeke, W., ed. *Cinema and Cultural Identity*. Lanham, Md.: University Press of America, 1988.

Dorfman, Ariel. "The Invisible Chile: Three Years of Cultural Resistance." In Armand Mattelart and Seth Siegelaub, eds., *Communication and Class Struggle. Vol. 2: Liberation, Socialism*. New York: International General, 1983.

Dorman, William. "Iranian People vs. U.S. News Media: A Case of Libel." *Race and Class* 21 (Summer 1979).

——, and Mansour Farhang. *The U.S. Press and Iran*. Berkeley: University of California Press, 1987.

Dorraj, Manochehr. *From Zarathustra to Khomeini: Populism and Dissent in Iran*. Boulder, Colo.: Lynne Reiner, 1988.

Downing, John. *Radical Media*. Boston: South End Press, 1984.

Dowmunt, Tony, ed. *Channels of Resistance*. London: BFI, 1993.

Eagleton, Terry. *The Function of Criticism*. London: Verso, 1988.

Eisenstadt, S. N. "Communication Patterns in Centralized Empires." In H. Lasswell et al., eds., *Propaganda and Communications in World History*, vol. 1. Honolulu: University Press of Hawaii, 1980.

Eisenstein, Elizabeth. *The Printing Press as an Agent of Change*. Cambridge: Cambridge University Press, 1979.

Elwell-Sutton, L. P. "The Press of Iran Today." *Journal of the Royal Central Asian Society* 35 (1948).

——. "The Iranian Press, 1941–1947." *Journal of the British Institute of Persian Studies* 8 (1968).

Enayat, Hamid. *Modern Islamic Political Thought*. London: Macmillan, 1982.

Enzensberger, Hans Magnus. "Constituents of a Theory of the Media." *New Left Review* 64 (November-December 1970).

Fanon, Frantz. *Studies in a Dying Colonialism*. New York: Monthly Review Press, 1965.

Fathi, Asghar. "The Role of the Islamic Pulpit." *Journal of Communication* 29, no. 3 (Summer 1979): 102–5.

——, ed. *Iranian Refugees and Exiles since Khomeini*. Costa Mesa, Calif.: Mazda Press, 1991.

Fischer, Michael. *Iran: From Religious Dispute to Revolution*. Cambridge: Harvard University Press, 1980a.

——. "Becoming Mullah: Reflections of Iranian Clerics in a Revolutionary Age." *Iranian Studies* 13, nos. 1–4 (1980b).

——. "Imam Khomeini: Four Levels of Understanding." In J. Esposito, ed., *Voices of Resurgent Islam*. New York: Oxford University Press, 1983.

——, and Mehdi Abedi. *Debating Muslims: Cultural Dialogues in Postmodernity and Tradition*. Madison: University of Wisconsin Press, 1990.

Floor, William. "The Revolutionary Character of the Ulema: Wishful Thinking or Reality?" In Nikkie Keddie, ed., *Religion and Politics in Iran*. New Haven: Yale University Press, 1983.

Forgacs, David, ed. *An Antonio Gramsci Reader*. New York: Schocken, 1988.

Foucault, Michel. "The Subject and Power." In Brian Wallis, ed., *Art after Modernism*. New York: New Museum of Contemporary Art, 1988. 417–34.

Frank, Andre Gunder. *Latin America: Underdevelopment or Revolution*. New York: Monthly Review Press, 1969.

Frederikse, Julie. *South Africa: A Different Kind of War*. Boston: Beacon Press, 1986.

Ganley, Gladys, and Oswald Ganley. *Global Political Fallout: The VCR's First Decade*. Norwood, N.J.: Ablex Press, 1987.

Ganley, Oswald, and Gladys Ganley. *To Inform or to Control?* New York: McGraw-Hill, 1982.

Gauhar, Altaf. "Free Flow of Information: Myths and Shibboleths." *Third World Quarterly* 1, no. 3 (July 1979): 53–74.

Geertz, Clifford. *The Interpretation of Cultures*. New York: Basic Books, 1973.

Gellner, Ernest. *Nations and Nationalism since 1780*. Oxford: Basil Blackwell, 1983.

——. "Foreword." In Said Amir Arjomand, *From Nationalism to Revolutionary Islam*. Albany: State University of New York Press, 1984.

Germani, Gino. *The Sociology of Modernization*. New Brunswick, N.J.: Transaction Press, 1981.

Gerth, H. H., and C. Wright Mills. *From Max Weber*. London: Routledge Kegan Paul, 1974.

Giddens, Anthony. *The Nation State and Violence*. Cambridge: Polity Press, 1985.

——. *The Consequences of Modernity*. Stanford: Stanford University Press, 1990.

Glucksman, Andre. *Le Nouvel Observateur* (July 11, 1979).

Goldstone, Jack. "Theories of Revolution: The Third Generation." *World Politics* 32 (1980).

Gonzalez, Hernando. "Mass Media and the Spiral of Silence." *Journal of Communication* 38, no. 4 (Autumn 1988): 33–49.

Gouldner, Alvin. *The Dialectic of Ideology and Technology*. New York: Seabury Press, 1976.

——. *The Future of Intellectuals and the Rise of the New Class*. London: Macmillan, 1979.

Graham, Robert. *Iran: The Illusion of Power*. London: Croom Helm, 1978.

Gramsci, Antonio. *Prison Notebooks*. London: Lawrence and Wishart, 1973.

Green, Jerrold. *Revolution in Iran*. New York: Praeger, 1982.

Gurr, Ted. *Why Men Rebel*. Princeton: Princeton University Press, 1971.

Habermas, Jürgen. "The Public Sphere." *New German Critique* 3 (Fall 1974).

——. *The Structural Transformation of the Public Sphere*. Cambridge: Polity Press, 1989.

Halliday, Fred. *Iran: Dictatorship and Development*. London: Penguin, 1979.

——. "The Iranian Revolution: Uneven Development and Religious Populism." In F. Halliday and H. Alavi, eds., *State and Ideology in Middle East and Pakistan*. New York: Monthly Review Press, 1988. 31–63.

Hamelink, Cees. *Cultural Autonomy in Global Communications*. New York: Longman, 1983.

Hanaway, William, Jr. "The Symbolism of Persian Revolutionary Posters." In Barry Rosen, ed., *Iran since the Revolution*. Boulder, Colo.: Social Science Monographs, 1985.

Hannerz, Ulf. "Notes on the Global Ecumene." *Public Culture* 1, no. 2 (1989).

Hanson, Brad. "The 'Westoxification' of Iran." *International Journal of Middle East Studies* 15 (1983).

Harlow, Barbara. *Resistance Literature*. London: Methuen, 1987.

Harris, Nigel. *The End of the Third World*. London: Penguin, 1987.

Harvey, David. *The Condition of Post-Modernity*. Oxford: Basil Blackwell, 1989.

Head, Sydney. *World Broadcasting Systems*. Belmont, Calif.: Wadsworth, 1985.

Hegland, Mary. "Two Images of Hussein: Accommodation and Revolution in an Iranian Village." In Nikkie Keddie, ed., *Religion and Politics in Iran*. New Haven: Yale University Press, 1983.

Herman, E., and N. Chomsky. *Manufacturing Consent: The Political Economy of the Mass Media.* New York: Pantheon, 1988.

Hill, Christopher. *Society and Puritanism.* London: Panther, 1964.

Hillman, Michael. *Iranian Culture.* Lanham, Md.: University Press of America, 1990.

Hiro, Dilip. *Iran under the Ayatollahs.* London: Routledge Kegan Paul, 1985.

Hobsbawm, Eric. *Primitive Rebels.* New York: W. W. Norton, 1959.

——. *The Age of Revolution.* New York: Sphere, 1977.

——, and Terence Ranger. *The Invention of Tradition.* Cambridge: Cambridge University Press, 1984.

Holzner, Burkart, and Roland Robertson. "Identity and Authority: A Problem Analysis of Processes of Identification and Authorization." In Roland Robertson and Burkart Holzner, eds., *Identity and Authority: Explorations in the Theory of Society.* New York: St. Martin's Press, 1980.

Hooglund, Eric. *Land and Revolution in Iran, 1960–1980.* Austin: University of Texas Press, 1982.

Hooglund, Mary. "Rural Participation in the Revolution." *MERIP Reports* 87 (May 1980).

Huntington, Samuel. *Political Order in Changing Societies.* New Haven: Yale University Press, 1968.

Hurst, David. "Radicals Again in the Ascendant in Iran." *Manchester Guardian Weekly* (February 26, 1989).

Innis, Harold. *Empire and Communications.* Toronto: University of Toronto Press, 1950.

——. *The Bias of Communication.* Toronto: University of Toronto Press, 1951.

"Inside Iran." *Index on Censorship* 21, no. 3 (March 1992): 7–29.

Iran Yearbook 1977. Tehran: Keyhan Research Associates, 1977.

The Iranian Bulletins. London: Index on Censorship, 1979.

Issawi, Charles, ed. *The Economic History of Iran, 1800–1914.* Chicago: University of Chicago Press, 1971.

Jameson, Frederic. "Post-modernism; or, The Cultural Logic of Late Capitalism." *New Left Review* 146 (1984).

Jankowski, Nick, Ole Prehn, and James Stappers. *The People's Voice: Local Radio and Television in Europe.* London: John Libbey, 1992.

Jazani, Bijan. *Iran: The Socio-Economic Analysis of a Dependent Capitalist State.* Tehran: The Iran Committee, 1973.

Johnson, Chalmers. *Revolutionary Change.* Stanford: Stanford University Press, 1966.

Kato, Hidetoshi. "A Cultural Balance Sheet of Big Media." East-West Seminar on Media and Society: A Review of Unanswered Questions. Honolulu, 1977.

Katouzian, Homa. *The Political Economy of Modern Iran, 1926–1979.* London: Macmillan, 1981.

Katz, Elihu, and Dov Shinar. "The Role of Broadcasting in National Development: Iran Case Study." *Craft Report* (limited ed.). Jerusalem: Communication Institute, The Hebrew University, 1974.

——, and George Wedell. *Broadcasting in the Third World.* Cambridge: Harvard University Press, 1978.

Kazemi, Farhad. *Poverty and Revolution in Iran.* New York:New York University Press, 1980.

Keddie, Nikkie. *Religion and Rebellion in Iran: The Tobacco Protest of 1891–2.* London: Frank Cass, 1966.

——, ed. *Iran: Religion, Politics, and Society.* London: Frank Cass, 1980.

——, ed. *Religion and Politics in Iran.* New Haven: Yale University Press, 1983.

Khomeini, Ayatollah Rouhollah. "Islamic Government (1970)." In Imam Khomeini, *Islam and Revolution,* trans. H. Algar. Berkeley: Mizan Press, 1981. 27–149.

——. "Message to the Pilgrims (February 1971)." In Imam Khomeini, *Islam and Revolution,* trans. H. Algar. Berkeley: Mizan Press, 1981. 195–200.

——. "The Incompatibility of Monarchy with Islam (October 13, 1971)." In Imam Khomeini, *Islam and Revolution,* trans. H. Algar. Berkeley: Mizan Press, 1981. 200–208.

Kifner, John. "Rumanian Revolt, Live and Uncensored." *New York Times* (December 28, 1989): 1, 12.

Kimiachi, Bijan. "History and Development of Broadcasting in Iran." Unpublished Ph.D. dissertation, Bowling Green University, 1978.

Kottak, Conrad. *Prime-Time Society*. Belmont, Calif.: Wadsworth, 1990.

Laclau, Ernesto. *Politics and Ideology in Marxist Theory*. London: New Left Books, 1977.

Lambton, A. K. S. "Quis Custodiet Custodes?" *Studia Islamica* 5, no. 2 (1956).

——. *Landlord and Peasant in Persia*. London: Oxford University Press, 1969.

Landes, Joan B. *Women and the Public Sphere in the Age of the French Revolution*. Ithaca: Cornell University Press, 1988.

Larkin, Ralph. "Revolution." In *International Encyclopedia of Communication*. Oxford: Oxford University Press, 1989.

Laroui, Abdallah. *The Crisis of the Arab Intellectuals*. Berkeley: University of California Press, 1976.

Lasswell, Harold, and Abraham Kaplan. *Power and Society*. New Haven: Yale University Press, 1965.

Lerner, Daniel. *The Passing of Traditional Society*. New York: Free Press, 1958.

——, and Wilbur Schramm. "Looking Forward." In *Communication and Change: The Last Ten Years—and the Next*. Honolulu: University of Hawaii Press, 1976.

Lewis, Bernard. *The Political Language of Islam*. Chicago: University of Chicago Press, 1988.

Liebes, T., and E. Katz. *The Export of Meaning*. Oxford: Oxford University Press, 1990.

Liu, Michael Tien-Lung. "Explaining the Revolutionary Outcomes in Iran and Poland." *Theory and Society* 17, no. 2 (March 1982).

Luke, Tim. "Televisual Democracy and the Politics of Charisma." *Telos* 70 (Winter 1986).

Lull, James. *China Turned On*. London: Routledge, 1991.

MacBride Report: Many Voices, One World. International Commission for the Study of Communication Problems. London: Kogan Page; New York: Unipub; Paris: UNESCO, 1980.

Mahdavy, Hossein. "Patterns and Problems of Economic Development in Rentier States: The Case of Iran." In M. A. Cook, ed., *Studies in the Economic History of the Middle East*. Oxford: Oxford University Press, 1970.

McMurray, David, and Ted Swedenburg. "Rai Tide Rising." *MERIP Report* (March-April 1991).

McNeely, Connie, and Yasemin Muhoglu Soysal. "International Flows of Television Programming: A Revisionist Research Orientation." *Public Culture* 2, no. 1 (Fall 1989): 136–45.

Mattelart, Armand, ed. *Communicating in Popular Nicaragua*. New York: International General, 1986.

——, and Seth Siegelaub, eds. *Communication and Class Struggle. Vol. 2: Liberation, Socialism*. Paris: International General, 1983.

Meadows, Robert. *Politics as Communication*. Norland, N.J.: Ablex Publishing Corporation, 1980.

Media Development. Special issue on "Group Communication in Different Cultures." 27, no. 2 (1981).

——. Special issue on "Alternative Media in South Africa." 32, no. 3 (1985).

——. "Communication: People's Power" (theme issue). 35, no. 1 (1988).

Mehrdad, Hormoz. "Political Orientations and the Style of Inter-group Leadership Interactions: The Case of Iranian Political Parties." Unpublished Ph.D. dissertation, Ohio State University, 1979.

Menzel, Herbert. "Quasi-mass Communication: A Neglected Area." *Public Opinion Quarterly* (Fall 1971): 406–9.

MERIP Reports. "Iran in Revolution: Fear Reigns in Abadan." (March-April 1976): 75–76.

Milbrath, L. W., and M. L. Goel. *Political Participation*. New York: Rand McNally, 1977.

Moghadam, Val. "The Left and Revolution." In Houshang Amir-Ahmadi and Parvin Manouchehr, eds. *Post-Revolutionary Iran*. Boulder, Colo.: Westview Press, 1988.

Mohammadi, Ali. "Development Support Communications and Instructional Learning Centres for Rural Areas in Iran." Doctoral dissertation, Teachers College, Columbia University, 1975.

——. "One Hundred Exile Publications under the Islamic Republic." Unpublished manuscript, 1989.

Moore, Barrington, Jr. *Injustice: The Social Bases of Obedience and Revolt.* London: Macmillan, 1978.

Mortimer, Edward. "Introduction." In *The Iranian Bulletins.* London: Index on Censorship, 1979.

Motamed-Nejad, K. *The Impact of Mass Media on Iranian Society.* Honolulu: East-West Institute, 1977.

Mowlana, Hamid. *Journalism in Iran: A History and Interpretation.* Unpublished doctoral dissertation, Northwestern University, 1963.

——. "Technology versus Tradition: Communication in the Iranian Revolution." *Journal of Communication* 29, no. 3 (Summer 1979): 107–13.

Naficy, Hamid. "The Development of an Islamic Cinema in Iran." In *Third World Affairs 1987.* London: Third World Foundation. 447–63.

Naraghi, Ehsan. "Iran's Cultural Identity and the Present-Day World." In J. Jacqz, ed., *Iran: Past, Present and Future.* New York: Aspen Institute for Humanistic Studies, 1976.

National Iranian Radio and Television. *NIRT.* Tehran: NIRT Publications, 1974.

Nimmo, Dan D., and Keith R. Saunders, eds. *Handbook of Political Communication.* Beverly Hills: Sage, 1981.

Nirumand, Bahman. *Iran: The New Imperialism in Action.* New York: Monthly Review Press, 1969.

Nobari, Ali-Reza, ed. *Iran Erupts.* Stanford: Iran-America Documentation Group, 1978.

Norton, Anne. *Reflections on Political Identity.* Baltimore: The Johns Hopkins University Press, 1988.

Olivera, Omar Souki. "Brazilian Soaps Outshine Hollywood—Is Cultural Imperialism Fading Away?" ICA conference, Dublin, June 1990.

Ong, Walter. *The Presence of the Word.* Minneapolis: University of Minnesota Press, 1967.

——. *Orality and Literacy.* London: Routledge, 1982.

Pahlavi, Mohammad Reza. *Mission for My Country.* London: Hutchinson, 1961.

——. *Answer to History.* New York: Stein and Day, 1980.

Perlmutter, Amos. *Modern Authoritarianism.* New Haven: Yale University Press, 1981.

Petrossian, Vahe. "A New Cultural Revolution." *The Guardian* (London) (September 29, 1988).

Phillipe, Lucien. "Voices That Cannot Be Ignored." *Index on Censorship* 17, no. 1 (January-February 1978).

Pliskin, Karen. "Camouflage, Conspiracy, and Collaborators: Rumors of the Revolution." *Iranian Studies* 13, nos. 1–4 (1980).

Pool, Ithiel de Sola. *Technologies of Freedom.* Cambridge: Belknap Press, 1983.

Pye, Lucian. "Models of Traditional, Transitional, and Modern Communications Systems." In Lucian Pye, ed., *Communications and Political Development.* Princeton: Princeton University Press, 1963.

——. "Identity and the Political Culture." In L. Binder et al., eds., *Crises and Sequences in Political Development.* Princeton: Princeton University Press, 1971.

Rajaee, Farhang. *Islamic Values and World View: Khomeyni on Man, the State and International Politics.* Lanham, Md.: University Press of America, 1983.

Ranganath, H. K. "Not a Thing of the Past: Functional and Cultural Status of Traditional Media in India." *International Commission for the Study of Communications Problems* 92. UNESCO, 1980.

"Report of the Patriotic Muslim Students of Tabriz on the Tabriz Uprising." RIPEH (*Review of Iranian Political Economy and History*) 2, no. 2 (June 1978): 60–71. [Translated documents.]

Rogers, Everett, and Livia Antola. "Television Flows in Latin America." *Communication Research* 11, no. 2 (1984).

Roosevelt, Kermit. *Countercoup.* New York: McGraw-Hill, 1979.

Rose, Gregory. "The Thought of Khomeini." In Nikkie Keddie, ed., *Religion and Politics in Iran.* New Haven: Yale University Press, 1983.

Rothschuh Villanueva, Guillermo. "Notes on the History of Revolutionary Journalism in Nicaragua."

In Armand Mattelart and Seth Siegelaub, eds., *Communication and Class Struggle. Vol. 2: Liberation, Socialism.* Paris: International General, 1983.

Runciman, W. J. *Relative Deprivation and Social Justice.* Berkeley: University of California Press, 1966.

Said, Edward. *Covering Islam.* London: Routledge Kegan Paul, 1981.

Saikhal, Amin. *The Rise and Fall of the Shah.* Princeton: Princeton University Press, 1980.

Sanche, Don. In *International Herald Tribune* (January 16, 1979).

Schlesinger, Philip. *Media, State and Nation.* London: Sage Publications, 1991.

Scholl, Inge. *The White Rose: Munich 1940–43.* Trans. A. R. Schultz. Hanover, N.H.: University Press of New England, 1983.

Schramm, Wilbur. *Mass Media and National Development.* Stanford: Stanford University Press, 1964.

——. *Big Media, Little Media.* Washington, D.C.: Information Center on Instructional Technology, 1972.

Shain, Yossi. *The Frontier of Loyalty: Political Exile in the Age of Nation State.* Boulder, Colo.: Westview Press, 1989.

Shariati, Ali. *On the Sociology of Islam.* Trans. H. Algar. Berkeley: Mizan Press, 1979.

——. *Marxism and Other Western Fallacies.* Trans. R. Campbell. Berkeley: Mizan Press, 1980.

Shibutani, Tamotsu. *Improvised News.* New York: Bobbs-Merrill, 1966.

Shils, Edward. *Tradition.* Chicago: University of Chicago Press, 1981.

Shinar, Dov. "The 'Myth of the Mighty Media': Communication Networks in Processes of Social Change." Unpublished paper, 1980.

——. *Communications and Nation-Building on the West Bank.* Boulder, Colo.: Lynne Reiner, 1988.

Shirazi, Manny. *Siege of Azadi Square.* London: The Women's Press, 1991.

Sibeko, Alexander. "The Underground Voice." In Armand Mattelart and Seth Siegelaub, eds., *Communication and Class Struggle. Vol. 2: Liberation, Socialism.* Paris: International General, 1983.

Simon, Herbert. *Persuasion.* New York: Addison-Wesley, 1976.

——, and Elizabeth W. Mechling. " The Rhetoric of Social Movements." In Dan D. Nimmo and Keith R. Saunders, eds., *Handbook of Political Communication.* Beverly Hills: Sage, 1981.

Simpson, John. *Inside Iran.* New York: St. Martin's Press, 1987.

Skocpol, Theda. *States and Social Revolution.* Cambridge: Cambridge University Press, 1979a.

——. "State and Revolution: Old Regimes and Revolutionary Crises." *Theory and Society* 7, nos. 1–2 (1979b).

Soley, Lawrence. *Clandestine Radio Broadcasting.* New York: Praeger, 1987.

Speier, Hans. "Historical Development of Public Opinion." *American Journal of Sociology* 55, no. 4 (1950).

Sreberny-Mohammadi, Annabelle. "The Power of Tradition: Communication and the Iranian Revolution." Unpublished doctoral dissertation, Columbia University, 1985.

——. "Small Media for a Big Revolution: Iran." *International Journal of Politics, Culture and Society* 3, no. 3 (1990): 341–69.

——. "Media Integration in the Third World: An Ongian Look at Iran." In Bruce Gronbeck et al., eds., *Media, Consciousness and Culture: Explorations of Walter Ong's Thought.* Newbury Park, Calif.: Sage Publications, 1991. 133–46.

——, and Maryam Mahloudji. "News from Somewhere: Foreign News in the Iranian Press." *Communications and Development Review* 2, no. 2 (Summer 1978).

——, and Ali Mohammadi. "Post-revolutionary Iranian Exiles: A Study in Impotence." *Third World Quarterly,* special issue on "The Politics of Exile." 9, no. 1 (January 1987): 108–29.

——, and ——. "Hegemony and Resistance: Cultural Politics in the Islamic Republic of Iran." *Quarterly Review of Film and Television* 12, no. 4 (1991): 33–59.

Stempel, John. *Inside the Iranian Revolution.* Bloomington: Indiana University Press, 1981.

Stewart, Charles, Craig Smith, and Robert E. Denton, Jr., eds. *Persuasion and Social Movements*. Prospect Heights, Ill.: Waveland Press, 1984.

Stone, Lawrence. *The Causes of the English Revolution, 1529–1642*. London: Routledge Kegan Paul, 1972.

Straubhaar, Joseph. "Estimating the Impact of Imported versus National Television Programming in Brazil." In S. Thomas, ed., *Studies in Communication and Technology* 1. Norland, N.J.: Ablex Press, 1981.

Sykes, Brig.-General Sir Percy. *A History of Persia*. 2 vols. London: Macmillan, 1915.

Taheri, Amir. *Noosepepper: A Study of the Persian Press in a Period of Turmoil*. London: International Press Institute, 1980.

Tehranian, Majid. *Communication Policies—A White Paper*. Tehran: Iran Communications and Development Institute, 1977.

——. "Communication and Revolution in Iran: The Passing of a Paradigm." *Iranian Studies* 13, nos. 1–4 (1980).

——. *Socio-Economic and Communication Indicators in Development Planning: A Case Study of Iran*. Paris: UNESCO, 1981.

Therborn, Goran. *The Ideology of Power and the Power of Ideology*. London: Verso, 1980.

Tilly, Charles. *From Mobilization to Revolution*. Reading, Mass.: Addison-Wesley, 1978.

Tiryakian, Edward. "From Durkheim to Managua: Revolutions as Religious Revivals." In Jeffrey C. Alexander, ed., *Durkheimian Sociology: Cultural Studies*. Cambridge: Cambridge University Press, 1988.

Tocqueville, Alexis de. *The Old Regime and the French Revolution*. Trans. S. Gilbert. New York: Anchor Press, 1955.

Tomaselli, Keyan, Ruth Tomaselli, and Johan Muller. *Studies on South African Media: The Alternative Press*. London: James Currey, 1989.

Tracey, Michael. "Popular Culture and the Economics of Global Television." *Intermedia* 16, no. 2 (1988).

Trinh Minh-Ha. "Of Other Peoples: Beyond the 'Salvage' Paradigm." In Hal Foster, ed., *Discussion in Contemporary Culture* 1. Seattle: Bay Press, 1987.

Tunstall, Jeremy. *The Media Are American*. New York: Columbia University Press, 1977.

UNESCO Statistical Yearbooks. Paris: UNESCO, various dates.

UNESCO: Press, Film, Radio 4. Paris: UNESCO, 1950.

UNESCO World Communication Report. Paris: UNESCO, 1975, 1989.

Vaghefi, Mohammad Reza. *Entrepreneurs of Iran*. Palo Alto: Altoan Press, 1975.

Varis, Tapio. "The International Flow of Television Programs." *Journal of Communication* 34 (1984): 143–52.

Verba, Sidney. "Sequences and Development." In Leonard Binder et al., eds., *Crises and Sequences in Political Development*. Princeton: Princeton University Press, 1971.

Wade, Graham. "Community Video: A Radical Alternative." *Media Development* 27 (1981).

Weber, Max. "On the Sociology of Charismatic Authority." In *Max Weber: On Charisma and Institution Building*. S. N. Eisenstadt, ed., Chicago: University of Chicago Press, 1968.

Wilson, Clint C., II, and Felix Gutierrez. *Minorities and Media*. Beverly Hills: Sage, 1985.

Wright, Denis. *The English amongst the Persians*. London: Heinemann, 1977.

Zabih, Sepehr. *The Mossadeq Era*. Chicago: Lake View Press, 1982.

Zonis, Marvin. *The Political Elite of Iran*. Princeton: Princeton University Press, 1971.

Zubaida, Sami. "Components of Popular Culture in the Middle East." In Georg Stauth and Sami Zubaida, eds., *Mass Culture, Popular Culture, and Social Life in the Middle East*. Boulder, Colo.: Westview Press, 1987.

Persian References

Aflatouni, Homa. *Bar resi-ye Towlid va Taksir-e Navar-e Kasett dar Tehran*. (A survey of the production and distribution of cassette tapes in Tehran). Tehran: Iran Communications and Development Institute, 1978.

Alavi, Bozorg. *Panjah-e-Se Nafar* (Fifty-three People). Tehran: Amir Kabir Publications, 1978.

Arbabzadeh, Mehdi. *Bar Resi-ye Afkar-e Umumi-ye Iran* (Analysis of public opinion in Iran). Tehran: Audience Research Institute, NIRT, 1977.

Ardekani, Hosein Mahbubi. *Ketab va Matbuat dar Iran* (Books and printed materials in Iran). Tehran: Plan and Budget Organization, 1352/1973.

——. *Tarikh-e Moassesate Tamadoni Jadid dar Iran* (History of new civic organizations in Iran). Tehran: Moasseye Entesharat va Chape Daneshga Tehran, 1368 (1988–89; vols. 1–3).

Asnad va Tasavir-e az Mobarezat-e Khalq Mosalman-e Iran (Document and pictures of struggles of Moslem people in Iran). Entesharat-e Abu Zar, n.p., 1358/1979.

Assadi, Ali, and Hormoz Mehrdad, eds. *Naqsh-e Rasanehha dar Poshtibani-ye Tause'a-ye Farhangi*. Tehran: Iran Communications and Development Institute, 1355/1976.

Bakhtiari, Pezhman M. *Tarikhe Post, Telegraph va Telephon* (History of Post, Telegraph, and Telephone). Tehran: Chapkhane va Ketabfrushi Ali Akhbar Elmi, n.d.

Barnameye Avale Tosa'e Ekhtesadi-Ejtemai'-Farhagni Jomhuriye Eslamiye Iran 1362–1366 (The first economic, social and cultural development plan of the Islamic Republic). Tehran: Sazmane Barname va Budje, 1368/1989.

Barzin, Massoud. *Matbuate Iran* (The Iranian press). Tehran: Ketab-Khane Behjad, 1354/1975.

Fashahi, Mohammad Reza. *Gozareshe Kutah az Tahavolat-e-Fekri va Ejtemaii Dar Jameei Feodaliye Iran* (A concise report of the social and intellectual changes in the feudal society of Iran). Tehran: Gutenburg, 1354/1976.

Ghanune Khate Masheye Koli va Osule Barnamehaye Sazmane Seda va Simaye Jomhuriye Islamiye Iran (The planning and production objectives and philosophy of voice and vision of the Islamic Republic). Tehran: VVIR, n.d.

Haj Seyyed Javadi, A. A. *Nameh-ha* (Letters). Tehran: Modaress, 1357/1978.

Hamelzoo, Bijan. *Gozareshe Grouhaye Siyasi* (A report on political groups). Tehran: Iran Communications and Development Institute, 1357/1978.

Jamalzadeh, Mohammad Ali. *Ganj-i Shaigan* (The plentiful treasure). Berlin: Kaveh, 1335; Tehran: Ketab-e-Tehran, 1362/1983.

Malekzadeh, Mehdi. *Tarikh-e Englabe Mashrutiyate Iran* (History of the constitutional revolution in Iran). Vol. 1. Tehran: Entesharate Ibn Sina, 1328/1949.

Mowlana, Hamid. *Seyre Ertabatat, Ejtemaie dar Iran*. Tehran: Entesharate Daneshkade-ye-Olume-Ertebatate Ejtemaie, 1357/1978.

Najafi, Mohammad Bagher. *Bahaiian dar Iran* (Bahaii in Iran). Tehran: Amir Kabir, 1357/1978.

Najafi, S. M. B. "Appendix on Religious Media, Centers, and Organizations." In Ali Assadi and Hormoz Mehrdad, eds., *Naqsh-e Rasanehha dar Poshtibani-ye Tause'a-ye Farhangi*. Tehran: Iran Communications and Development Institute, 1355/1976.

Nedaye-Hagh (The message of truth). Vol. 1. Society of Islamic Students in Europe and America, 13 Dey 1357/3 January 1979.

Pahlavi, Mohammad Reza. *Besu-ye Tammaddon-e-Bozorg* (Toward the Great Civilization). Tehran, 1978.

"Peyke Seda va Sima" (The messenger of VVIR). No. 153. Tehran: Publications Office, VVIR, 1368.

Pezhman, Hussein. *Tarikhe Post, Telegraph va Telephone* (History of Post, Telegraph, and Telephone). Tehran: Vezarate Post, Telegraph va Telephone, 1948.

Qiyam-e Hamaseh Afarinan-e Qom va Tabriz va digar Shahr-ha-ye Iran (The uprising of people in

Qom, Tabriz, and other parts of the country). 3 vols. Tehran: Nehzat-e Azadi-ye Iran, n.p., 1356/1978.

Ra'in, Esmail. *Faramushkhaneh va Framasoneri dar Iran* (The house of oblivion and freemasonry in Iran). 3 vols. Tehran: Amir Kabir Press, 1968.

Sadr-Hashemi, Mohammad. *Tarikhe Jarayed va Majalat Iran* (A History of newspapers and magazines in Iran). 4 vols. Isfahan: Entesharate Kamal, 1327/1948.

Seminare Barnamerisi Tolid va Pakhsh Seda va Simaye Jomhuriye Islami Iran (Seminar on policy of production and programming of voice and vision of the Islamic Republic). Tehran: *Soroush*, 1360/1981.

Shoraye Markazi-ye Hamhangi-ye Sazmanhaye Dowlati va Melli (Central Coordinating Committee of Governmental and National Institutions of Iran). Tehran, 10 Azar 1357/1978.

Syndikaye Moshtarak-e Karkonan Sanate Naft (9 Azar 1357; October 1978).

Touran, Alef (Bagher Momeni). *Masale-ye Arzi va Jange Tabaqati dar Iran* (The problems of land and class struggle in Iran). Tehran, 1978.

Index

Compiled by Eileen Quam and Theresa Wolner

tions, 22; and national identity, 11; as political discourse, xiii, 9–10, 13–15, 106–7; as public communication, 4; as public space, 26, 85; and retraditionalization, xviii, 94; rise of in Iran, 88–89; and small media, 35–37; and social solidarity, 35; and traditional identity, 9, 94, 95–96. *See also* Ceremonies; Clergy; Mosque; Shiism
Religious Corps. *See Sepah-e-Din*
Religious tax. *See Khoms*
Resalat, 211
Resistance Corps, 142
Review of Iranian Political Economy and History, 118, 126, 127, 129, 140, 141
Revolution: as communicative process, xxii, 19; as emotional, xi; as evolving process, 19; as political process, xxii, 19, 20; as psychological, xi; Third World model of, xix
Revolutionary Committee of the Islamic Republic, 66
Ritual. *See* Ceremonies
Robertson, Roland, 110
Roche, Daniel, 20
Romania: economics in, 23; mass demonstrations in, 22; mediated communication and revolution in, xix
Rose, Gregory, 116
Rosvakhiz, 128
Rouhani Mansur, 64
Rouleau, Eric, 168
Rowzeh, 86, 87, 121, 199; *Rawda*, 88
Rowzeh khan, 86, 199
Royal ceremonies: broadcasting of, 68–69
Rumor, 125, 131–32
Rushdie, Salman, 112, 179, 186
Russia: political control in, 24; revolution slogan, 118
Ruzbe, Chosro, *101*

Sabet Pasal, Habibollah: and television, 61–62, 63, 65, 66
Sabeti, Parviz, 64
Sackur, Stephen, 187
Saddoughi, Ayatollah, 124
Saderat Bank, 128–29, 140
Saedi, Gholam-Hossein, 102, 195n
Safavids, 11
Sahm-e Imam, 82, 195n, 199
Said, Abdul Aziz, xii
Said, Edward, 135
Salaffiya, 118

Samizdat, 24, 27, 103
Sanche, Don, 90
Sanjabi, Karim, 99–100, 147, 152, 158
Sassanids, 50
Satanic Verses, The (Rushdie), 112
Satellite dishes: and international communication, 29, 30, 68, 186, 187; social impact of, 193; in Soviet Union, 26
SAVAK (Sazman-e Etela'at va Amniyat-e Keshvar): brutality of, 143; and Cinema Rex fire, 126, 145; communiqués, 129; defined, 199; elimination of, 99, 128, 158; fear of, xxi, 32; and guild courts, 82; and Islamic Republic, 170; and military consolidation, 65; role of, 24, 25; and Tabriz events, 141; television programming of, 69; workings of, 150
Sazman-e-Melli Daneshgaian, 130
School. *See Madraseh; Maktab*
Schramm, Wilbur, 20, 191
Secular opposition, xvi, 9, 98–100, 195n; clergy vs., 108–9; communiqués, 125; identity of, 39, 107–9; and middle class, 100, 108–9; and tradition, 38; and Westernization, 108
Sepah-e-Din, 81, 199
Sermons. *See Khotbehs*
Shab-i khun (television series), 187
Shab-nameh, 121, 122, 199. *See also* Communiqués; *Elamieh*; Leaflets; Open letters
Shah, xiii, xv, xvi, *91–93*; antipathies toward, xvii; coronation, 38; despotism of, 22; legitimacy of, 15; media use by, 7; and patriotism, 51; power of, xxi, 65; revolution against, xix; as *Shahanshah*, 68; and single party development, 24; wealth of, 63–64
Shah, Mohammad Reza, 13, 57, 58, 59, 71, 76, 86, 106; and television, 62, 71
Shah, Reza, 49–51, 52, 53–54, 56, 67, 68, 81, 86, 95
Shahanshahi calendar, 146
Shahbanou Farah Foundation, 97
Shahed (newspaper), 56
Shahnameh of Ferdowsi, 50
Shame (Rushdie), 179
Sharghzadeh, xii
Shariat-Madari, Ayatollah: authority of, 112; communiqués of, 124, 140, 147; invasions upon, 146; and oil production negotiations, 159; recordings of, 121; regional identification with, 83; on tyrannical regime, 143, 147, 159

Annabelle Sreberny-Mohammadi is Professor and Director of the Centre for Mass Communication Research, University of Leicester, England. She taught sociology and communications at National University and Damavand College in Tehran during the Iranian revolution, and was the editor of the English-language quarterly *Communications and Development Review*, based at Iran Communications and Development Institute from 1977 to 1979. She is a coeditor of *Questioning the Media* and of the UNESCO/IAMCR study *Foreign News in the Media: International Reporting in Twenty-nine Countries*. Her current interests concern globalization theory and the political economy of media industries; tactical media as an alternative global public sphere; media, gender, and social space in the Middle East; and gender politics and public knowledge in Britain.

Ali Mohammadi is Reader in international communication and cultural studies at Nottingham Trent University, England. He was the head of the graduate program in culture and communication studies at Farabi University in Tehran both before and after the Iranian revolution. He is a coeditor of *Questioning the Media* and has written on Iranian exile, on foreign images and cultural policy of the Islamic Republic, and on communication policy in the Persian Gulf region. His major interests are cultural imperialism and national identity in the context of the developing world, particularly the Persian Gulf region.